46

Social History of Canada

Allan Greer and Craig Heron, general editors

Gender Conflicts
New Essays in Women's History

In the early 1970s, when women's history began to claim
attention as an emerging discipline in North American universities, it was dominated by a middle-class Anglo-Saxon bias.
Today the field is much more diverse, a development reflected
in the scope of this volume. Rather than documenting the experiences of women solely in a framework of gender analysis,
its authors recognize the interaction of race, class, and gender
as central in shaping women's lives, and men's.

Some of the topics covered in these essays have received little attention in the context of women's history: consumption
and leisure, crime and the courts, and social welfare in the
1950s. Others are addressed in new ways: intellectual history
of first-wave feminism, sexuality, women in the labour force,
and women on the left.

These essays represent an exciting breakthrough in women's
studies, expanding the borders of the discipline while breaking
down barriers between mainstream and women's history.

FRANCA IACOVETTA is a member of the Department of History, Scarborough Campus, University of Toronto.
MARIANA VALVERDE is a member of the Department of Sociology, York University.

Gender Conflicts
New Essays
in Women's
History

Edited by

*Franca Iacovetta and
Mariana Valverde*

UNIVERSITY OF TORONTO PRESS
Toronto Buffalo London

© University of Toronto Press 1992
Toronto Buffalo London
Printed in Canada

ISBN 0-8020-2734-2 (cloth)
ISBN 0-8020-6773-5 (paper)

Printed on acid-free paper

Canadian Cataloguing in Publication Data

Main entry under title:
Gender conflicts: new essays in women's history
(The Social history of Canada; 46)
ISBN 0-8020-2734-2 (bound)   ISBN 0-8020-6773-5 (pbk.)

1. Women – Canada – History.   2. Women – Ontario –
History.   I. Iacovetta, Franca, 1957–   .
II. Valverde, Mariana, 1955–   . III. Series

HQ1453.G45 1992   365.4'C971   C92-093397-1

Front cover: 'Hallelujah Lasses': Captain Cowan and Fanny
Robin, courtesy of The Salvation Army, G.S.R. Heritage Centre,
Toronto (248)

Social History of Canada 46

This book has been published with the help of a grant from the
Social Science Federation of Canada, using funds provided by the
Social Sciences and Humanities Research Council of Canada.

In memory of Daniel Valverde

Contents

Contributors

KAREN DUBINSKY, who has published articles on contemporary anti-feminism, teaches women's history at the University of Toronto. This article is derived from her recently completed dissertation, 'Improper Advances: Sexual Danger and Pleasure in Rural and Northern Ontario, 1880–1929' (Queen's University).

RUTH FRAGER teaches history at McMaster University and has published articles on immigrant and working-class women, and on the history of the Jewish left. She is the author of *Sweatshop Strife: Class, Ethnicity, and Gender in the Jewish Labour Movement in Toronto, 1900–1939* (Toronto: University of Toronto Press, forthcoming).

FRANCA IACOVETTA is a specialist in immigration and women's history and is the author of *Such Hardworking People: Italian Immigrants in Postwar Toronto* (Montreal and Kingston: McGill-Queen's University Press 1992). She teaches history at the Scarborough Campus of the University of Toronto.

LYNNE MARKS, who will soon take a teaching position with the history department at the University of Victoria, completed her dissertation on working-class religion and leisure in small-town Ontario at York University. She has published articles in women's history and labour history and contributed to volume 3 of the

Historical Atlas of Canada (Toronto: University of Toronto Press 1991).

JANICE NEWTON teaches political science at York University. She has published articles on women in the early Canadian left, and is currently completing a book on the topic.

CAROLYN STRANGE is a specialist in the history of women, sexuality, and crime. She is doing postdoctoral work on capital crime and mercy in Australia, after completing her dissertation, 'The Perils and Pleasures of the City: Single Wage-Earning Women in Toronto, 1880–1930,' at Rutgers University.

MARIANA VALVERDE teaches social theory and feminist issues in the sociology department at York University. She has published articles in British and Canadian social history, feminist theory, and sexual politics. She is the author of *Sex, Power, and Pleasure* (Toronto: Women's Press 1985) and *The Age of Light, Soap, and Water: Moral Reform in English Canada, 1885–1925* (Toronto: McClelland and Stewart 1991).

CYNTHIA WRIGHT is a doctoral candidate at the Ontario Institute for Studies in Education, where she is finishing her thesis on Eaton's College Street store. She has taught women's studies at the University of Toronto and works part-time in the Archives of the Law Society of Upper Canada.

Introduction

Consider this scene from the past. A Salvation Army preacher in a red silk dress, leading a revival meeting in a small Ontario town in the 1890s. The sight of this working-class 'girl' addressing a crowd of emotionally charged youths is sufficiently provocative to evoke the stern disapproval of the local gentry. Another scene, also in small-town Ontario, occurs in a courtroom. Here, too, a woman is the centre of attention as her father, having determined to bring an end to his daughter's sexual liaison with a boarder, lays criminal charges of 'seduction' against him. How different this courtroom drama from the celebrated trial of Clara Ford, a 'mulatto' seamstress acquitted of murdering the son of a prominent Toronto family despite an earlier confession in police court. In this scene, set in 1895, Ford performs brilliantly on the witness stand and her lawyer convinces an all-white, all-male jury that a black woman who shoots a rich white man should be set free.

Although Ford won her case, her race had excited considerable commentary. Twenty years later, in 1912, concerns about race as well as class prompted the feminists of the Women's Political League, a Toronto suffrage organization, to refuse an invitation to support striking Jewish immigrant women at Eaton's garment factory in the city. While claiming sympathy for the 'girls,' these middle-class Anglo-Saxon women remained unwilling to risk tarnishing the suffrage cause for 'only a strike of Jews.' In contrast, social workers employed in an immigrant aid agency in Toronto tried to avoid pandering to the racism of their day when, in 1958, they suppressed a sexual assault case involving a Hungarian refugee who had raped a female compatriot living in the same boarding-house. Assuming that such publicity would only encourage anti-immigrant sentiment, the caseworkers bought the woman's silence, offering her better housing in exchange for not pressing charges.

These scenarios were set in social arenas that women inhabited but about which we still know very little: the revival meeting, the courtroom, the social worker's office. The women present contrasting and conflicting images that speak to the diversity of the Canadian female experience. They were women from different class, racial/ethnic, and religious backgrounds whose behaviour was not always exemplary. By hinting at the wide array of relationships that women either forged or were thrust into, the incidents also shed light on the crucial role played by gender relations – that is, the formation of femininity, masculinity, and the relations between these two constructs – in shaping people's lives in the past.

These images, and many others, emerge in this collection of articles in the history of women in English Canada. Taken together, the essays represent some of the new directions in Canadian women's history, tackling such hitherto neglected fields as heterosexual relations among rural youth, bourgeois women and the rise of the department store, immigrant women's experience of violence, and the racial politics of Anglo-Saxon feminists. The essays explore what we call gender conflicts. By this we mean not only the conflicts and tensions that characterized relations between men and women, but also conflicts among women of different racial, class, and cultural backgrounds. These tensions historically have resulted in various groups of women having different and, at times, conflicting gender experiences. The articles also help to fill some glaring gaps in various sister subdisciplines – the histories of religion, labour, and the left, politics, business and consumption, intellectual life, crime and the law, and immigration – as well as contribute to a fuller understanding of gender relations. We hope they offer a point of departure for integrating women's history into mainstream history.

Some of the most exciting recent work in social history has been in the history of women and of gender relations. Over the past two decades, the writing of women's history in Canada has flourished and the field itself has undergone profound changes as scholars have continually discovered new topics, explored new sources, and raised new issues and questions. Like most recent work in the field, the essays in this volume owe a great debt to the contributions made by feminist historians in Canada who, during the 1970s and early 1980s, produced a vast amount of scholarship in women's history. Heavily influenced by the new social history, with its emphasis on recording the lives of ordinary people and writing history 'from the bottom up,' and bolstered by a vibrant women's movement, women's historians writing in that period sought to break away from the older, male defined tradition of history, with its focus on war and diplomacy, elitist institutions, and male heroes and 'nationbuilders.' In so doing, they faced hostility and contempt from many within the academy, and were repeatedly told that the topics they had chosen were trivial and the sources unavailable. Their persistence and devotion to feminist projects need to be recalled now that at least some universities have been forced to pay attention to women's history in hirings and in course offerings.[1]

Many of the earlier studies of women in Canada detailed the rise of women's reform-oriented organizations and women's political struggles to gain entry into the professions and to secure the vote. These discoveries of women long hidden from history were significant in themselves, but they also encouraged further research in the field. That the work on first-wave feminism in Canada continues to generate enormous debate among scholars in this country – a debate continued here with Mariana Valverde's analysis of the racial notions underlying the sexual politics of first-wave feminism – is a testament to the importance of the groundwork in women's history.[2]

Few people, however, would dispute the claim that from the

start women's history in Canada revealed a strong preoccupation with articulate, white, middle-class women. This was by no means a uniquely Canadian perspective. American and British historians of women began in this period to produce a largely white and middle-class women's history, and in this, as in other areas of Canadian intellectual life, Canadians were strongly influenced by the politics and methods of our colleagues in more powerful countries. But the biases, even if largely imported, also reflected the predominant class and ethnicity of the practitioners who dominated the field in its early stages as well as the relative accessibility of sources. The written records left behind by well-educated women – political speeches, recorded minutes of organizational meetings, private diaries and letters – offered a comparatively straightforward entry into the lives of some women.[3]

And yet, even while it is true that the field has been, and in some respects continues to be, characterized by certain liberal and middle-class biases, it is also true that from its origins women's history in Canada attracted scholars with diverse forms of feminist politics. It incorporated some innovative research on women who fell outside the mainstream, such as native women in fur-trade society,[4] farm women, and working-class women and girls. In considering working women, scholars were influenced by labour history and by traditions of historical materialism. By a careful charting of women's paid work and their unpaid labours within the household, feminists sought to explore the lives of working-class and poor women who left few written records and who might never have captured the public eye. In recent years, working-class women have received far greater attention than in the past.[5]

By the early 1980s, feminist historians had laid a firm intellectual and political foundation for the writing of women's history in this country. Without such a foundation, our current research would not be possible. Earlier feminist scholarship presented the first real challenge to the profession and, moreover, helped to create an intellectual and social environment conducive to doing women's history in the academy. However, even though overt hostility to feminist history may have waned or been disguised during the last decade, a recent survey of history departments shows that most male faculty are convinced that women's history already has everything it needs, but that their women colleagues generally believe that a great deal must be done to rectify institutional marginalization. Women graduate students doing feminist research similarly experience hostility, as another recent survey shows.[6]

In opening up the field of women's history, feminist scholars felt compelled to emphasize the contributions of women in the past. In the process, however, their work at times neglected the class bias and xenophobic views and practices of some of the women they studied. This was particularly true of many studies of middle-class suffragists and first-wave feminists. Here, there was a tendency to see a racist ideology as a minor slip in an otherwise progressive platform. Similarly, in earlier studies of working-class women, little attention was paid to immigrant and minority women who composed a significant proportion of the female working classes.[7]

Like any discipline, however, history is an evolving one and, as part of this evolution, the range of topics being explored by feminist and gender-conscious historians in Canada, as elsewhere, has expanded enormously in recent years. As scholars today delve into new topics and ask broader questions about gender, they are enlarging the parameters of the subdiscipline. In many cases, their research is informed by contemporary debates and international perspectives, and thus they are bringing into the discipline of history methodological and theoretical insights from other fields.[8] That some of the contributors to this volume are not strictly speaking historians is perhaps a sign of the times: scholars trained in related disciplines, such as political science, sociology, and cultural studies, are doing historical research, while many historians are sympathetic to interdisciplinary perspectives. Feminist historians from working-class and non-Anglo-Saxon backgrounds have also opened up new areas of research, including the study of minority women and feminist analyses of racism and anti-immigrant sentiment.[9]

All this activity has led us to approach the issue of femininity from new angles, by considering alternative sources and moving beyond the narrow confines of women on the political stage, in the factory, or in the household. Certainly, the labour market, the family household, and the political arena remain key areas for gender formation. However, as the essays presented here reveal, there is a great deal more to Canadian women's lives than work, the family, and formal politics. The experiences of women who did not live within family households, the organization of working-class women's leisure pursuits and religious activity, and the work/pleasure of consumption are all relatively new areas for feminist history. In this collection, Lynne Marks's paper shows the central role played by religion in many young women's lives and the way in which revivalist religion combined culture, leisure, and piety. Karen Dubinsky's examination of courtship patterns in rural and small-town Ontario and Cynthia Wright's analysis of the department store are also innovative studies of previously neglected 'female worlds.' Studying such fields involves tapping unconventional sources, such as court records and department-store floor plans.

Using new sources, as well as asking new questions of old sources, has made it possible to analyse the shifting interactions among race/ethnicity, class, and gender as objective structural factors and as subjective meanings. In women's history, class and race have been generally regarded as important for the study of working-class and immigrant women, native and black women, and other women of colour. Indeed, some of the essays presented here offer new research in the history of immigrant and refugee women. More importantly, however, although not all the essays specifically deal with racial or ethnic minority women, all use class and race or ethnicity as analytical categories. We want to suggest with our essays that, just as gender is equally, though distinctly, constitutive for men and women, so, too, class and race or ethnicity inform the lives of all women, including those of the relatively privileged. This is seen, for example, in Wright's consideration of the role of upscale department stores like Eaton's in the formation, through the culture of consumption, of a Canadian femininity with a specifically bourgeois character. In noting the class bias of Canadian women's history, we are not suggesting that middle-class white women have received too much attention from historians, but, rather, that their experiences should be analysed rather than celebrated.

Nor do we want to supplant the old model of middle-class heroines and working-class victims with a heroic model of working-class women. Without creating romanticized pictures of immigrant and working-class women, we want to suggest some of the ways in which those with limited power could nevertheless find ways of exercising a measure of control over their own and others' lives. Even socialist women, Janice Newton shows, were often limited in their politics by their race and class. Garment workers of both sexes, argues Ruth Frager, seldom managed to transcend racial (in this case, Jewish/gentile), gender, and political splits within the working class. It also has to be acknowledged that some working-class women could behave in manipulative and questionable ways. Especially to the point is Carolyn Strange's essay, which details how male-centred discourses on chivalry in the courts could facilitate the acquittal of female killers. Such a manoeuvre raises questions about the nature of oppression and of agency, and makes it impossible to generalize about 'bad guys' and 'good girls.' For their part, Franca Iacovetta and Karen Dubinsky show that, while rural and immigrant/refugee women were oppressed by state structures (the criminal courts, in Dubinsky's study, and the welfare apparatus, in Iacovetta's), not all of the women who appear in their records were paragons of virtue.

We resist creating heroines of any type. Indeed, in this collection we gladly abandon the unfruitful model that counterposes research on heroines (whether middle-class suffragists or working-class strikers) to research documenting the implacable force of socioeconomic structures. We are more interested in showing that generalizations about universal oppression or about glorious resistance erase the complexity of women's (and men's) lived experiences. The problem is disguised rather than solved by historians who merely juxtapose descriptions of structures of domination with examples of resistance, a tendency evident in the writings of some working-class historians.[10] The inadequacies of this juxtaposition suggest a need to rethink our fundamental assumptions about social power and human agency. Whether one accepts the philosophical challenge mounted by Foucault and other Nietzschean thinkers (and introduced into historians' discussion by Joan Scott and others),[11] it is timely and useful for historians to critique the assumption that power and resistance are located in distinct and mutually exclusive social sites. Power does not flow from a single source, and it is not the exclusive domain of those who are 'powerful.' While capital, patriarchy, Anglo-Saxon supremacy, and the state are the basic structures of oppression shaping the social relations analysed in this book, the actions of women or of labour often involve the operations of what one might call 'subpowers.' If we have learned anything definite from twenty years of women's history, it is that not all agency on the part of the oppressed can be characterized as resistance. Seeing the people we study as subjects does not imply celebrating them as morally pure. The historical past is far too complex, and people's lives shot through with too many contradictions and ambiguities, to be easily captured by this tired dichotomy of top-down domination versus bottom-up resistance.

These concerns lead us to another central issue: the way in which writing women's history can take us beyond the study of the subject 'woman' and provide us with analytical tools for exploring social relations as a whole. For example, Dubinsky's analysis of criminal prosecutions for seduction describes the 'female world' of courtship, but it also covers masculine discourses on honour, the role of geography in shaping sexual experience, and rural versus urban patterns in relations between children and parents. Similarly, Newton's study of women on the left goes beyond asking 'What did the left do for/to women?' and focuses attention instead on subtle processes of gender, such as the masculinization of socialism through its rejection of temperance.[12] The new feminist scholarship is continuing to map the majority's past, but it is simultaneously revising and critiquing sister subdisciplines, such as immigration history, cultural history, or the history of crime. We aim not only at a more complete history of women but also at developing feminist analyses in all areas of historical research.

As Gisela Bock notes in the lead article in the first issue of the journal *Gender and History*, women's history holds the possibility of doing much more than recovering a history of women's past lives. It can shed light on gender relations and provide new understandings of general history.[13] In Canada, the existing research has also revealed that women's lives are no less rich or complex than men's, and that women's lives do not necessarily share the same rhythms.

While we wholeheartedly agree that women's history is a legitimate field, it would be unfortunate to see the study of women and gender confined to a ghetto, while non-feminist historians (both male and female) pursue their 'mainstream' studies of labour, immigration, politics, culture, and so on. We have already seen that happen; in Canada, women's history has been isolated as a subdiscipline. Women's history, if it is to have a profound and irrevocable impact, cannot be isolated, as Gisela Bock suggests. For this reason, we aim at the integration of feminist perspectives into all subdisciplines and even other disciplines. As Wright notes, existing studies of the business of department stores in Canada barely mention women, and her piece can be seen as an attempt to rewrite business history as well as to describe women's role in consumption. Similarly, the essays by Frager, Iacovetta, and Valverde all suggest the importance of feminist perspectives to the study of immigration and race relations. Strange's work demonstrates that an integrated analysis of race, class, and gender is necessary to understand crime and the courts, while Marks locates her work at the intersection of the history of religion, working-class history, and women's history. Newton's article, finally, shows that the left, like other social movements, was gendered all the way through, even when 'the women question' was not on the formal agenda. As a whole, these articles pose challenging questions for Canadian history, not only for women's history.

We are thus committed both to enriching women's history and to encouraging feminist-minded scholarship on social relations that do not easily fit into the category of 'women.' Internationally, feminist historians have developed the concept of gender history as a way of making similar claims.[14] The purpose of gender history is to understand all social relations as gendered – which is very different from the search for previously neglected subjects. Gender history is a challenge both to women's history as first developed two decades ago and to traditional history, which can now be seen as men's history without an awareness of masculinity. Gender history does not avoid the study of wars or diplomacy, but it does suggest that the social construction of masculinity is a necessary concept in the full understanding of military or diplomatic history. Similarly, while some work has been done on relations among immigrant men or among male co-workers, the emphasis has been on the utility of these relations to the ethnic group or the class, and not on the organization of masculinity.[15]

We intend this collection as a contribution to this new agenda and, indeed, many of the essays are innovative in their understanding of the masculine social relations of honour and chivalry. We share Bock's concern, however, that 'gender history' may become a fashionable euphemism used by those who shun the study of women from a feminist perspective. We thus want to emphasize explicitly (as the essays do implicitly) that for us gender history is a deepening of the analysis already carried out by women's history, not a less political, more fashionable diversion.

Just as women's history was earlier shaped by issues and concerns raised by the women's movement of the 1960s and 1970s, feminist history today is informed by the present women's movement. Much of the interest in race or ethnicity and class, or in the history of sexuality, for instance, is grounded in current political discussions and debates. The impact of such debates on the writing of women's history in North America is clearly evident in the recent American text, *Unequal Sisters: A Multicultural Reader in U.S. Women's History*, edited by Ellen Carol DuBois and Vicki L. Ruiz (New York and London: Routledge 1990). All the contributors to *Gender Conflicts* share a basic commitment to a socialist, feminist, and anti-racist politic. In terms of field of study, methodology, and commitment to empirical research or theory, there is a great diversity in this collection, one we believe is healthy and productive. Underlying this diversity, however, is a commonality of political and ethical purpose, a common commitment to justice for all oppressed groups (not just women) that has kept us together as each other's trusted critics and colleagues.

As a group, we have reflected some of the recent changes that have taken place in the women's movement and among historians. When some of us began meeting in Janice Newton's kitchen in 1984, we were concerned with the struggles of working-class, labour, and left women. As time went on, and as new members joined the group and helped redefine its agenda, our interests expanded to include the fields described above.

It is this history of many years of reading and commenting on each other's work that explains the composition of the book, and in particular explains the Ontario focus of most of the articles. Apart from the glaring geographical bias of the collection, there are other omissions that are due to the idiosyncrasies of our group's membership. For instance, there are no articles that deal explicitly with state formation, even though this is a major area in the new feminist scholarship.[16] Work by and about women of colour (native, black, and Asian) would, of course, have been included if this were a 'representative' anthology.

This book reflects the collective discussions and preoccupations of one particular group of feminist scholars in Toronto with different disciplinary perspectives but sharing a history and a vision. We would like to acknowledge that some women formed part of this group for a significant length of time and contributed research, criticism, and food: Kathy Arnup, Joan Sangster, and Marg Hobbs. We hope that they, and the women and men across the country who see themselves as part of the new generation of gender-conscious social historians, will regard this volume, despite its flaws and omissions, as contributing to a broad-based collective effort to invigorate Canadian scholarship, and hence as more than the peculiar obsessions of eight scholars.

Karen Dubinsky, Ruth Frager, Franca Iacovetta, Lynne Marks, Janice Newton, Carolyn Strange, Mariana Valverde, Cynthia Wright

NOTES

We thank Linda Kealey, Ruth Pierson, and Ian Radforth for their comments on an earlier version of this introduction. Thanks also to Allan Greer and to Gerry Hallowell, Laura Macleod, and Rosemary Shipton of University of Toronto Press.

1 With the exception of Veronica Strong-Boag, *The Parliament of Women: The National Council of Women of Canada 1893–1929* (Ottawa: National Museum of Man 1976), Carol Lee Bacchi, *Liberation Deferred? The Ideas of the English-Canadian Suffragists, 1877–1918* (Toronto: University of Toronto Press 1983), and Ruth Roach Pierson, *'They're Still Women after All': The Second World War and Canadian Womanhood* (Toronto: McClelland and Stewart 1986), most published works in English-Canadian women's history have, until recently, appeared as journal articles and essays in edited collections. Widely used anthologies include Susan Mann Trofimenkoff and Alison Prentice, eds., *The Neglected Majority: Essays in Canadian Women's History*, vols. 1 and 2 (Toronto: McClelland and Stewart 1977 and 1985); Linda Kealey, ed., *A Not Unreasonable Claim: Women and Reform in Canada 1880–1920s* (Toronto: Women's Press 1979); Barbara Latham and Cathy Less, eds., *In Her Own Right: Selected Essays on Women's History in B.C.* (Victoria, BC: Camosun College 1980); and Joy Parr, ed., *Childhood and Family in Canadian History* (Toronto: McClelland and Stewart 1982). Recent additions include Veronica Strong-Boag and Anita Clair Fellman, eds., *Rethinking Canada: The Promise of Women's History* (Toronto: Copp Clark Pitman 1986; 2nd ed. 1991); Mary Kinnear, ed., *First Days, Fighting Days: Women in Manitoba History* (Regina: Canadian Plains Research Centre 1986); Linda Kealey and Joan Sangster, eds., *Beyond the Vote: Canadian Women and Politics* (Toronto: University of Toronto Press 1989).

There has also been a proliferation of bibliographies, such as Beth Light and Veronica Strong-Boag, *True Daughters of the North: Canadian Women's History: An Annotated Bibliography* (Toronto: OISE Press 1980), and collections of historical documents intended as teaching tools and as guides to facilitate further research. These collections include Ramsay Cook and Wendy Mitchinson, eds., *The Proper Sphere: Women's Place in Canadian Society* (Toronto: Oxford University Press 1976); Alison Prentice and Beth Light, eds., *Pioneers and Gentlewomen* (Toronto: New Hogtown Press 1980); Joy Parr and Beth Light, eds., *Canadian Women on the Move 1867–1920* (Toronto: New Hogtown Press 1983); and, most recently, Ruth Roach Pierson and Beth Light, eds., *No Easy Road 1920s–60s* (Toronto: New Hogtown Press 1990).

2 For contrasting interpretations of first-wave feminism see Strong-Boag, *Parliament of Women*; her ' "Ever a Crusader": Nellie McClung, First-Wave Feminist,' in Strong-Boag and Fellman, eds., *Rethinking Canada*; T.R. Morrison, ' "Their Proper Sphere": Feminism, the Family, and Child-Centred Social Reform in Ontario, 1875–1900,' in *Ontario History* (1976); Bacchi, *Liberation Deferred?* and the essays in L. Kealey, ed., *A Not Unreasonable Claim.*

3 A valuable discussion of these themes is in Ruth Roach Pierson, 'Experience, Difference, Dominance and Voice in the Writing of Canadian Women's History,' in Karen Offen, Ruth Roach Pierson, and Jane Rendall, eds., *Writing Women's History: International Perspectives* (London: Macmillan 1991). See also the introduction in Ellen Carol DuBois and Vicki L. Ruiz, eds., *Unequal Sisters: A Multicultural Reader in U.S. Women's History* (New York and London: Routledge 1991).

4 Sylvia Van Kirk, *Many Tender Ties: Women in Fur-Trade Society in Western Canada, 1700–1850* (Winnipeg: Watson and Dwyer 1980); Jennifer S.H. Brown, *Strangers in Blood: Fur Trade Company Families in Indian Country* (Vancouver: University of British Columbia Press 1980). More recent work on native women includes Alicja Muszynski, 'Race and Gender: Structural Determinants in the Formation of the British Columbia Salmon Cannery Labour Force,' in G.S. Kealey, ed., *Class, Gender and Region: Essays in Canadian Historical Sociology* (St John's: Committee on Canadian Labour History 1988); Mary Crnkovich, ed., *Gossip: A Spoken History of Women in the North* (Ottawa: Canadian Artic Resources Committee 1990).

5 Widely cited earlier works, all but one of them articles, include the essays in Janice Acton et al., eds., *Women at Work, Ontario 1850–1930* (Toronto: Canadian Women's Educational Press 1974); D. Suzanne Cross, 'The Neglected Majority: The Changing Role of Women in 19th Century Montreal,' originally in *Social History/Histoire sociale* (1973) and reprinted in Prentice and Trofimenkoff, eds., *Neglected Majority* vol. 1; Ruth Pierson, 'Women's Emancipation and the Recruitment of Women into the Labour Force in World War II,' in Prentice and Trofimenkoff,

eds., *Neglected Majority*; Wayne Roberts, *Honest Womanhood: Feminism, Femininity and Class Consciousness among Toronto Working Women, 1896–1914* (Toronto: New Hogtown Press 1977); Joan Sangster, 'The 1907 Bell Telephone Strike: Organizing Women Workers,' *Labour/Le Travailleur* 3 (1978); Bettina Bradbury, 'The Family Economy and Work in an Industrializing City: Montreal in the 1870s,' *Historical Papers* (1979); Veronica Strong-Boag, 'The Girl of the New Day: Canadian Working Women in the 1920s,' *Labour/Le Travail* 4 (1979); Marilyn Barber, 'The Women Ontario Welcomed: Immigrant Domestics for Ontario Homes,' originally in *Ontario History* (1980) and reprinted in Prentice and Trofimenkoff, eds., *Neglected Majority* vol. 2; and the monograph, Joy Parr, *Labouring Children: British Immigrant Apprentices to Canada, 1869–1924* (London: Croom Helm 1980). For a valuable discussion of studies on working-class women's paid and unpaid labours published after 1980 see Bettina Bradbury, 'Women's History and Working Class History,' *Labour/Le Travail* 19 (1987); and the new essays reprinted in the second edition of Strong-Boag and Fellman, eds., *Rethinking Canada* (1991). On farm women see Linda Rasmussen et al., *A Harvest Yet To Reap: A History of Prairie Women* (Toronto: Women's Press 1976); Marjorie Cohen, *Women's Work, Markets, and Economic Development in Nineteenth-Century Ontario* (Toronto: University of Toronto Press 1988); and Veronica Strong-Boag, 'Pulling in Double Harness or Hauling a Double Load: Women, Work and Feminism on the Canadian Prairies,' *Journal of Canadian Studies* 21:3 (fall 1986).

6 Linda Kealey, 'Women Historians in Canadian Universities: A Report on the Canadian Historical Association Survey,' *Canadian Historical Review* 72:3 (1991); Lykke de la Cour et al., ' "Here's Where We Separate the Men from the Boys": Comments on Women's Experiences as Students in Graduate History Programmes in Canada,' paper presented to the Canadian Historical Association Annual Conference, University of Victoria, 1990.

7 It has only been in the past few years that the history of immigrant women, particularly non-British women, has attained a greater profile. The books and special journal issues that have helped to fill a long-existing lacuna include Jean Burnet, ed., *Looking into My Sister's Eyes* (Toronto: Multicultural History Society of Ontario 1986); Varpu Lindström-Best, *Defiant Sisters: A Social History of Finnish Immigrant*

Women in Canada (Toronto: Multicultural History Society of Ontario
1988); Makeda Silvera, *Silenced* (Toronto: Williams-Wallace 1983); special issues on immigrant and refugee women and women of colour in
Resources for Feminist Research 16:1 (1987); *Canadian Woman Studies* 8:2
(1985) and 10:1 (1989); *Polyphony* 8:1–2 (1986). See also Tamara Adil-
man, 'A Preliminary Sketch of Chinese Women and Work in British
Columbia 1858–1920,' in Barbara K. Latham and Roberta J. Pazdro,
eds., *Not Just Pin Money: Selected Essays on the History of Women's Work in
British Columbia* (Victoria, BC: Camosun College 1984); Frances Swyripa,
'The Ideas of the Ukrainian Women's Organization of Canada,' in
Kealey and Sangster, eds., *Beyond the Vote;* and Ruth Frager, 'Politicized
Housewives in the Jewish Communist Movement of Toronto,
1923–1933,' in Kealey and Sangster, eds., *Beyond the Vote.*
8 Even a brief list indicates the diversity of topics – ranging from life-
cycle approaches, to the history of medicine and sexuality, and to the
law and the criminal courts – that scholars have recently pursued. For
example, see Veronica Strong-Boag, *The New Day Recalled: Lives of Girls
and Women in English Canada* (Toronto: Copp Clark Pitman 1988); Angus McLaren and Arlene Tigar McLaren, *The Bedroom and the State: The
Changing Practices and Politics of Contraception and Abortion in Canada,
1880–1980* (Toronto: McClelland and Stewart 1987); James G. Snell, *In
the Shadow of the Law: Divorce in Canada, 1900–1939* (Toronto: University
of Toronto Press 1991); Wendy Mitchinson, *The Nature of Their Bodies;
Women and Their Doctors in Victorian Canada* (Toronto: University of Toronto Press 1991); Constance Backhouse, 'Involuntary Motherhood:
Abortion, Birth Control and the Law in 19th Century Canada,' *Windsor
Yearbook of Access to Justice* 3 (1983), and *Petticoats and Prejudice: Women
and Law in Nineteenth Century Canada* (Toronto: Women's Press 1991);
Carolyn Strange, 'From Modern Babylon to City upon a Hill: The Toronto Social Survey Commission of 1915 and the Search for Sexual Order in the City,' in Roger Hall, William Westfall, and Laurel Sefton
MacDowell, eds., *Patterns of the Past: Interpreting Ontario's History* (Toronto: Dundurn Press 1988); Mariana Valverde, *The Age of Light, Soap,
and Water: Moral Reform in English Canada, 1885–1925* (Toronto: Mc-
Clelland and Stewart 1991); Judith Fingard, *The Dark Side of Life in Victorian Halifax* (Porters Lake: Pottersfield Press 1989); Katherine Arnup,
Andrée Levesque, and Ruth Roach Pierson, eds., *Delivering Motherhood:*

Maternal Ideologies and Practices in the Nineteenth and Twentieth Centuries (London and New York: Routledge 1990); and Marianne G. Ainley, ed., *Despite the Odds: Essays on Canadian Women and Science* (Montreal: Véhicule Press 1989).

9 In Canadian as well as American historiography, anti-immigrant views and practices are usually described as nativism, a term coined by John Higham in his pioneer study, *Strangers in the Land: Patterns of American Nativism 1860–1925* (New York: Atheneum 1973). We suggest, however, that this term can perpetuate the construction of white Anglo-Saxons as the true 'natives' of North America, a construction which ideologically obscures the process of conquest. (To give but one example: the Methodist church for many decades categorized its missions to native peoples under 'foreign' rather than 'domestic' missions, a classification that speaks volumes.) 'Racism' and 'racial politics' are terms which, in the Canadian context, are useful not only to analyse black-white or native-white conflicts but also to examine French-English or Anglo-Saxon versus 'ethnic' conflicts, since these conflicts among peoples who are not necessarily of different colours have often been felt by the participants to be indeed racial.

10 For example, see Bryan D. Palmer, *A Culture in Conflict: Skilled Workers and Industrial Capitalism in Hamilton, Ontario, 1860–1914* (Montreal: McGill-Queen's University Press 1979).

11 For a discussion of these issues in the Canadian context see Mariana Valverde, 'Poststructuralist Gender Historians: Are We Those Names?' *Labour/Le Travail* 25 (1990).

12 Valuable studies on left woman include Linda Kealey, 'Canadian Socialism and the Woman Question, 1900–1914,' *Labour/Le Travail* 13 (1984); Janice Newton, 'Women and *Cotton's Weekly*: A Study of Women and Socialism in Canada, 1909,' *Resources for Feminist Research* 8 (1980); Frager, 'Politicized Housewives'; Joan Sangster, *Dreams of Equality: Women on the Canadian Left, 1920–1950* (Toronto: McClelland and Stewart 1989).

13 Gisela Bock, 'Women's History and Gender History: Aspects of an International Debate,' *Gender & History* 1 (1989).

14 For a Canadian work in this new tradition of gender history see especially Joy Parr, *The Gender of Breadwinners: Women, Men, and Change in Two Industrial Towns, 1880–1950* (Toronto: University of Toronto Press 1990). This book examines the work and family lives of female factory

workers in Paris, Ontario, as well as the ways in which masculine gender formation shaped management-labour relations in the all-male workplaces of Hanover, Ontario.

15 A recent, excellent study of masculinity in the Canadian context is Mark Rosenfeld, '"It was a hard life": Class and Gender in the Work and Family Rhythms of a Railway Town 1920–1950,' *Historical Papers* 1988. Little attention has been paid to the masculinity of immigrant men. For a consideration of this issue with respect to one group, working-class Italians, see, for example, Robert F. Harney's 'Men without Women: Italian Migrants in Canada, 1885–1930,' in Betty Boyd Caroli et al., eds., *The Italian Immigrant Woman in North America* (Toronto: Multicultural History Society of Ontario 1978), which predates the development of gender history or studies of masculinity, and, more recently, Franca Iacovetta, *Such Hardworking People: Italian Immigrants in Postwar Toronto* (Montreal and Kingston: McGill-Queen's University Press 1992).

16 Recent Canadian examples of research in this field include Ruth Roach Pierson, 'Gender and the Unemployment Insurance Debates in Canada, 1934–1940,' *Labour/Le Travail* 25 (1990); Lykke de la Cour, Cecilia Morgan, and Mariana Valverde, 'Gender and State Formation in Nineteenth-Century Canada,' in Allan Greer and Ian Radforth, eds., *Colonial Leviathan: State Formation in Mid-Nineteenth-Century Canada* (Toronto: University of Toronto Press 1992).

GENDER CONFLICTS

1 'When the Mother of the Race Is Free':

Race, Reproduction, and Sexuality in First-Wave Feminism

Mariana Valverde

That the vast majority of English-speaking first-wave feminists were not only ethnocentric but often racist is by now widely acknowledged. It is also acknowledged that this led to the exclusion of native women, immigrant women, and women of colour from a movement which claimed to be based on gender, with negative political consequences reverberating into our own day.[1] Racist strategies were not confined to situations in which topics such as immigration were directly at issue: they were integral to the movement as a whole. An aspect of this pervasive racial politic that has seldom been examined is the way in which racist assumptions and strategies were implicated in the reproductive and sexual politics of the movement. Because women without children or husbands, as well as those in traditional family situations, justified their claims to political and social rights by reference to their quasi-maternal public and private roles, ideas about sexuality and reproduction had an impact on all women, regardless of individual situations. The purpose of this article is thus to undertake a critical analysis of the racial specificity of that key figure in our past, 'the mother of the race,' and of the discourses on sex and reproduction within which this symbolic figure was constructed.

While most first-wave feminists believed that women deserved political and social rights as a matter of equal justice, they also used utilitarian and organicist arguments that grounded women's cause in an affirmation of their role in biological and social reproduction. In this sense, the conceptualization of women's work in reproduction was key to feminism as a whole. While today feminists tend to analyse reproductive politics in terms of individual women's rights and collective gender oppression, at the turn of the century reproduction was generally seen, by feminists as well as anti-feminists, as inextricable from racial and imperial politics.[2] Women did not merely have babies: they reproduced 'the race.' Women did not merely have just enough babies or too much sex: through their childbearing they either helped or hindered the forward march of (Anglo-Saxon) civilization.[3] Phrases such as 'race suicide,' or, in a feminist context, 'mothers of the race,' organize sexuality and reproduction under racial categories. Feminists challenged the sexist elements of the evolutionary theories of Darwin, Spencer, and other scientific and social Darwinists, but they did not, with one or two exceptions, question the fundamental racism of mainstream theories of social and biological evolution, and in many ways they reinforced racist theories of biological and social progress by adopting them for feminist purposes.

The international feminist debate on race, gender, sex, and reproduction was well publicized in English-Canadian feminist circles: Charlotte Perkins Gilman, Elizabeth Blackwell, and Frances Willard were widely respected and frequently quoted – more so than any homegrown feminist, in fact. The history of Canadian feminism has until the present been researched basically as a Canadian phenomenon, but first-wave feminism had an international dimension and some of its aspects – particularly its intellectual history – have to be understood in this international context.

The Meanings of 'Race' in International Feminist Thought

'The great menace to the race is the bar-room and its brood of ills in direct line with drinking customs [and] social impurity in all its forms.'[4]

That the ambiguity of the term 'race' provided a space in which silently (or not so silently) to deploy the racial privilege of white women seeking gender justice is clearly seen in the writings of Elizabeth Blackwell (1821–1910). Usually known only as the world's first woman physician, Blackwell was an important thinker and leader in both the feminist and the social purity movements, developing a thoroughly feminist and racist philosophy of sexuality that was influential in both movements. An Englishwoman educated in the United States and well known on both sides of the Atlantic, Blackwell believed there were two fundamental principles underlying human existence: first, the independence and perfection of the individual and, second, 'the preservation of the race.'[5] Blackwell elaborated the first principle, individual independence, in the political context of struggles to give women more autonomy over their bodies; it is clearly part of a long tradition that extends from Mary Wollstonecraft to today's pro-choice movement. The second principle, however, is more historically specific: Blackwell, like most anglophone intellectuals of her day, believed that reproduction, and therefore sexuality, were not only individual choices but collective and, more particularly, racial problems. In some cases racial progress took precedence over individual desire: for instance, she would counsel individuals of different races to refrain from expressing mutual sexual attraction because the 'congress of different races' will result in 'racial injury.'[6]

The obvious question to ask about such phrases as 'racial injury' or 'menace to the race' (as in the Canadian quote cited above) is whether 'race' means the human race, all people of a particular colour, or an ethnic group. The answer is complex, because 'race' meant different things simultaneously. The layers and ambiguities of meaning, far from demonstrating confusion, helped to legitimize and at the same time obscure the mechanisms of racial and imperial power.

In turn-of-the-century Anglo-Saxon thought, the paradigm of the human 'race' was the Anglo-Saxon Protestant ruling bloc, with other groups (from the Irish of Manchester to the Zulus of South Africa) being regarded as human only by analogy.[7] These 'others' were human only in so far as they were perceived to share the essentially human feature of rationality, conceived ethnocentrically as the English ability to use reason and morality to master (sic) one's 'base' impulses. John Stuart Mill's assertion that the English were furthest from the state of nature than any other people, and hence had the most 'civilization and discipline,' went unquestioned.[8] This superiority was regarded by most people (apart from a few extreme biological determinists) as rooted not only in genetic purity but also in old social traditions of reason-ableness, self-control, morality, and diligence. Blackwell typically uses a synthesis of hereditarian and environmental arguments when she states that the habits cultivated by reason can overcome heredity, while good genes do not suffice to ensure progress. 'Race after race has perished from blind or wilful ignorance,' she warned, adding that the ignorance that threatens 'the race' can be dispelled through the combination of science and morality implied by the term 'moral reform.'[9]

The feminist claim to control over one's body, to autonomy, is thus in Blackwell's thought linked to performing one's (that is, white women's) duty to 'the race.' Moral autonomy is perceived as an Anglo-Saxon trait. Arguing against the compulsory medical examination of alleged prostitutes, Blackwell does not say that all women need to control their own bodies; rather, she states that 'we should uproot our whole national life, and destroy the characteristics of the Anglo-Saxon race, if we gave up this natural right of sovereignty over our own bodies.'[10] Control over one's own body is thus an Anglo-Saxon women's issue; it would follow that only Anglo-Saxon women are predisposed to feminism. Women of colour are in fact described by Blackwell as either victims or corrupters, or both, but never as active subjects of a cross-racial gender-based feminism. Asian women, for instance, are seen through the mythical lens of 'Orientalism':[11] the 'east' is said to be 'barbarous,' 'polygamous and sensual.'[12] Lumping together all women of colour, and explaining their situation as due to racial characteristics rather than to patriarchy, Blackwell declares, using the imperial 'we': 'We find amongst these races, as the result of their sexual customs, a want of human charity.'[13] Neither Blackwell nor English feminists involved in the campaign to ban the compulsory medical examinations of prostitutes working for the British army in India would have gone as far as to claim that Indian women were so different from English women that they had no rights over their bodies; but the emphasis on the Anglo-Saxon origins of habeas corpus and personal autonomy tends to construct the feminist struggle for legal and physical autonomy as intrinsically Anglo-Saxon. The extensive literature produced by Protestant women's foreign missionary societies tended to construct abuses against Third World women as akin to cruelty against children or animals, and thus as qualitatively different from the self-emancipation sought by Western women.

Racial and class privilege were woven together in arguments, made by feminists as well as anti-feminists, about the similarities between the 'lower' classes and the 'lower' races. Frances Power Cobbe assumed that the popular Anglo-Saxon classification of races, with blacks at the bottom, and groups such as Greeks and Jews in slightly higher spots, indicated a moral as well as a physical 'chain of being'; the racial hierarchy in turn mirrors the English class system. That the upper classes, male as well as female, are morally superior to the working classes is taken for granted in Cobbe's widely read essay 'Wife Torture in England.' Cobbe, who wrote primarily on theological issues but was also a feminist of an elitist, Tory variety, poses the question of wife abuse in such a way as to create disunity among women. Irish and English working-class women are described as follows: 'the women of the class concerned are, some of them woefully [sic] unwomanly, slatternly, coarse, foul-mouthed – sometimes loose in behaviour, sometimes madly addicted to drink. There ought to be no idealising of them, as a class.'[14]

Evolution and Race 'Degeneration'

When the mother of the race is free, we shall have a better world, by the easy right of birth and by the calm, slow, friendly forces of social evolution.[15]
Charlotte Perkins Gilman

It was an article of faith among the Anglo-Saxon ruling classes in England, the United States, and English Canada that the ambiguous entity 'the race' was, at the turn of the century, in imminent peril of what was equally ambiguously known as 'degeneration.' Feminist intellectuals participated in the debate about who was responsible for degeneration and who was to take a leadership role in 'regeneration,' elaborating complex theories of women and evolution countering the misogynist assumptions of male-stream evolutionists. Feminist evolutionism, however, not only failed to question the racist presuppositions of evolutionary thought, but produced a profoundly racist form of feminism in which women of 'lower' races were excluded from the specifically Anglo-Saxon work of building a better world through the freeing of 'the mother of the race.'

Male evolutionary theorists used sexist assumptions about gender roles in their debates about the mechanisms of natural and sexual selection (mechanisms which, prior to the acceptance of Mendelian genetics in the second quarter of the twentieth century, occasioned much speculation). One of these assumptions was that women did not contribute to natural selection because conservatism was inscribed in their very eggs, while the male sperm was not only quick but 'progressive.' A popular book on heredity stated, in 1883, that 'the male element is the originating and the female the perpetuating factor; the ovum is conservative, the male cell progressive.'[16] The 'male element' was responsible for evolution, because, as it was generally believed, there was more genetic variability among men than among women. Women's bodies were mere storage bins, unable to generate new and potentially progressive mutations. Females were thus portrayed as in an analogous position to the so-called less evolved races – they were dragged along the evolutionary path rather than marching at the head. Darwin himself had drawn a parallel between women's role in evolution and that of 'lower' (that is, less evolved) races: 'It is generally admitted that with women the powers of intuition, of rapid perception, and perhaps of imitation, are more strongly marked than in man; but some, at least, of these faculties are characteristic of the lower races, and therefore of a past and lower state of civilization.'[17]

Women of all races, then, were the passive conservers of past biology. What was in Darwin a description (however invented) quickly became, in the hands of male writers on social evolution, a prescription. Thus, the famous American psychologist, G. Stanley Hall, wrote, in his 1904 magnus opus *Adolescence*, that single (white middle-class) women had a duty to use their scant biological energies for the reproduction of the race, not for the pursuit of careers or other individual goals. Using the discourse of banking, he wrote:

> The bachelor woman is an interesting illustration of Spencer's law of the inverse relation of individuation and genesis. The completely developed individual is always a terminal representative in her line of descent. She has taken up and utilized in her own life all that was meant for her descendants, and has so overdrawn her account with heredity that, like every perfectly and completely developed individual, she is also completely sterile. This is the very apotheosis of selfishness from the standpoint of every biological ethics.[18]

Feminist intellectuals challenged the misogynist consequences of evolutionary theories, but without questioning the overall shape of evolutionary argument or its reliance on racist categories. Olive Schreiner, for instance, questioned Hall's interpretation of the 'New Woman' not be rejecting the concept of women's duty to the race but by claiming that New Women were in fact fulfilling this duty. In polite, defensive tones she wrote:

> In the confusion and darkness of the present, it may well seem to some that woman in her desire to seek for new paths in life is guided only by an irresponsible impulse, or that she seeks selfishly her own good, at the cost of that of the race which she has so long and faithfully borne onward. But, when a clearer future shall have arisen and the obscure mists of the present shall have been dissipated, it may then be manifest that not for herself alone, but for her entire race, has woman sought her new path.[19]

As a South African, Schreiner was less inclined than English or Canadian feminists to forget that there was a difference between the fortunes of the Anglo-Saxon race and the progress of humanity. She believed that different races and cultures demanded different roles for women: simpler societies needed strong women performing social and biological reproduction while men hunted or fought, while modern European culture diminished domestic labour and domestic production and hence allowed, and indeed needed, women's paid work. Despite this attempt at cultural relativism, she nevertheless believed that the situation of white Anglo-Saxon women was of higher world-historical significance than that of women of other times and places: 'We, the European women of this age, stand today where again and again, in the history of the past, women of other races have stood; but our condition is yet more grave, and of wider import to humanity as a whole, than theirs was.'[20]

Schreiner is here countering the sexism of evolutionary theory with the argument that women are indeed leaders in social evolution (a statement without a racial bias); but she is simultaneously tying this feminist view to the deeply ethnocentric belief that European women are the paradigm (and paragon?) of womanhood in general, and that the specifically European women's movement is the vanguard of civilization. European women were regarded, as we saw above, as more morally evolved than other women, and insofar as women's contribution to 'the race' was seen to lie in moral reform and education as well as in childbearing, then it was European women who led both their own race and the human race. Even when Schreiner's careful specification ('We European women') is absent, the ethnocentric social construction of womanhood as moral teacher left no doubt about which women were most suited to lead feminism as well as world progress.

White women's contribution to world progress was not limited to their private role in bringing up their children as good Christians and citizens. Some Protestant women participated in foreign missions with the idea that, as 'mothers of the race,' they had a particular role to play in evangelism, especially in Eastern societies, where sexual segregation, as Ruth Brouwer's study shows, was exaggerated by women missionaries in order to ensure a demand for their services.[21] Women missionaries envisioned Third World women as downtrodden victims of cultural practices more sexist than anything existing in Christian countries. A text written by a man but used by many women's missionary societies stated as a trite fact that 'we have been accustomed to speak of the disabilities of women in India, her degraded position, seclusion and illiteracy. It is true that the women of India have been among the greatest obstacles to progress in that land.'[22] Third World women may have been mothers in their own right, and occasionally they were addressed as 'sisters': but the role assigned to them by the foreign female missionary was really that of devoted daughter, as a missionary poem entitled 'Work in the Zenana' vividly illustrates:

Do you see those dusky faces
Gazing dumbly to the West —
Those dark eyes, so long despairing,
Now aglow with hope's unrest?
They are looking, waiting, longing
For deliverance and light;
Shall we not make haste to help them,
Our poor sisters of the night?[23]

In this poem as well as in countless descriptions of widow-burning and other 'primitive' practices found in missionary and travel literature produced by women,[24] Third World women's own mothering is unacknowledged. Third World women are presented as either too victimized or too corrupt to qualify as real mothers. Rather, they need to be themselves mothered – by wiser Anglo-Saxon Protestant women.

While Canadian women saw their domestic and international mothering in primarily moral terms, some English and American feminists debated anti-feminist male intellectuals on their own terrain. Claiming not just moral but even biological equality or superiority, they tried to turn the discourse of biological evolu-

tion to their own advantage. One of the most systematic attempts
to build a feminist social theory by adapting evolutionism was
made in the United States by Antoinette Brown Blackwell. She
did not challenge the view that women's and men's bodies, and
female and male social abilities, were totally different, admitting
that male and female in each species evolve 'not in parallel but
in adapted diverging lines.'[25] She even admits that men have
larger brains than women; but she argues that for every male
superiority there is a corresponding inferiority. A chart in her
1875 book, *The Sexes throughout Nature*, shows that men are superior in size and strength, but inferior in 'endurance,' 'direct
nurture,' and 'structure' (the latter meaning that women's physical structure is more complex than men's). As a whole, then,
gender traits balance each other, so that although claiming equality for women would be biologically incorrect, the changes due
to evolution have never and will never alter the fundamental
'equivalence' of the genders.[26]

Some English feminists went further than the 'equivalence'
thesis, arguing that women were not simply equivalent but actually superior in the work of social/physical evolution. Frances
Swiney countered male and governmental complaints about middle-class women's role in 'race suicide' with an inventive argument for the moral and biological superiority of women. She
argued that male lust was responsible for the spread of venereal
disease, which in turn was responsible for modern women's physical troubles (including menstrual cramps and the pains of labour); even men not infected with VD were physically harmful
to women because sperm, Swiney believed, was toxic for women
except when women wanted to conceive a child. Women were
thus charged with the sacred mission of evolutionary progress,
and should begin, Swiney counselled, to make eugenic choices
among male partners for reproductive purposes, avoiding heterosexuality at all other times.[27]

The radical suffragette Christabel Pankhurst also argued that
it was men, not women, who were to blame for the sexual excesses
that caused social/racial degeneration, and, like Swiney, she
warned women against sexual contact with males. 'Syphilis is the

prime cause of race degeneration,' Pankhurst stated, criticizing the gender bias of medical men who blamed prostitutes for venereal disease while leaving the concept of race degeneration intact.[28]

Although Swiney's and Pankhurst's radical attacks on male heterosexual privilege were the extreme of the feminist continuum, many feminists who were more orthodox sexually and intellectually contributed to the attempt to turn the panic about racial degeneration to feminist advantage by arguing that it was men, not women, who were, through their vices and their innate lust, hurrying the downfall of the race. Elizabeth Blackwell, for instance, argued in measured tones that 'Nature has laid upon women the more important share in the great work of continuing the race. It is not therefore pity, but justice which requires that reverent and grateful aid should be rendered by men, in the grand duty of creating an even nobler race.'[29]

The feminist critique of the gender bias of evolutionism was a fairly narrow one. The same anti-feminist writers who deplored that college-educated women were not bearing children in large numbers usually also – and often more centrally – used the concept of racial degeneration to attack lawbreakers, the mentally ill, and people of colour. White feminists attacked only the gender bias of evolutionary and eugenic thought, leaving its basic framework intact. This was tantamount to creating a new hierarchy among women, with nefarious consequences for women who were stigmatized and oppressed not only through gender but also through their labelling as 'feeble-minded,' 'unfit,' or 'primitive.' Some women – of 'healthy' middle-class Protestant stock – claimed a spot higher up the evolutionary scale, but the majority of the world's women were in an ambiguous position between hapless victims of their own cultures and active agents of the dreaded process of 'degeneration.'

'Degeneration,' a term originally referring to the decay of nerve tissue, was in the 1880s and 1890s appropriated to refer to wider social processes of decadence and decay. As George Moss and Robert Nye have argued for Germany and for France, respectively, anxieties about urban crime and political upheavals were welded to fears about mad people, criminals, anarchists, and the racially 'other.'[30] There was in particular a fear about the reproductive excesses of 'degenerates,' whose numbers were perceived to be swelling at the expense of those of the more reproductively cautious middle classes.

Sometimes the term 'degeneration' was simply a synonym for 'biologically and morally inferior.' At other times, however, the term had a more specific meaning, and was used primarily to refer to Asian cultures. While Africans were regarded as 'primitive' – as not sufficiently evolved – Asians (most notably the Chinese, but also the vague category of 'Oriental') were seen as belonging to a civilization long past its prime, to a race that was overly evolved, decadent. When Roosevelt described the Chinese as 'an ancient and effete civilization,'[31] while Sir John A. Macdonald labelled them 'a mongrel race,'[32] they were saying that 'the Orient' (which since Marco Polo could hardly be regarded as primitive by Europeans) had had its glorious epoch in the long-ago past, but was now decayed and had lost its virility, just like Oscar Wilde.[33] The North American panic about the role of Chinese men in so-called 'white slavery,' a panic in which feminists played a major role, was justified by reference to this general theory of racial evolution and degeneration. Black men were perceived as primitive, as unable to control their instincts; Chinese men, by contrast, were perceived as decadent perverts in need of opium and other drugs to fuel their flagging sexual energies. These mythological differences account for the varying modes of racist persecution: while black men were constantly suspected of impulsively raping or wanting to rape white women, Chinese men were suspected of hatching intelligent but devious plots, such as luring young white women into apparently harmless 'chop suey palaces' and opium dens, and from there into the 'white slave traffic.' The anti-Chinese and other racist agitations that took place in Canada in the 1920s were legitimized partly through sexual and reproductive myths.[34] Many of these myths were, unfortunately, not challenged but rather supported by Canadian maternal feminists.

Canadian Feminism and the Question of Racial Degeneration

A leading first-wave Canadian feminist, the magistrate and popular writer Emily Murphy, published an exposé of the drug trade entitled *The Black Candle*, which raised the spectre of white women being lured to (perverted) sex through opium. This book, published in 1922, was part of a wider anti-Chinese campaign that was particularly virulent in western Canada. The book's sensationalist pictures of drugged individuals (mostly Chinese men) included a photo of a *black* man apparently in bed with a white woman. The connection between that photo and drug trafficking is not explained, but it is clear that white readers had their anti-black racism fuelled by the book, along with their anti-Chinese prejudices.[35] That Murphy's feminism was designed for white women only is equally clear, since, gender divisions aside, she believed that the 'Nordic' races were inherently superior: 'I think the proximity of the magnetic pole has something to do with the superiority of the Northmen. The best peoples of the world have come out of the north, and the longer they are away from the boreal regions in such proportion do they degenerate.'[36]

Murphy's sense of racial superiority was by no means unique. In the work and discourses of the largest grassroots feminist organization in turn-of-the century Canada, the Woman's Christian Temperance Union (WCTU), one can see that the white ribbon worn by female temperance activists was a symbol not only of the healthy pure milk they would substitute for alcohol but also of the kind of racial composition they favoured for Canada. The WCTU did not, at least in the 1880s and 1890s, exclude women of colour: in fact, there were a few local 'coloured unions' in southern Ontario (whose activities need to be researched by local historians). Nevertheless, the scant mentions of women of colour in the WCTU press are condescending and maternalistic, in keeping, with missionary societies' portrayal of 'natives' in Canada and 'heathens' abroad.

The WCTU was by no means impervious to the new, 'scientific' racism promoted in the later nineteenth century by anthropologists and writers on social evolution, and in the first few decades of the twentieth century by the eugenics movement. As early as 1889, the dominion WCTU had organized a separate department of 'Heredity and Hygiene' which evidenced some activity at least in Ontario and Quebec, where provincial department superintendents produced irregular reports. The Quebec coordinator, Maria G. Craig, explained in July 1891 that the original reason for the department's existence was a concern for the 'hereditary effects of alcohol and tobacco,' but that it quickly broadened its mandate to include 'all hereditary tendencies, the beautiful and the pure as well as diseased conditions.' Craig and her colleagues were not strict biological determinists, however; they put much stress on the need for WCTU members to create healthy environments for their children through healthy food, dress reform, and other elements of what Craig (following Frances Willard) called a 'religion of the body.'[37] An early report from the Ontario Heredity and Hygiene Department also stressed women's, specifically mothers', active agency in shaping children not only through proper childrearing but through 'prenatal influences.'[38] While promoting addresses to local unions by physicians, the leaders of this department were obviously not interested in a strictly determinist view of genetics; such a view would have led to resignation and passivity, or possibly to joining the eugenic campaign for sterilization of the unfit. (The National Council of Women of Canada, a less evangelical and more state-oriented organization, put more work into investigating the 'problem' of 'feeble-minded women.') The WCTU preferred to leave medical and scientific strategies to others; in its own work it promoted a cheerful validation of the ability of Christian mothers to overcome genetic obstacles.[39] In calling on women to 'uplift the race,' the WCTU was arguing that mothers (actual and symbolic) could do a great deal to shape both their children and the future of the nation – a contribution which would have been negated if a strict genetic-determinist argument had been accepted. That women could shape the genetic pool was a necessary premise in the WCTU's argument for political rights: 'Governments rise and fall by votes, and until women have electoral value, their reforms, their labours, their dreams of an uplifted race, a purified country with 'protected' homes, will lack fulfilment.'[40]

The WCTU, however, did not directly challenge biological determinism. Some of their members, such as Mrs (Dr) Wickett, Wentworth County superintendent of heredity and hygiene, were firm believers in the reality of 'race suicide.' She warned that Canadian Anglo-Saxons were in peril of being overcome by the 'less moral' but more prolific French Canadians, 'and all because we women, for various reasons, shrink from the duty and the joy of motherhood.' As wealthy women pursued careers and other selfish goals, 'among the outcast, the feebleminded and the criminal, reproduction will still go on.'[41] It is clear that in Mrs Wickett's eyes not all actual mothers qualify as 'real' mothers.

The WCTU journal's editors sporadically included articles from determinists such as Dr Helen MacMurchy in their journal. In December 1906 MacMurchy, Ontario's superintendent of the feeble-minded and Canada's leading propagandist for the eugenic cause, gave a sensationalistic speech to the Ontario WCTU on the dangers of the 'survival of the unfit,' in order to enlist support for her campaign for the institutionalization of 'feeble-minded' children.[42] The same convention, however, heard long reports on the work of WCTU departments such as social purity eduction, but nothing on the work, if any, of the Heredity and Hygiene Department, so it is possible that MacMurchy's rhetoric met a lukewarm reception.[43]

The strongest call for eugenic measures was heard at the Ontario WCTU 1911 convention, which passed a resolution asking the government to investigate the problem of 'the marriage of moral degenerates'; an editorial in the dominion journal followed this up with a call for compulsory pre-marital medical exams. Even this contribution to the panic about the prolific 'unfit,' however, had a certain ambiguity absent from the work of Canada's scientific racists, in so far as the term 'moral degenerates' was not clearly race-based.[44]

WCTU leaders, then, were aware of developments in genetic and eugenic theory and occasionally endorsed these scientific discourses on race and heredity, but they seemed relatively lukewarm about them, in contrast with the enthusiasm for eugenics shown by Canada's physicians, especially public health doctors. This was not because of the quantity of racism present in eugenics: in 1906 the WCTU journal began to publish inflammatory articles on the vices of immigrant men and their relative worthlessness as voters compared with Anglo-Protestant women, and into the 1920s articles raising the spectre of Jewish control over the liquor trade used anti-Semitism to fuel the fire of prohibition.[45] If the WCTU did not prioritize its 'heredity and hygiene' departments, and even within those departments stressed hygiene over heredity, it was rather because of a conflict between scientific determinism and the WCTU's optimistic evangelism. A typical compromise is found in an editorial entitled 'The Law of Heredity,' published in the same issue in which Dr Helen MacMurchy waxes eloquent on the evils of genetic degeneration. This editorial acknowledges that inherited *tendencies* are important, since it is clear that pipe-smoking fathers, for instance, often have sons who take up the cigarette habit. (Cigarettes were the second most important target of WCTU anger, after alcohol.) After painting a pessimistic picture of a father passing on his acquired tastes to his children, the writer quickly introduces a more prominent and brighter figure: a heroic mother who countered a hereditary taste for alcohol among her offspring through careful childrearing. The conclusion, that 'environment in this instance prov[ed] itself stronger than heredity,' was in keeping with the WCTU's practical work in mothers' groups.[46] Shortly afterwards, an editorial on 'Patriotism' concluded that, despite Canada's mixed genetic inheritance, a pure and Christian nation could be produced through hard work, because 'heredity doesn't count for much in the presence of good environment.'[47]

This is not to say that the WCTU was necessarily less racist than the female and male advocates of science. The discourse of evangelism allowed ample opportunity to decry the wrongdoings of 'heathens' who insisted on selling ice-cream and candy on Sundays in defiance of Sunday observance laws, and of male 'aliens' who were allowed to vote although they did not own as much property as white Canadian women. In respect to Sunday observance, the WCTU thundered: 'Every decent Canadian citizen should make up his mind that the foreign hosts that are sweeping down on this country shall obey its laws, or find it a decidedly uncomfortable abiding place';[48] and in respect to the vote, the spectre of hordes of 'Assyrians, Italians, and others' is invoked as the WCTU asks: 'Why should the ballot be given to these aliens, who own not a tithe of the property owned by Canadian women who are without the ballot?'[49]

The WCTU's form of racism, although influenced by the scientific discourse of eugenics, was primarily shaped by an older religious tradition labelling people of colour as 'heathens' – as culturally and morally inferior – and not necessarily as genetically inferior. The shopworn allegory equating Europe with light/ morality and Africa with darkness/sin was the dominant trope utilized by WCTU women in their conceptualization of race and culture, as evidenced in the use of 'light' as a metaphor both of Christianity and of freedom in the missionary poem quoted above. The exercise suggested for young people by a British missionary textbook published in 1906 was one familiar to Canadian church-goers of both sexes in this time period: 'Contrast the darkness of Africa with the light of civilization in England. Show how applicable the title "the Dark Continent" is to Africa, as inhabited by the Negro race, as the "Great Unknown Land" and as the country that, more than any other, has been given over to the Works of Darkness.'[50]

The WCTU's approach to race, culture, and heredity was, in conclusion, somewhat contradictory, but it tended to rely on old missionary ideas about darkness and light more than on the new scientific racism. This evangelical perspective was less rigid and had the potential to view all people, whatever their race, as potentially useful members of society – as long as they followed Christian morality, identified by the WCTU with Canadian mores. Putting the missionary zeal at work, the WCTU proselytized among the black communities in Chatham and Windsor; in St Catharines there was a committee to recruit black women, and in Hamilton there was a 'coloured' local union.[51] The contradictory position in which black women found themselves in a movement characterized by metaphors of whiteness is clear in the following passage, in which a white WCTU member reports on a conversations she had with a black mother: 'With eyes flooded with tears, one [black] woman said, "Our children are precious and although their faces are black, yet we want their lives to be white. We do not know how to combat a terrible sin that is prevalent in our school." '[52] The black mother is not a 'real' mother, since she is quite unable to prevent her children from falling into sin. Again, here race marks the adult woman as a non-adult, as a tearful girl in need of guidance.

Although an evangelical perspective differs from a genetic-determinist one in not automatically precluding black women or children from being 'pure,' the fact that purity was equated with whiteness,[53] and hence indirectly with European culture, made it difficult if not impossible for Canada's women of colour to identify with the brand of feminism elaborated by the WCTU, and in general by the overwhelmingly Protestant women of first-wave Canadian feminism. First-wave feminism was envisaged as the freeing of 'the mothers of the race': but not all adult women, even if they had children, qualified to mother either their own children or 'the race.'

The irony of the evangelical feminist theorization of race and culture may have been that, had they emphasized women's strictly biological role in reproduction, there might have arisen a potentially cross-racial sense of women's work in reproducing the human race. The heavy emphasis on women's role as moral teachers of children, however, privileged those women whose cultural and racial background marked them as more adult, more evolved, more moral, and better 'mothers of the race.' By proclaiming that 'the standard of morality is in the keeping of our woman,'[54] the WCTU indirectly narrowed the scope of feminism to women from dominant cultures/races, since, as seen in the first section, women of colour were usually regarded as less moral and maternal and as more corrupted by their culture. Women of colour were largely invisible, making cameo appearances only as grateful recipients of the moral reform message, never as potential active agents of the feminist project.

Since the consequences of the racism and ethnocentrism of first-wave feminism are still being felt in the 1980s, it is important to understand not only that many suffragists were racist, but exactly how they were racist. As Canadians become aware of the shady past of the eugenics movement in Canada, it is important to note that racism was not the exclusive province of biological determinists. Different discourses (evangelism, science, tourism) produce specific varieties of racism performing distinct functions in the Canadian social imaginary. The WCTU employed both scientific and evangelical discourses on race in their conceptualization of 'the mother of the race,' but as a rule the latter predominated over the former. The feminist theorization of race, finally, was not only evident in their views on immigration but was also centrally implicated in their thoughts about what they saw as the core of women's gender identity and hence of the feminist project – biological and social reproduction.

NOTES

Many thanks to my friends in the feminist history group, especially Lynne Marks, and also to Himani Bannerji.

1 Angela Davis, *Women, Race, and Class* (New York: Vintage 1983); Carol Bacchi, *Liberation Deferred? The Ideas of the English-Canadian Suffragists 1877–1918* (Toronto: University of Toronto Press 1983); Angus Mc-Laren, *Our Own Master Race: The Eugenics Movement in English Canada* (Toronto: McClelland and Stewart 1990). My thanks to Angus McLaren for allowing me to read his book in manuscript.

2 Anna Davin, 'Imperialism and Motherhood,' *History Workshop* no. 5 (1978): 1–75; Lucy Bland, *Banishing the Beast: Feminism, Sex, and Morality 1885–1918* (forthcoming 1992). My thanks to Lucy Bland for sharing her work with me.

3 See Hazel V. Carby, ' "On the Threshhold of Woman's Era": Lynching, Empire, and Sexuality in Black Feminist Theory,' in H.L. Gates, Jr, ed., *Race, Writing, and Difference* (Ithaca: Cornell, University Press 1986), 301–16; Jacquelyn Dowd Hall, 'The Mind That Burns Each Body: Women, Rape, and Racial Violence,' in A. Snitow et al., eds., *Powers of Desire* (New York: Monthly Review 1983), 328–49.

4 *Canadian White Ribbon Tidings* (*CWRT*), 15 Dec. 1904, 182. This magazine succeeded the *Woman's Journal* as the official organ of the Canadian Woman's Christian Temperance Union (WCTU); an almost complete set of both is found in the WCTU collection at the Archives of Ontario (AO) in Toronto.

5 Elizabeth Blackwell, *Essays in Medical Sociology* (London: Ernest Bell 1902), vol. 1, 14

6 Ibid., 94–5

7 A similar point is made by Nancy Stepan, *The Idea of Race in Science: Great Britain 1800–1960* (London: Macmillan 1982), 6–12. See also Douglas Lorimer, *Colour, Class and the Victorians: English Attitudes to the Negro in the Mid-Nineteenth Century* (Leicester: Leicester University Press; New York: and Holmes-Meier 1978), and Stephen Jay Gould, *The Mismeasure of Man* (New York: W.W. Norton 1981).

8 J.S. Mill, *On the Subjection of Women* (1869; Cambridge, Mass.: MIT Press 1970), 67

9 That the evangelistic racism of Blackwell and other moral reformers was not as pernicious as that of the scientific determinists who became dominant in the 1920s and 1930s can be seen in Robert Proctor, *Racial Hygiene: Medicine under the Nazis* (Cambridge, Mass.: Harvard University Press 1988), chaps 1 and 2; see also McLaren, *Our Own Master Race*.

10 Blackwell, *Essays*, vol. 1, 125

11 Edward Said, *Orientalism* (New York: Pantheon 1977)

12 Blackwell, *Essays*, vol. 1, 235

13 Ibid. On English perceptions of Indian women see Lata Mani, 'The Production of an Official Discourse on *sati* on 19th Century Bengal' in F. Barker et al., eds., *Europe and Its Others* (Colchester: Proceedings of the University Essex Conference on the Sociology of Literature 1985), 107–27. On the perceived link between darkness and excess sexuality see Sander L. Gilman, 'Black Bodies, White Bodies: Toward an Iconography of Female Sexuality in late 19th Century Art, Medicine, and Literature,' in Gates, ed., *Race, Writing, and Difference*, 223–61, and Joanna de Groot, ' "Sex" and "Race": The Construction of Language and Image in the Nineteenth Century,' in S. Mendes and J. Rendall, eds., *Sexuality and Subordination* (London: Routledge 1989), 89–128.

14 Frances Power Cobbe, 'Wife Torture in England,' in S. Jeffreys, ed.,

The Sexuality Debates (London: Routledge 1987), 224; see also Frances
Power Cobbe, *Darwinism in Morals and Other Essays* (London: Williams
and Norgate 1872) and *The Hopes of the Human Race* (London: Williams
and Norgate 1880). For an account of Cobbe's wife-torture campaign
that ignores the blatant racism and classism of Cobbe's feminism, see
Carol Bauer and Lawrence Ritt, ' "A Husband Is a Beating Animal":
Frances Power Cobbe Confronts the Wife Abuse Problem in Victorian
England,' *International Journal of Women's Studies* 6: 2 (1983): 99–118. My
thanks to Karen Dubinsky for the last reference.

15 Charlotte Perkins Gilman, *Women and Economics* 1898; New York Harper & Row 1966), 340

16 W.K. Brooks, *The Law of Heredity*, quoted in Cynthia E. Russett, *Sexual
Science: The Victorian Construction of Womanhood* (Cambridge Mass.: Harvard University Press 1989), 94. See also Eveleen Richards, 'Darwin and
the Descent of Woman,' in D. Olroy and I. Langham, eds., *The Wider
Domain of Evolutionary Thought* (Dordrecht and London: Reidel 1983),
57–111.

17 Darwin, *The Descent of Man*, quoted in Flavia Alaya, 'Victorian Science
and the "Genius" of Woman,' *Journal of the History of Ideas* 38: 2 (1977):
261. This passage is also quoted by Richards, 'Darwin and the Descent
of Woman'; Richards points out that Darwin explicitly rejected J.S.
Mill's argument about the socialization of women in favour of biological
determinism.

18 G. Stanley Hall, quoted in Russett, *Sexual Science*, 120. It was widely
believed that sterility was the necessary result of breaking the laws of
social/biological evolution; many nineteenth-century anthropologists,
for instance, believed that the offspring of black-white marriages were
sterile.

19 Olive Schreiner, 'The Woman Question,' reprinted in *An Olive Schreiner
Reader* (London: Pandora 1987), 83–4. Schreiner's record on racial politics was probably the best among leading white Anglo-Saxon feminists;
she resigned from South Africa's suffrage organization when it resolved
to seek equal suffrage (that is, suffrage for white women) rather than
universal suffrage for men and women of all races. See Ruth First and
Ann Scott, *Olive Schreiner* (New York: Schocken 1980).

20 Schreiner, 'The Woman Question,' in *An Olive Schreiner Reader*, 100

21 Ruth Compton Brouwer, *New Women for God: Canadian Presbyterian Women and India Missions, 1876–1914* (Toronto: University of Toronto Press 1990), 97–101

22 Canadian Council of the Missionary Education Movement, *Canada's Share in World Tasks* (np 1921), 90

23 Quoted in Brouwer, *New Women*, 87

24 A good example is Lucy Guiness, *Across India at the Dawn of the Twentieth Century* (London: Religious Tract Society 1902). The engravings in this book create a sharp contrast between the literally dark and frightening images of Indian 'superstitions' with the well-lit portraits of virtuous Anglo-Saxon women playing hymns at the piano.

25 Antoinette Brown Blackwell, *The Sexes throughout Nature* (New York: Putnam's Sons 1875), 25

26 Chart in Blackwell, *Sexes*, 58, arguments 177 and 14. Blackwell is implicitly challenging the common masculine view that as human and social evolution unfold, the genders become increasingly differentiated. Emil Durkheim, founder of academic sociology, typically believed that while among 'primitives' men and women had roughly equal brain sizes, educated European women had much smaller brains than their male counterparts; see E. Durkheim, *The Division of Labour in Society* (1893; Toronto: Macmillan 1933), 60–1.

27 A long excerpt from Swiney's *The Bar of Isis* (1912) is found in S. Jeffreys, ed., *The Sexuality Debates* (London: Routledge 1987); for Swiney's life see Sheila Jeffreys, *The Spinster and Her Enemies* (London: Pandora 1985).

28 Christabel Pankhurst, *Plain Facts about a Great Evil* (New York: Medical Review of Reviews 1913), 37. This anti-venereal disease pamphlet was published in Britain under the title *The Great Scourge and How to End It*.

29 Blackwell, *Essays*, vol. 1, 165

30 George Mosse, *Nationalism and Sexuality* (New York: Fertig 1985); Robert Nye, *Crime, Madness and Politics in Modern France* (Princeton: Princeton University Press 1984); and Frank Mort, *Dangerous Sexualities: Medico-Moral Politics in England since 1800* (London: Routledge 1987)

31 Roosevelt quoted in Richard Hofstadter, *Social Darwinism in American Thought* (Philadelphia: University of Pennsylvania Press 1945), 155

32 Macdonald quoted in Donald Avery, 'Canadian Immigration Policy and

the 'Foreign Navvy' 1896–1914,' in M. Cross and G. Kealey, eds., *The Consolidation of Capitalism 1896–1929* (Toronto: McClelland and Stewart 1983), 52

33 For an attack on Wilde, Nietzsche, impressionist painters, and other intellectual degenerates, see the influential work by Max Nordau, *Degeneration* (New York: Appleton 1895).

34 Mariana Valverde, *The Age of Light, Soap, and Water: Moral Reform in English Canada, 1885–1925* (Toronto: McClelland and Stewart 1991), chap. 4

35 Emily Murphy, *The Black Candle* (Toronto: Thomas Allen 1922). Murphy played a leading role in the passing of provincial laws allowing 'eugenic' sterilization. See Angus McLaren, 'The Creation of a Haven for 'Human Thoroughbreds': The Sterilization of the Feeble-Minded and the Mentally Ill in British Columbia,' *Canadian Historical Review* 67:2 (1986).

36 Emily Ferguson [Murphy], *Janey Canuck in the West* (Toronto: Cassel 1910), 38

37 Maria G. Craig, *Woman's Journal*, July 1891, 2–3

38 *Woman's Journal*, Jan. 1891, supplement, no page number

39 See, for instance, the article 'Hygiene and Heredity' by the local superintendent of this department in Oxford County, Ontario, in CWRT 15 April 1907, 879–80; and the untitled article on hygiene by WCTU leader Dr Amelia Yeomans in ibid., 1 May 1907, 886.

40 'Woman's Franchise,' *Woman's Journal*, Feb. 1892, 7

41 'Race Suicide,' CWRT, 15 Aug. 1908, 1221

42 Speech by MacMurchy reported in CWRT 1 Dec. 1906, 721; article by MacMurchy entitled 'Heredity' in CWRT 15 April 1907, 870. On MacMurchy's ideas and career see Angus McLaren, *Our Own Master Race*, chap. 2.

43 Occasional departmental reports in the minutes of the dominion WCTU tend to be brief and to deplore the lack of interest of WCTU members in this department. See AO, WCTU collection, minutes of dominion WCTU.

44 CWRT, 1 March 1911, 1861. See McLaren, *Our Own Master Race*.

45 An article reprinted from the Ford publication, *The Dearborn Independent*, entitled 'Aspects of Jewish Power,' claimed that governments were

reluctant to implement prohibition because of the undue influence of Jews controlling the liquor traffic; *CWRT*, Dec. 1924, 256. My thanks to Lynne Marks for this reference.

46 Editorial, 'The Law of Heredity,' *CWRT*, 15 April 1907, 874–5

47 *CWRT*, 15 June 1908, 1184

48 Editorial, *CWRT*, 15 June 1907, 938

49 *CWRT*, 15 March 1905, 228. Note the obviously literary reference to the ancient Assyrians, who are here typically mixed with the more plausible Italians. The WCTU women, like other reasonably educated Anglo-Saxons of their time, saw racial and ethnic groups through the filters of both learned and popular texts and images of 'the Orient.' The *Thousand and One Nights* imagery is seldom explicitly invoked, but it would have been employed by both writers and readers of such allegedly 'factual' pieces as the description of immigrant men's drunkenness in *CWRT*, 1 May 1905, 251–2.

50 Quoted in Lorimer, *Colour, Class and the Victorians*, 76. A similar racial hierarchy, expressed in somewhat more benevolent terms, is found in Canadian texts such as William T. Gunn, *His Dominion* (Canadian Council of the Missionary Education Movement 1917), and John R. Mott, *The Decisive Hour of Christian Missions* (New York: Student Volunteer Movement for Foreign Missions 1911). Mott's book was used as a textbook by Canadian Presbyterians.

51 A Miss Phelps, whose race is not indicated, was active among St Catharines blacks in the early 1890s. See AO, WCTU Collection, minutes of Ontario WCTU for 1894 annual convention. The existence of a 'coloured union' in Hamilton has been pointed out to me by Lynne Marks, whose own work will shed further light on some of the issues raised in this paper. Lynne Marks, 'Religion and Leisure in Three Ontario Towns, 1880–1902' (PhD thesis in progress, Department of History, York University).

52 *CWRT*, 15 March 1904, 50. The 'terrible sin' is probably masturbation, vigorously denounced by Arthur W. Beall, the WCTU's paid sex hygiene educator for boys.

53 In its first issue, the *Woman's Journal* (July 1885, 1) declared: 'The distinctive badge of the WCTU Union is a white ribbon, denoting purity in the heart, in the home, is society.'

54 Ibid., Nov. 1885, 3

2 'Maidenly Girls' or 'Designing Women'?
The Crime of Seduction
in Turn-of-the-Century Ontario
Karen Dubinsky

Sex makes fascinating politics. Issues such as pornography, workplace sexual harassment, lesbian and gay rights, prostitution, and reproductive choice have all become the stuff of government inquiry, academic treatises, and popular political organizing in recent years. These topics raise a host of unsettling questions, such as the relationship between sexual representation and practice, censorship and other forms of state sexual regulation, the connections between male sexuality and violence, and the processes by which our sexual desires (and anxieties) are brought into being.[1]

It is not coincidental that historians have played central roles in many of these debates, nor is it happenstance that most of them argue strongly for a 'social construction' approach to sexuality.[2] To suggest that the meaning, politics, and experience of sexuality is constructed socially, rather than being essentially or biologically determined in men and women, is to open the sexual past to historical scrutiny. To take just one example: if we accept that heterosexual male sexuality has developed in such a way that sex is a realm of power and privilege, that the right to express oneself sexually contains fewer risks for men than for women, then we want to know how this came to be. What historical and political forces have shaped male sexuality to bring about the link between sex, power, and conquest? Similarly, if we accept that, for women, sexuality has been constructed around the twin poles of pleasure and danger, of autonomy and victimization, again we want to know about the many forces that have shaped this tension.

Explorations in the history of sexuality have been helpful in understanding a number of current questions. Feminists concerned about the rising tide of sexual conservatism emanating from both the right and some sections of the women's movement have attempted to illustrate the results of a one-sided analysis of sexuality by examining the often problematic sexual politics of the first wave of feminism. Others, attempting to understand contemporary moral panics that link 'deviant' sexuality with disease, have investigated the roots of medical and moral regulation in the nineteenth century.[3] These debates have also shaped new historical questions and suggested new uses of historical sources.

Within feminism, one of the most controversial issues that has emerged from the sex debates is the 'pleasure/danger' analysis of female sexuality. To simplify, the main question is, To what extent can we speak of female agency, autonomy, and self-assertion in the realm of sexuality? Feminist social theorists of all persuasions have agreed that control over women's bodies is a major element of patriarchal domination. Those in the radical feminist tradition have tended to be sceptical about the possibility of sexual agency for women under present social arrangements. Indeed, American radical feminist Andrea Dworkin, a chief proponent of what is understatedly known as 'sexual pessimism,' states bluntly that 'sexuality is the stuff of death, not love.'[4]

A more complex position is taken by others. Arguing that radical feminist theory views women's experience of sexuality exclusively 'through the lens of the oppressors,' other feminists stress the complex range of forces that support patriarchal domination, of which sexual violence is one part.[5] Patriarchy, like capitalism, has its 'coercive apparatus,' and women ignore this at their peril. There is no question that sexuality is gendered; women experience sex in much more complicated and troubled ways than men. However, it is too simple to suggest that patriarchy is maintained by coercion alone, or that sex holds only danger for women. To conclude that is to deny the many ways in which women have carved out sexual territory, often in less than hospitable surroundings.

How does one pursue these questions historically? Are topics as elusive as sexual autonomy, courage, domination, or passion even possible to glimpse in the past? Victorian era sexual prescriptions have a familiar historical ring. Men were thought to have a voracious sexual appetite, which needed to be kept in check by passionless and pure women. First-wave feminists fashioned an entire movement around asserting the 'civilizing' influence of women in campaigns to win social purity, temperance, even suffrage. How can we examine the every-day experience of passion and sociability to determine the practice of such ideas? How can we determine the extent to which hegemonic sexual ideologies informed the lives of the dominated? I shall attempt in this article to show that the legal records of prosecutions for some sexual offences allow historians to study a hidden aspect of social life in the past: heterosexual intimacy. At their richest, court records provide a window into instances of personal life. Through these documents we learn about romantic and sexual expectations, and how these differ between women and men; and we can hear men and women arguing with each other about love, emotional and sexual intimacy, about betrayal and broken promises.

The particular 'crime' I shall focus on is seduction. Perhaps the key insight of those who advocate a social construction approach to sexuality is that the meaning assigned to human acts, values, and behaviour is constantly shifting.[6] In today's sexual discourse, seduction does not exist as a criminal category. Rather, in the language of popular culture, seduction conjures up images of erotic flirtation, a sexual adventure in which one party is 'in charge' but the other surrenders at her or his will. In the hands of nineteenth-century moral reformers and the legal system, however, the distinction between coercive, forced sex and sexual play was not so clear. In a culture that denied full political and economic citizenship to women, it is not surprising that women were denied cultural and legal control over their sexuality. Then, as now, women and men did not face each other as equals in the bedroom (or, in our context, the berry patch or the kitchen) any more than they did in the workplace, the state, or the street.

The criminalization of voluntary sexual activities between women and men reveal something of the force of the double standard of sexual behaviour, a cultural imperative of remarkable durability. But the sexual double standard was more than a powerful social prejudice. Legislation that made certain types of sex illegal, whether it was coercion, age, or relationships that prohibited such activity, was always framed to prevent men from acting against women. Men do, of course, act against women's physical wishes, often. But the entire weight of Anglo legal tradition rests on the patriarchal assumption that, as Rosalind Coward has put it, 'only men have an active sexuality, therefore, only men can actively seek out and commit a sexual crime.'[7]

The double standard of sexual behaviour is thus linked to the historical construction of desire. Female desire has rarely been legislated or regulated overtly; it was men, after all, who were forbidden to have sex, under certain conditions, with women. State sexual regulation, premised on such assumptions about women's and men's differing sexual natures, helps on the one hand to construct, channel, or, sometimes, limit male sexual desire, while on the other hand leaves vague questions of female desire.[8] Women's bodies are indeed regulated, but this tends to take place in a diffused and indirect fashion. Women are more immediately regulated by families and husbands, and, at the level of the state, policies as varied as those on birth control, abortion, even welfare act to shape women's sexual possibilities.

Such an appreciation of the gendered complexities of sexual regulation and desire will help us to understand why certain types of voluntary sexual relations between women and men became the subject of legislative debate and criminal prosecution in late nineteenth-century Canada. Laws that regulated seduction were, in their conception and application, based on an assumption of the oppositional sexual natures of men and women. The doctrine of female purity and passionlessness, however, served to increase the stakes for women. The higher one was on the moral pedestal, the further one had to fall.[9] Women who brought their seduction complaints to court learned this lesson painfully and publicly.

I shall begin with an overview of the legislative campaign in favour of the seduction law, which was waged by one firebrand MP, supported by the moral reform movement and the labour movement, and passed into law by the late 1880s. The rest of this article will focus on criminal prosecutions for one type of voluntary sexual activity: seduction.[10] I will first examine how these cases were handled by the legal system, and use this material to make some preliminary remarks about the social and sexual mores that governed heterosexual coupling in this period. Prosecutions under the law allow us to contrast the intentions of moral reformers with the opinions of legal authorities and the experience of young heterosexual couples. We shall go further than a simple contrast between intention and experience, however, by exploring how the criminalization of voluntary sexual activity served to entrench the legal and parental regulation of women, and to punish women who transgressed cultural prohibitions of female desire.

The Campaign against Seduction

> The name of John Charlton, as orator, economist, financier, moral reformer and deadliest foe of vice, is a household word in every Canadian family. There is no citizen in the country at large who does not regard his life, his property, his privileges and above all his sacred family ties, as more safe, more assured and more free from touch, by reason of that honoured name.[11]

This tribute to Charlton, delivered in 1897 by the Norfolk County Liberal Association on the occasion of Charlton's twenty-fifth anniversary as MP, perhaps overstates his fame, but it certainly does capture Charlton's sense of himself and his political mission. Charlton was an MP for the Ontario riding of Norfolk North and a successful entrepreneur. During his tenure as MP (1872–1904), he piloted an amazing array of 'moral legislation' through the House of Commons. Sabbath observance, temperance, censorship of 'obscene' literature, and opposition to abortion and birth control were all causes embraced by Charlton, but it is in the area of the criminalization of certain sexual offences that, as he opined in a published collection of speeches, his 'name will be remembered.'[12] In this instance, hyperbole was not without substance. Charlton was so associated with seduction offences that it was common for both criminal indictments and newspaper accounts of trials to refer to seduction as 'offences against the Charlton Act.'

Charlton's diaries and unpublished autobiography reveal no particular insights into why except for deeply held religious convictions, the cause of moral legislation was so important to him. His constant and often stated concern was to 'protect' women, especially young women, from unspecified moral danger. He was more alert to the consequences of immorality. 'It is surely a crime,' he told the House of Commons in his second attempt to introduce seduction legislation in 1883, 'to blight a home, to ruin a life; to make an innocent person an outcast of society, and to drive her to prostitution, when this is done by the exercise of wiles and false promises.'[13] Thus Charlton, like other moral reformers of his day, had a dramatic and paternal vision of the lives of 'seduced' women.

Another constant theme in his speeches, one which united his major moral preoccupations – seduction and sabbath observance – was the relationship between a strong morality and a strong state. In a major address on sabbath observance in the House of Commons, for example, he argued that by bringing more people 'under religious influence,' a strong sabbath observance bill would reduce crime, win the favour of the working class, and, by placing Canada 'on a higher moral plane ... will strengthen the nation and make it more powerful and prosperous.'[14] Similarly, in another speech in the House of Commons on seduction, he put the issue in melodramatic terms: 'The degradation of women is a crime against society. The pure Christian home is the only safe foundation for the free and enlightened State. Vice in the shape of social immorality is the greatest danger that can threaten the state, and the duty of the Legislature, the duty of the Government, is to take measures, so far as it can, to punish infractions of morality and to conserve the morality of the public.'[15] Claims such as these, made around issues such as the publication of Sunday newspapers or sexual relations outside matrimony, appear exaggerated and absurd. However, if one sets these issues in an expanded conception of the meaning of moral regulation, Charlton's grand statements make more sense. Historians have tended to interpret the turn-of-the-century social purity movement as an Anglo-Saxon, middle-class response to increasing fears about immigration, the growth of the working class, and changes in social and family life brought on by industrialization and urbanization.[16] Yet, as other commentators have recently argued, moral regulation also involved the creation of a particular kind of citizen. The emerging state in nineteenth-century Canada was concerned not just with the formation of political and economic 'subjectivities,' but also with 'the formation of a moral subjectivity that would not only be congruent with but also would provide the psychological basis for what was known as nation-building.'[17] Nations required factories, workers, and transportations systems, but they also required citizens, subjects with 'character.'

Indeed, the link between 'moral building' and 'nation building' can be glimpsed in the way Charlton chose to express his opinion on the Pacific Scandal. Never a fan of Sir John A. Macdonald (a 'bad old man' whose morals were 'not above reproach,'),[18] he blamed the prime minister and the Tories for 'betraying the interest of a young nation for the benefit of a body of speculators and capitalists.'[19] In Charlton's view, young nations, like young women, needed protection lest the strong (speculators, capitalists, or blackguardly men) betray the weak.

An expanded definition of the meaning of moral regulation also helps make sense of another of Charlton's favourite themes – Canada's moral reputation or standing in the world. A peculiar form of 'moral boosterism' was common when people reflected on incidents of sexual crime in their midst. Judges at Assize court, for example, would congratulate or condemn an entire community, depending on the number of sexual crimes on the docket. When reporting on serious sexual crimes in Britain or the United

States, Canadian newspapers would often smugly point out that
Canada's 'purer moral atmosphere' would make the commission
of such a crime unlikely here. Alternatively, when sensational
crimes did 'happen here,' commentators would find convenient
scapegoats in geography; border towns would blame their proximity to the United States, rural areas would blame nearby towns,
towns would blame cities, and all would blame immigrants. So,
when Charlton, in making his case against the publication of
Sunday newspapers, argued that 'we do not want this American
institution in Canada,' he spoke in a language common to other
moral reformers, designed to blend community or patriotic fervour with good behaviour.[20] Moral standing was thus not simply
a matter of individual reputation. A common standard of morality was a community concern, and the community – in concert
with the state and the legal system – had an interest in ensuring
the maintenance of that standard by all. Yet morality, conceived
of in abstract national or geographic terms, was applied to existing communities with rigid social hierarchies, and often served
to reproduce those hierarchies in new ways.

What were the specific moral offences Charlton aimed to correct through the seduction law? Charlton introduced his bill in
1882, and by 1886 a version of it became law.[21] The salient features of the bill were that it introduced the concept of seduction
– as opposed to forcible, coercive attack – into Canadian law.
Consent was not an issue in seduction cases. The law proclaimed
that in certain situations there could be no consent to sexual
relations. The situations specified changed throughout the period
under investigation, but in general they applied when the female
was between the ages of fourteen and sixteen; to all women under
the age of twenty-one when sex had been accompanied by the
promise of marriage; and to all women under twenty-one who
were the wards or employees (in factory, mills, or workshops) of
their 'seducers.' In all of these cases, the law only applied to
women 'of previously chaste character.' The maximum penalty
for those found guilty of seduction was two years in prison. There
were many amendments throughout the 1880s and 1890s. Even
after the law was passed, Charlton continued the campaign to

expand its scope, mainly by attempting to increase the age limits for women. These provisions in the criminal law accompanied an already existing civil seduction law. The right to sue one's 'seducer' for damages predated the criminalization of seduction and existed throughout this period. Unlike the criminal law, however, civil seduction suits could not be initiated by the woman involved; rather, her father would have to seek damages himself. This resulted in different patterns of both prosecutions and verdicts, which we will contrast below.

Charlton's bill was initially ignored in the House, but as he persisted, the arguments against criminalizing seduction became vociferous. The fear that women would use the law to blackmail men was repeated by many through the years of debate on this topic, and when the workplace seduction provisions were introduced, this concern reached new heights. Many MPs seized on the popular stereotype of the 'designing woman' to make their case against the bill. According to one MP, employers would be at the mercy of a 'designing woman, who would throw herself very much in his way, and who would do what has been done again and again in the history of the world. namely, seduce him.' The promise-of-marriage provision might prove tempting for women, who 'might find it profitable to fall.' Others worried that even the stipulation requiring previous chastity would not guarantee that the law would be used to help respectable girls, since 'chastity, like the phases of the moon, is very changeable.' Still others spoke candidly as men, arguing that 'we have the right to protect ourselves; and it is our duty to see, not for ourselves alone, but as representative men, that legislation is not placed upon our statutes which is unfair or unjust, and likely to lead young men into trouble improperly.'[22]

Charlton's bill was supported by one of the major players in the moral reform movement, David Watt of the Montreal Society for the Protection of Women and Girls. Like Charlton, the Montreal Society had a far-reaching concern with protecting women from all moral dangers, though Watt's own preoccupations, revealed in his voluminous correspondence with the federal Department of Justice, were in the area of prostitution and procuring

offences. The Montreal Society did advance one significant criticism of the seduction bill. In reference to the employer/em-
ployee section of the legislation, the society argued that a woman's
'previously chaste character' should not be a criterion for successful prosecution. An employer, they argued, 'should not be in
a position to take advantage of the weakness or previous faults
of those whose moral welfare he should be in an important sense
the custodian.'[23] This suggestion was not acted upon by government, but it is an interesting reversal of the more typical discourse
of the period in which fallen women fell permanently. In this
articulation of the 'moral obligations' of employers, Watt also
gave voice to the protective practices of many nineteenth-century
factory owners, who attempted to protect the 'good name' of
female employees by 'claiming common cause with their fathers
and husbands.'[24]

The seduction law also had a less well-known source of support,
one generally not regarded as a participant in the movement for
social purity. The nineteenth-century labour movement displayed a significant concern for the 'moral hazards' of women's
working lives. The Ontario branch of the Knights of Labor was
a staunch supporter of the seduction law, and was credited by
the minister of justice, John Thompson, with convincing him to
introduce legislation prohibiting seduction in the workplace. Unlike middle-class proponents of seduction legislation, the labour
movement had a precise notion of the sorts of moral dangers
requiring protection.

In Hamilton, for example, a Knights of Labor stronghold, the
Knights were first drawn to the problem of seduction through
the case of Maria McCabe, an Irish immigrant convicted of the
murder of her illegitimate infant. The Knights read this case as
a clear sign of the vulnerable position of working-class women,
and participated in a successful community campaign to commute
McCabe's death sentence. Katie McVicar, one of the most active
women in the Canadian branch, added the McCabe case to her
arsenal of arguments in favour of women's suffrage, noting that
at present 'girls have nothing to do with the making of the laws
by which they are governed.'[25]

McCabe's case served as a local springboard for an even more sensational incident which captured Canadian Knights' attention a few years later. The Knights followed the story of William Stead and his 'Maiden Tribute to Modern Babylon' in Britain with avid attention. Stead's discovery of a huge network of 'white slavery' in Britain, consisting primarily of working-class 'daughters of the people,' as well as his subsequent prosecution for abduction confirmed for the Knights that capitalism and morality were incompatible. As labour journalist Phillips Thompson explained: 'The main cause of the moral rottenness of the English upper classes – and of the same class everywhere – is the inequalities of conditions which prevail; the corrupting influence of unearned wealth and idleness on the one hand, and on the other the degradation caused by overwork, poverty and wretched homes.'[26] For Thompson, aristocratic exploitation of young women was simply an extension of capitalist domination of workers: 'Sensuality is naturally begotten by luxury, overfeeding and laziness, and fostered by the entire spirit of English institutions which make the poor slaves of the rich.'[27] Thompson's words were more than good polemics. This argument, which located vice in the upper class, was the opposite of the dominant association of immorality with the working class.[28]

Both the McCabe story and the Maiden Tribute revelations served to make the Ontario Knights keen supporters of Charlton's attempts to introduce seduction legislation. Hamilton's *Palladium of Labor* drew attention to the 'special interest' workers had in Charlton's bill, since working women's dependent position 'places them at the mercy of lecherous employers.' The labour press also reminded its readers that if women had the vote, 'as they rightfully should,' the issue would be dealt with quickly. In the wake of Stead's findings, it seemed clear to the Knights that Canadian legislators were stalling Charlton's bill. The 'notorious libertines' on Parliament Hill, claimed the Knights, had 'strong personal reasons for wishing the defeat of the measure.'[29] This time, however, the workers had the government's ear. In 1889 the Canadian Legislative Committee of the Knights met with justice minister John Thompson and convinced him to include a limited amendment on workplace seduction in the next round of changes to the Criminal Code.

The Knights saw one of the particular ways in which the power relations of capitalism victimized women. Sparing themselves the painful business of self-reflection, they overlooked the distribution of power between men and women in the working class. The men, as historian Barbara Taylor has argued in another context, were often as bad as their masters.[30] This construction of sexual danger clearly let working-class men 'off the hook.' Furthermore, like others in the progressive wing of the social purity movement (including most feminists), the Knights continued to reproduce the dichotomy of good and bad womanhood, and offered little space for positive or autonomous female sexuality.[31] Yet, unlike some social purity activists, the Knights did not blame working-class women themselves for their proximity to 'vice.' Rather, they located the problem in women's dependent economic and political position, and used this issue to reiterate their support for female suffrage. They also made a significant discovery: notions of female purity, passionlessness, and innocence were clearly out of reach for most women, especially working-class women. It seemed to the Knights that capitalism forced working women into daily battle with vice: in fending off advances from employers, in the 'temptations of sin' that grinding poverty created, or even in the simple act of walking home at night from work. As such, these women were denied their 'right' to chastity and morality. A seduction law provided an opportunity to claim these virtues for all, to democratize morality.

Such were the expectations of the proponents of the seduction law. Whether one saw the issue in class terms or not, seduction law advocates expected that their legislation would help innocent and victimized 'maidens' claim redress against wilful men who came bearing gifts, not guns. The law was constructed such that age or economic relationships, not force, were the determinants of the sorts of sexual liaisons women were to be protected from. Once seduction entered the realm of the legal system, however, some very different stories emerged.

The 'Seduction Story': Prosecutions under the Law

Canadian legal historians have done valuable research reconstructing and interpreting the legislative framework of nine-
teenth- and early twentieth-century sexual morality. John
McLaren studied the seduction law in the context of a larger
examination of the movement against 'white slavery' in Canada,
and explained seduction in terms of the generalized concern of
the middle-class moral reform movement to regulate the sexual
activities of the working class.[32] Constance Backhouse looked at
seduction in the context of rape and other sexual assault legislation. While she does note the overwhelmingly paternal nature
of the criminal seduction law, she locates it in the general movement towards the consideration of sexual assault as a crime against
women themselves, rather than the earlier notion that rape dam-
aged women only in so far as they were considered property of
their fathers.[33] Graham Parker studied seduction along with other
sexual crimes in which physical force was not a criterion, such as
'carnal knowledge' of young girls and abduction. According to
Parker, laws which governed voluntary sexual behaviour served
to reinforce the double standard of sexual morality and the cult
of chastity for women.[34]

My survey of seduction prosecutions reaches similar conclusions. Studying the law from this perspective allows us to view
the sorts of sexual entanglements that were thought to require
punishment, as well as how the legal system determined guilt or
innocence in these situations. This approach yields different results from studies that rely primarily on legal commentary and
interpretation. In this sample, seduction was not primarily about
rape or other nonconsensual sexual acts, nor was it about prostitution or commercial sexual exchange. Well over one-half of
the seduction cases in this survey were the result of ongoing and
mutual relations between two lovers. As such, the seduction law
often acted to contain the sexual behaviour of women as well as
men.[35]

The sexual situations which resulted in prosecutions reveal

that the law was interpreted by many complainants as a means of channelling sexual behaviour into 'appropriate' institutions, namely marriage; it was about ensuring childbirth in wedlock. Seduced women, and often the parents of seduced daughters, attempted to use the law to enforce what historian Christine Stansell calls the barter system between the sexes, in which 'women traded sexual favours for a man's promise to marry.' But as Stansell also notes, this was not an exchange between two equals. A woman 'delivered on her part of the bargain – and risked pregnancy – before the man came through with his.'[36] The power that male 'seducers' held did not arise primarily from their advanced age or their economic relationship to their conquest; their power resulted from their more favoured position in this system of sexual exchange. These men had power because they were men, in a society in which the dominant moral climate punished pre- or extra-marital sexual activity on the part of women. The seduction law did not change or improve women's standing in the sexual barter system because, despite the chivalrous rhetoric advanced by proponents of the new law, women's stories of sexual betrayal were simply not believed by the courts.

Over fifty Ontario women who had been wronged by their lovers took the law at its word and presented the court with stories in which consent to sex arose from false or unmet promises. A typical case was that fifteen-year-old Charlotte S and her boyfriend Henry S.[37] They met when Henry, a farmer's son in Fitzroy Township near Ottawa, came to Charlotte's father's farm in the fall of 1889 to help with the threshing. According to Charlotte, Henry 'appeared to desire to induce me to be his companion.' Henry began to visit regularly, and they 'kept company' in the kitchen of Charlotte's family home while the rest of the family was upstairs asleep. Charlotte's mother, Jane, saw 'nothing improper in their company keeping' because she presumed that his 'object was marriage.' After a time, Henry 'coaxed' Charlotte into having sex. In a grand declaration of love, Henry told her that 'if he owned the whole world ... he would not think it too much to give it to her,' and asked for her hand in marriage. The family kitchen continued to be the site of their visits; they would lay down on the bench and have sex at the kitchen table. This arrangement lasted until Charlotte got pregnant, and her mother began to hear 'stories' about her. When questioned, Charlotte confessed her situation to her mother. Charlotte's parents confronted Henry at his father's farm and, standing in a cow field, the two families had it out. At first, Henry denied any responsibility for Charlotte's pregnancy, but, when pressed, he admitted that 'he could not put hand to heart and answer to God that he had no freedom with Charlotte.' He insisted, however, that he would not and had not promised to marry her. Charlotte's distraught mother begged him to do 'what was right,' and offered him a home in a neighbouring farm. At this, Henry relented and promised to return to the woman's parents later that week, but his father disagreed. Telling the parents to 'go to hell,' Henry's father refused to let Henry leave, saying there was too much work to do on his farm. Thus the affair ended up in court, where Henry was found not guilty.

Reading seduction charges from the 'bottom up' – from the complaints filed by women that they thought demanded legal punishment – reveals two general categories of seduction. Contrary to the intention and language of the legislation, seduction charges were laid both when sex was physically forced and when it was voluntary. Why were seduction charges laid in instances of physically coerced sex, when there were a number of other charges (rape, attempted rape, indecent assault) that would have been appropriate? This confusion in legal categorization reflects in part the uneven development of the justice system in this period, particularly in rural areas. The difference between, for example, what might be called rape, indecent assault, and attempted rape was (and is) always a judgment call on the part of authorities, and there was a great deal of regional variation in legal classification. Such confusion cut both ways. Even after the seduction law was well in place, rape charges continued to be laid in cases which 'read' like seduction tales – for example, pregnant women who stated quite clearly that they consented to sex after their boyfriends promised to marry them. Yet, as American historian Mary Odem has pointed out in her study of statutory rape prosecutions, the practice of categorizing stories of physical coercion alongside stories of seduction also reveals the ambivalence of the legal system in accepting the assumptions behind the seduction law. In a sexual climate that drew rigid lines between 'good girls' (who were not sexual) and bad, any woman who admitted to sexual relations outside proscribed boundaries was suspect.[38] The sexual culture of turn-of-the-century Ontario, which informed the opinions of judges and the decisions of juries, held little sympathy for a girl who had the misfortune to fall voluntarily for the 'wrong' sort of man.

Stories of forced, unwanted sex, sometimes between strangers (what we would today call 'pickup' situations), more often between neighbours or household members, form a minority of cases in this study, fewer than 20 per cent of all charges filed under the seduction law. Such sexual encounters usually occurred only once or twice, and, according to the women, male physical force was what led to sex. Even when women used the language of seduction to tell their story, it is clear they were often describing acts of rape. As fifteen-year-old Edith H from Parry Sound described here story, her neighbour, William J, came by to borrow a drill one afternoon and, finding her alone in the house, he 'shoved me up against the door and seduced me.'[39] Such cases were sometimes accompanied by other charges, such as rape, attempted rape, or indecent assault. These types of cases have two elements in common: they were rarely the result of sexual relations between lovers and they were much more likely to be believed than seduction stories. Most such incidents resulted in guilty verdicts. The exception to this rule was the pick-up situation, which never resulted in a guilty verdict.

The voluntary incidents always involved sexual relations between lovers, often those who had dated for a period of one or two years. These could be neighbours, co-workers, boarders, farm hands, or old friends. The women in these situations admitted to having sexual relations with their boyfriends, usually claiming that a promise of marriage was what led them to consent to sex. These are stories of courtship gone awry, because the woman got pregnant and the man reneged on his commitment to marriage, because the man ended the relationship in favour of pursuing another, or because the woman discovered the man was already married. Many of these cases were pursued when the woman discovered she was pregnant, and often the complainant's parents played a significant role in the prosecution. In these situations, the men involved were rarely found guilty.

Charlotte S's case was typical of seduction stories in which the young man's refusal to marry his pregnant girlfriend was the main reason the case went to court. The case of Kenneth C and Margaret F was typical of a second type of voluntary case, in which courtship ended when the man's previous marriage was discovered.[40] Kenneth and Margaret were co-workers at the Martin Manufacturing Company in Whitby in 1917. They dated regularly, every Wednesday and Saturday evening, and he would also pick her up from nightschool on other evenings. They usually had sex in his vehicle. Margaret began hearing rumours in the factory that he was married, which he laughed off. When her mother got wind of the same rumours, she forbade any more contact between the two. Their attempt to run off to Toronto (to marry, according to Margaret) was stopped when Margaret's mother caught them in a hotel room in Oshawa and immediately laid charges against him. Kenneth wrote to his wife from jail, telling her she would be surprised about the 'scrape' he had gotten into and asking for her help. He requested that she bring along their son to court, saying 'if you and him come it will help me out,' and he also asked for money. The crown attorney was outraged by the case. Margaret may have acted 'imprudently,' he told the judge, but 'the law was made to protect young girls from men like him.' Kenneth's cavalier attitude irked the jury; he was found guilty, but received a suspended sentence.

These cases share many similarities with other seduction stories. The principals appear to be relative social equals, and sex took place in the context of a romantic relationship. Most of the men and women involved in these cases were from similar working-class or farm backgrounds. A few domestic servants charged their employers, but no cases involved employers in the specified 'factories, mills or worshops.' There were no cases in which the 'seducer' matched the Knights of Labor vision of aristocratic libertine. This is not to suggest that the nineteenth-century work-place was free of what we would today call sexual harassment. As American labour activist, Rose Cohen, remembered, the first words of English she learned in her job in the garment industry were 'keep your hands off me, please.'[41] Then, as now, women used both individual and collective strategies to negotiate their way past unwanted sexual attention at work. Yet, given women's often precarious position in the labour force, it is hardly sur-prising that the criminal court system was not how they chose to deal with these problems.[42]

These cases reveal that young men and women were relatively free to pursue a relationship that included a sexual component; it was only when they got caught, either by an unplanned preg-nancy or by breaking the rules of monogamous marriage, that the relationship came to an unhappy conclusion. Often, it was then up to the woman's parents to determine how to proceed. These cases reveal a variety of patterns of parental involvement in their children's sexual lives. Charlotte S's case is one in which parents took the side of their wronged daughter. Similarly, Eliz-abeth S told the court that her mother was 'managing' her case against her boyfriend, George D, for her. Elizabeth testified that she 'thought enough' of George to marry him still, even though he had 'used her so mean,' reneging on his promise of marriage after she became pregnant. Elizabeth's mother freely admitted that she laid charges against George 'to compel him to marry my daughter.'[43] At other times the interests of parents and chil-dren conflicted, and the legal system might be used to assert parental authority in other ways.

In some cases, parents clearly undermined their daughters' desires. In 1903, fifteen-year-old Mary Ellen T became romant-ically involved with Patrick C, an iron worker and boarder at Mary Ellen's family home in Oshawa.[44] Their sexual affair be-came known when Patrick took a half-day off from work to go berry picking with Mary Ellen and bragged about the 'good time' he had had with here to his co-workers the next day. News of his sexual exploits reached Mary Ellen's father Hiram, who then began to watch the couple. He told the court the story that he watched them one evening having sex in the kitchen. 'I saw him sitting on her knee with his arm around her neck and they were kissing each other. In a few minutes they changed places and he raised her clothes and unbuttoned his trousers ... he accomplished the act ... he seduced her.' Hiram did not interrupt them that night, because he 'wanted to keep cool until I had my man arrested.' This he did, the next morning. It is unlikely that Mary Ellen was a party to the prosecution; it does not appear that she was pregnant, and her father took his story to the police without telling her. The court heard no testimony from her. Prosecution thus acted to punish Patrick, as well as his 'wayward' girlfriend, by ending what appears to have been a mutually desired relationship and by exposing her intimate life to public scrutiny.

Like Mary Ellen's father, the parents of Beatrice A of Woodstock used the legal system to challenge their daughter's relationship with a man they disapproved of. This case also illustrates the double standard of justice delivered to blacks in late nineteenth-century Ontario. Beatrice, a 'prepossessing mulatto,' had been dating a 'coloured' labourer named Thomas M for a year and a half. She became pregnant after several sexual encounters with Thomas, most of them taking place outside her father's house after their evening walk. Thomas wrote Beatrice's father a letter, apologizing for his 'indiscretion' and asking his permission for marriage. Mr A had long objected to this courtship, however, and he refused permission, opting instead to take Marshall to court. Clearly Beatrice would have preferred marriage; in a melodramatic rendering of the story, the Woodstock press described how, in court, the 'wronged girl fell upon the neck of her lover, and he, in turn, clasped her in a fond embrace.' The scene was referred to in a jocular and breezy tone, which contrasts with the tragic language used to describe most other seduction trials, as 'full of pathos and not without a tinge of humour.' Thomas's colour likely also accounts for the verdict; despite his admission of responsibility, Beatrice's admission that she consented to sex, and Thomas's willingness to 'fulfill his obligation' by marrying Beatrice, his case resulted in a guilty verdict.[45]

Thus the seduction law could be used to regulate the sexual behaviour of both parties, sometimes by putting an end to a relationship not sanctioned by a woman's parents, other times by channelling sexual activity into its only acceptable form – conventional marriage. The desire to avoid unwed motherhood was clearly what fuelled many prosecutions for seduction. Historians have termed illegitimacy the 'moral litmus test' of Victorian society.[46] While some studies suggest a degree of community and family tolerance for unwed mothers in Canada, these cases reveal that this was not a fate that young women, or their families, accepted willingly.[47] In several of these cases, the threat of court proceedings served to force the men involved to uphold their part of the sexual bargain by marrying the woman. Three days before his trial for the seduction of Alice M in 1917, Thomas L of Thessalon ensured that the proceedings were halted by marrying her. In this case, however, marriage did not mean the end of their troubles. Five years later, Thomas was back in court, pleading guilty to assaulting his fifteen-year-old niece.'[48] Despite the low conviction rate, the law gave some women a degree of bargaining power to make men uphold their part of the sexual bargain.

Was the stipulation requiring 'previously chaste character' on the part of the woman one reason why so few seduction cases resulted in guilty verdicts? This clause, unique in Canadian law, certainly provided an out, which accused men used to their advantage. Graham Parker notes that the meaning of this clause was subject to a continuing debate among judges and other legal commentators. Some judges interpreted it narrowly, and simply looked for evidence of whether women had previous sexual relations. Others interpreted it more broadly, and allowed evidence on all 'acts and that disposition of mind which constitute an unmarried woman's virtue or morals.'[49] A wide interpretation was allowed in many of these cases. The most common defence was to suggest that the man charged was not the first or only man to have been involved with the woman. William W, for example, successfully defended himself against seduction charges laid by

Beatrice M by producing two other men in court who, according to the Orangeville *Sun*, 'with brazen and brassy faces, told of their illicit relations with the girl.'[50] In other cases, the mere suggestion of other boyfriends seemed to be enough to raise doubts about women's previous chastity. Many women were cross-examined about their past relationship with men, and even when there was no evidence to suggest these relationships had involved sexual intimacy, their stories were rarely believed.

A woman's sexual history was not the only criterion for determining 'character.' When it was alleged that sex was consented to under promise of marriage, women were asked to reconstruct carefully the precise timing of the proposal. If it came after their first sexual liaison, clearly they had not been seduced. The courts were also curious about how long a woman had dated before consenting to sex. Being 'coaxed' is how many women described this process, and here they could display marked degrees of morality. Elizabeth admitted she had sex with John H on their second or third date, but hastened to add, 'I required a great deal of coaxing.'[51] Mary C, of Sault Ste Marie, insisted that her boyfriend, Paul C, faithfully promised to marry here before sex took place, but in court she also pointed out his stature: 'Do you think I could fight a big fellow like that?'[52]

Other areas of cross-examination show how broadly conceived nineteenth-century notions of morality could be. Women who pressed seduction charges were interrogated about their church or school attendance, their employment history, and, sometimes, their parents' moral conduct. William T, for example, produced as his witness a previous employer of Margaret V, who testified that he had dismissed her two years previously from domestic service at his home in Stratford because she repeatedly stayed out past her 10 PM curfew.[53] Elizabeth P's mother Lydia was subject to a barrage of questions: regarding her own illegitimate child, her poor supervision of her daughter (for letting her stay downstairs along with her boyfriend), and for allegedly flirting with the defendant herself.[54] Similarly, Mary S's mother Martha was repeatedly grilled about the extent of supervision and control she exercised: Did she ever attempt to stop her daughter from going out? Did she have a lot of friends? Did she warn her to be careful with boys?[55]

Finally, financial transactions could be used to suggest poor character on the part of the woman or her family. This took two forms, one suggesting prostitution, the other hinting at blackmail. Women were regularly asked if they accepted money from their boyfriends, before or after sexual relations. None of these cases involved outright commercial exchange for sex between strangers. But Ontario had its share of women Kathy Peiss calls 'charity girls,' who agreed to sexual relations with men in return for money or gifts.[56] Celestine L admitted to accepting five dollars from Emile C, whom she had been dating for three months. She used the money to buy herself new boots and stockings. Bob C swept young Henrietta M off her feet: he bought her clothing, jewellery, paid for her music lessons, and even settled some of her father's debts.[57] Accused men used such instances to allege prostitution, a sure defence against previous chastity. Yet it seems more likely, given that in all situations where money or gifts changed hands the couple had been romantically involved, that money was simply a part of the barter system, particularly when women were taking the risk of premarital sex.

Many men accused of seduction attempted to exploit the cultural stereotype of the 'designing woman.' Sometimes a conspiracy on the part of the woman's family was suggested. When Margaret V's father, Moore, took the stand in the case he was pursuing against William T, the first question he was asked was whether he brought this action 'for the purpose of getting money.' He denied this, and further denied having any knowledge that William's father was a wealthy man. Margaret B no doubt increased her moral standing as a noble wronged woman (and helped secure a rare guilty verdict against her seducer) by returning the money her boyfriend's wife had offered her for silence, and pressing criminal charges instead.[58]

The courts frowned on financial negotiations, interpreting such bartering as evidence of extortion. Yet private financial transactions after a sexual argument were not necessarily sinister, but rather part of the extra-legal community traditions that regulated social life and gender relations. As Bryan Palmer has argued with respect to one such ritualized system of regulation, charivaris, there were, in nineteenth-century North America, 'obscure corners of everyday life where the rule of law could or would not intervene.'[59] In this period, particularly in sparsely settled communities such as rural and northern Ontario, the battle between the state and traditional means of problem-solving had not yet been settled decisively in favour of the state. This applied at the level of ideology as well as of material resources. In small communities, the legal system was not yet entrenched as an impersonal bureaucracy. As one crown attorney in Ontario complained to the provincial attorney-general in 1881, a lack of time and money, as well as the 'unpleasant nature of their duties in having examinations and committing their neighbours for trial,' prevented the smooth functioning of local magistrates.[60]

Criminal seduction prosecutions hovered precariously between traditional moral enforcement mechanisms, which might include financial exchange, charivaris, or tarring and feathering, and the more modern use of the state to right sexual wrongs. Calling the police, hiring a lawyer, and going to court were learned processes. Fears of the 'designing woman,' who might take matters into her own hands, arose from misogynist stereotypes of female sexuality. But this also revealed the apprehensions of an imperfect legal system, charged with the task of constructing itself as the sole place of sober authority.

This argument that financial negotiations were not the malicious plots they were made out to be by the courts is strengthened when we recall that the right to take civil action for monetary reward in cases of seduction existed throughout this period. Similarly, women whose boyfriends backed out of a commitment to marriage could and did take them to civil court under the 'breach-of-promise' law, which also provided monetary compensation.[61] Even when women pursued their legal right to sue a man for damages *within* the courtroom, cultural stereotypes about women's maliciousness loomed. Judges and legal commentators vilified women who brought breach-of-promise actions, casting them, as one judge put it, as 'hungry spinsters and designing widows.'[62]

Despite these prejudices against 'designing women,' civil prosecutions for seduction were both popular and remarkably successful. Constance Backhouse has demonstrated that seduction cases were the most litigated cases involving women, and an average of 90 per cent of cases between 1820 and 1900 in Ontario went to the plaintiff.[63] In civil trials, 'previous chastity' was not a condition of successful prosecution, although Backhouse found that it could determine the amount of the award. John McLaren has calculated that, across Canada, the average yearly conviction rate in criminal cases of seduction between 1900 and 1910 was 9.1 per cent, and increased to 34.14 per cent yearly between 1911 and 1917.[64] The conviction rate in my sample is approximately 45 per cent, decreasing to 35 per cent if we remove incidents of physical coercion. Why were seduction stories believed so much more readily in the civil courts?

Civil courts are, of course, different from criminal courts. Owing to differing requirements of proof, 'wronged parties' generally receive a more sympathetic hearing in civil than in criminal courts.[65] Backhouse interprets the success rate in civil trials strictly in gender terms. The law stipulated that actions must be brought by the woman's father; women could not bring suit themselves. The tort of seduction was, she argues, a relic of feudal ideology, which held that some individuals (men) hold property interests in others (women, children, and serfs). Backhouse does not compare the success rate in civil versus criminal seduction trials, but she does contrast the high success rate of civil seduction prosecutions with the much lower rate of convictions in rape trials, which, for the 1880s, she calculated at 34 per cent. 'The stark difference,' she argues, 'relates to the visible presence of the woman's father in the seduction trial, a factor which turned the competition into one between two males.'[66]

We have seen, however, that fathers often played prominent roles in criminal seduction prosecutions, and the presence of a father or mother did not appear to increase the chances of a guilty verdict. The direct and overtly paternal role of the father as a 'wronged party' in civil trials was no doubt part of the reason for its higher rate of success for the plaintiff. One suspects that traditional differences between civil and criminal courts, the relatively 'softer' punishment in civil cases, and the lack of the previous chastity requirement also came into play.

Class differences also shaped prosecutions in the two court systems. Backhouse notes that in the civil courts, defendants tended to be wealthier than the plaintiffs. There would be little point, of course, in suing a poor man. In the criminal cases, it appears that the men were more often of similar economic circumstances to the women. In the case of men who were farm hands, boarders, or co-workers, they were usually young and less financially established than the woman's family. Criminal charges were the poor woman's alternative; it is unlikely that many of the farm and labouring families who peopled the criminal courts could have undertaken the expense of hiring a lawyer to initiate private civil proceedings. Time in prison (when one was in fact convicted) was the poor man's alternative. The low conviction rate in criminal trials should also serve to underscore that those who did choose to press charges took their experiences seriously. Clearly many of these women (or their families) felt they had been dealt with unfairly by men, and brought their cases to the criminal court system in order to right a wrong.

The Parlour or the Kitchen: Rural and Working-Class Romance

We have seen how politicians and social reformers created the law, we have seen how it was applied by the criminal court system, and we have seen how women and their families attempted to use it to redress certain grievances. This survey of seduction cases also suggests some new ways of thinking about past romantic and sexual mores, particularly among rural and working-class populations.

There is a limited historiography of courtship, and little in a Canadian context.[67] The few accounts we possess have tended

*limited
sources?*

to rely on letters, diaries, and personal reminiscences, and are thus confined to the Anglo-Saxon middle and upper classes. A reliance on personal memoirs skews the history of intimate life in favour of the literate. It also tends towards sentimentality, presenting a universal picture of happy, contented couples who pass though courtship as the natural progression towards wedded bliss. Heterosexual coupling is taken as a given, rather than a structured process that could result in happy married life but could also go awry at many turns. Not everyone lived happily ever after. Conflict, betrayal, and recriminations were as much a part of social life as successful marriage. Whiggish interpretations of courtship should be placed in a larger context, one which not only takes into account the experience of all classes and races, but also sees the broader meaning of sexuality and gender relations as a realm of power and, often, conflict.

One cannot read the records of criminal prosecutions as 'authentic' stories of sexual or romantic truth. Like all historical sources, these texts are mediated by many factors. The involvement or non-involvement of parents, the objective in bringing charges, and the fact that these stories were told in a public, all-male, often hostile courtroom might determine the way the tale unfolded. With this caution in mind, we can use these cases to make some preliminary remarks about the intimate lives of rural and working-class people who have tended to pass through history – when they have been recognized at all – only as builders of railroads, organizers of strikes, or settlers of new lands.

Feminist historians have begun to document the turn-of-the-century moral panic around the recreational lives of single working-class women in urban areas.[68] Northern Ontario and rural southern Ontario also bore distinct social reputations. These two regions fell on opposite poles of the recreation controversy of the period. The north was perceived to be a place of too much fun; the south, of too little. The predominantly male, immigrant population of the north was associated with such rough entertainments as gambling, drinking, prostitution, and other forms of sexual licentiousness, so much so, for example, that northern schools had trouble attracting young female teachers because of their parents' concern for their moral safety.[69] For some women in the north, however, the gender imbalance gave them a high degree of popularity and social choice. As one woman remarked to historian Varpu Lindström-Best, remembering her arrival in Timmins, 'It took me four hours to find a man, there was no need to look for them, just pick and choose. I arrived on the four o'clock train, and at eight I left to dance.'[70]

The reverse problem was perceived in the rural south. A steady stream of commentators on the turn-of-the-century 'rural problem' identified the crisis of rural depopulation as stemming at least in part from the inferior opportunities for social life, recreation, and companionship. An uncreadited poem penned (presumably by a woman) in Norfolk County in 1880, titled 'An Ontario Girl's Complaint,' expressed this sentiment clearly, if badly:

I make of complaint of a plaguey pest
That's known by the name of the great North West
For this wondrous land of the setting sun
Has taken my beaux away, every one.

Yea, one by one have they all cleared out,
Thinking to better themselves, no doubt;
Caring but little how far they may go,
From the poor lone girl in Ontario.

The author went on in this vein, and should perhaps be given credit for attempting to find rhymes for 'Winnipeg' and 'Keewatin.' She ended with a stirring declaration:

I'll sling my goods in a carpet sack;
I'll off to the west and won't turn back,
I'll have a husband and a good one too.
If I have to follow to Cariboo.[71]

This research suggests, however, that while the pastimes and social life of rural and small-town youth may have been different from their urban counterparts in form, there were not always great differences in content. Changes in family life and economic relations in this period allowed many women the opportunity to leave their homes (whether permanently or for a few hours daily), meet new people, and make new choices.

Outside work allowed many women a degree of social freedom. Mary C, for example, met Paul C while she was working as a waitress at the Algonquin Hotel in Sault Ste Marie. Hotel chambermaids and cooks met a succession of men new to their communities, store clerks flirted with their customers, and factory workers often worked alongside a number of eligible men.

Even that supposedly respectable and closely supervised form of female employment, domestic service, allowed some women the opportunity to make friends with men. Two domestic servants in this study formed relationships with the sons of their employers, and several more met men as they were walking home from their jobs. The rural and small town setting of these cases adds a new dimension to relations between servants and their employers.[72] In most cases, the two families knew each other. The families of Herman M and Mary S, for example, had been neighbours near Wallaceburg for ten years, so when Herman's mother needed domestic help while she was ill, she called Mary in for a few weeks. In such cases, employment as a domestic also allowed women the freedom to get to know a neighbouring man, and gave the couples some new sexual possibilities. Mary testified that she and Herman had sex regularly while she was employed by his mother, both in the barn and a couple of times in the house.

Women also found freedom while visiting married siblings. Older sisters in particular allowed visiting younger sisters quite a bit of independence. Some couples met at parties given by elder sisters, and Margaret B's sister even allowed her and Alexander F to have sex (in the privacy of the kitchen) while she visited. Finally, single parenthood also seemed to loosen the reins of parental supervision; in one case, a father sent his daughter to live with her grandparents after the death of her mother, where she began a relationship with her cousin.[73] In other cases, living with one parent (most often a mother) might increase the chances of regular nights out with boys.

Even the most innocent and respectable courtship ritual might become a sexual adventure. Activities such as picnics, berry picking, skating, dances, and, in towns, commercial amusements such as movie theatres and restaurants were common. Sexual privacy could be found to and from all such outings. Going 'out walking' or sometimes driving (in a buggy or, later, a car or motorcycle) was the most common way to socialize, get picked up, or flirt. Kathy Peiss has suggested that, among New York working-class youth, a pick-up on the street was 'an accepted means of gaining companionship for an evening's entertainment.'[74] In rural areas, this often was the evening's entertainment. The sexual dimension of some walks or drives presents some wonderful incongruities – and perhaps speaks volumes about the real effect of movements for moral regulation. Several couples had sex in the woods while walking home together from church, and Sam S and Hilda R would make love in his buggy after he drove her home from Salvation Army meetings.[75]

For couples who desired (or, sometimes, when the man desired) to make sex part of their courtship, space and opportunity could be found. Contrary to the fears of the social purity movement, which conceptualized only cities as sources of sexual danger to women, the decision to become sexual had more to do with negotiations around the balance of power between the sexes than with geography. For some, even that most staid Victorian social ritual, paying a house call, might result not in a chaperoned tea in the parlour, but rather a late night tryst in the kitchen.

How did couples get caught? Sexual life in this period was regulated by a shifting combination of families, communities, and the state. We have already seen, in the case of Patrick C and Mary Ellen T of Oshawa, that Patrick's bragging to his co-workers was what tipped Mary Ellen's father off to their relationship. In several other cases, male sexual bravado got them in trouble. A neighbour of Herman M testified that Herman told him he had 'gone down to graft the mare' with Mary S and had 'got such a hard on' he 'didn't care if he got a year [in prison] for it.' Sometimes, sexual gossip reached the ears of anxious parents; at other times the woman involved found out, and this indiscretion may have added to her resolve to press criminal charges. Emma F of Haileybury, for example, told here mother about the flirtation she had been having with their boarder Frank B, after she heard him telling her uncle he'd been 'trying to have a little fun with her.'[76] One of the rules of non-marital sexual activity was silence, and when this was broken both parties might suffer.

An intriguing case of gossip as a form of regulation was the relationship between twenty-three-year-old George A and his fourteen-year-old sister-in-law, Mary R. It appears that George and Mary had been seeing each other for some time; they left their home in Picton together for a couple of weeks and, shortly after returning, Mary died, apparently from a botched abortion. No one in Mary's family was interested in pressing criminal charges against George, but her parents testified at the coroner's inquest that they had been subject to extreme community pressure for tolerating Mary's relationship, which they continued to deny, even after her death. Witness after witness testified to seeing them together, however, including one alert railroad switchman who saw them lying down together in the train station in Trenton, on their way out of town. 'We have to keep our eyes open for anything like that ... to see that nothing improper takes place,' he said in court. 'That's what we are paid for.'[77] Even while the state was creating new and stricter categories of criminal sexual behaviour, communities continued to keep watch over 'suspicious' actions.

This was especially true in the rural areas and small towns from which these stories emerge. We must keep in mind that the women in this survey are mostly the ones who 'stayed home.' These are not the independent wage-earning women who strutted the streets of Toronto and so concerned the police and social reformers of the day.[78] Most of the women in this study lived at home with their parents during their courtship. In rural and small-town Ontario, working 'out' might mean taking a series of short-term domestic jobs a few farms down the road, and going out on the town might involve a walk to the post office or home from church. Even in these constrained settings, however, dominant social conventions regarding dating, sex, and romance were contested. In rural Ontario, the berry patch could provide the same opportunity for sexual danger or sexual pleasure as the most raucous urban dance hall.

Relatively few young couples in Ontario fought out their problems in criminal court. It is difficult, especially given the absence of Canadian studies of working-class courtship, to say how typical these cases were. We do not know how many other women took the risks involved in allowing a sexual component to their relationships. Nor do we know much about what happened, beyond these criminal trials, to those who got caught. We will never know if seduced and abandoned women lived the 'ruined and blighted' lives Charlton and others warned of, or whether the romantic desires of fifteen-year-old girls resulted in happy adult marriages. The problem of unwed motherhood continued to vex moral reformers, particularly those in the expanding field of social work. The Ontario government tacitly admitted the failure of the seduction law to solve the problem of illegitimate children in 1921, when it took the decision to pursue charges against fathers out of the hands of the woman involved.[79]

We do know, however, that the criminal law was unhelpful, both in punishing men who reneged on romantic promises and in changing the social ethos which made premarital sex such an enormous risk for women. Protection, especially of the powerless, slid easily into surveillance. The suppression of women's sexuality historically has taken many forms. The legal regulation of seduction was one of the 'good cops,' but patriarchal power was not unleashed by sexual brutality alone. Through the limitation of women's sexual autonomy, the creation of artificial categories such as 'maidenly girls' and 'designing women,' or in more obvious forms of abuse such as rape, patriarchal ideas and practices about sexuality, desire, and gender were entrenched. Rather than the rhetoric of the seduction legislators, women in this period would have benefited more from the candid sentiment about sexuality expressed in 1921 by Canadian socialist feminist Alice Chown: 'I am convinced that, once we are willing to be frank and truthful, we shall find our way out of this morass of falsehood, hypocrisy, and illicit relations, with their heart-breaking results. Henceforth I hope I shall be brave and not try to cover my own or any other person's sex experience with moral platitudes.'[80]

NOTES

I would life thank the other contributors to this collection for their helpful comments on this paper. Thanks also to Roberta Hamilton and Bryan Palmer for their support of the project of which this is a part, and to Nancy Adamson and Anne Molgat for providing elegant and much needed privacy while I began writing.

1 See, for example, Kate Ellis et al., eds., *Caught Looking* (Seattle: Real Comet Press 1988); Dorchen Leidholdt and Janice Raymond eds., *The Sexual Liberals and the Attack on Feminism* (New York: Pergamon 1990); Joan Nestle, *A Restricted Country* (New York: Firebrand 1987); Ann Snitow et al., eds., *Powers of Desire* (New York: Monthly Review 1983); Carol Vance, ed., *Pleasure and Danger* (Boston: Routledge and Kegan Paul 1984); and Jeffrey Weeks, *Sexuality and Its Discontents* (London: Routledge and Kegan Paul 1986). Canadian contributors to this debate include Laurie Bell, ed., *Good Girls/Bad Girls* (Toronto: Women's Press 1987); Varda Burstyn ed., *Women against Censorship* (Toronto: Douglas and McIntyre 1985); Susan G. Cole, *Pornography and the Sex Crisis* (Toronto: Amanita 1989); Gary Kinsman, *The Regulation of Desire* (Montreal: Black Rose 1987); and Mariana Valverde, *Sex, Power, and Pleasure* (Toronto: Women's Press 1985).

2 See, for example, John D'Emilio and Estelle Freedman, *Intimate Matters: A History of Sexuality in America* (New York: Harper and Row 1988); Ellen DuBois and Linda Gordon, 'Seeking Ecstasy on the Battlefield: Danger and Pleasure in Nineteenth Century Feminist Sexual Thought,' in Vance, ed., *Pleasure and Danger*, 31–50; Kathy Peiss and Christina Simmons, eds., *Passion and Power: Sexuality in History* (Philadelphia: Temple University Press 1989); Christine Stansell, *City of Woman: Sex and Class in*

New York *1789–1860* (New York: A.A. Knopf 1986); and Jeffrey Weeks, *Sex, Politics and Society: The Regulation of Sexuality since 1800* (London: Longmans 1981). Sheila Jeffreys, *The Spinster and Her Enemies* (London: Pandora 1985), is an exception; Jeffreys is one of the few historians of sexuality writing from a radical feminist perspective.

3 For a critique of first-wave feminist sexual politics see DuBois and Gordon, 'Seeking Ecstasy'; Mariana Valverde, 'When the Mother of the Race Is Free,' in this volume; and Judith Walkowitz, 'Male Vice and Female Virtue: Feminism and the Politics of Prostitution in Nineteenth Century Britain,' in Snitow et al., eds., *Powers of Desire*. On the medicalization of sexuality see Janice Irvine, *Disorders of Desire: Sex and Gender in Modern American Sexology* (Philadelphia: Temple University Press 1990), and Frank Mort, *Dangerous Sexualities: Medico-Moral Politics in England since 1830* (London: Routledge and Kegan Paul 1987).

4 Andrea Dworkin, 'Why So-Called Radical Men Love and Need Pornography,' in Laura Lederer, ed., *Take Back the Night: Women on Pornography* (New York: William Morow 1980), 152, quoted in Alice Echols, 'The Taming of the Id: Feminist Sexual Politics, 1968–83,' in Vance, ed., *Pleasure and Danger*, 59. See also Sheila Jeffreys recent remarkable assertion that 'it is difficult to imagine how heterosexual desire – considering the role playing in just about every relationship – could possibly be egalitarian.' Jeffreys, 'Eroticizing Women's Subordination,' in Leidholdt and Raymond, eds., *Sexual Liberals*, 134.

5 Carol Vance, 'Pleasure and Danger: Toward a Politics of Sexuality,' in Vance, eds., *Pleasure and Danger*, 7. See also the critique of radical feminist sexuality theory by Varda Burstyn, 'Anatomy of a Moral Panic,' *Fuse* (summer 1984): 30–7; Echols, 'The Taming,' and 'The New Feminism of Yin and Yang,' in Snitow, et al., eds., *Powers of Desire*, 439–60; Joan Nestle, 'My Mother Like to Fuck,' in Snitow et al., eds., *Powers of Desire*, 468–70; and Lynne Segal, *Is the Future Female? Troubled Thoughts on Contemporary Feminism* (London: Virago 1987), 70–116.

6 This is one of the central principles of D'Emilio and Freedman's overview, *Intimate Matters*.

7 Rosalind Coward, *Female Desires* (New York: Grove Press 1985), 42.

8 Mary Poovey, among others, argues that differences in sexual desire

were a key component of the Victorian construction of gender difference. See *Uneven Developments: The Ideological Work of Gender in Mid-
Victorian England* (Chicago: University of Chicago Press 1988), 6.

9 D'Emilio and Freedman, *Intimate Matters*, 70

10 In the Assize and County Court Judges Criminal Court (the top two levels of the criminal court system in Ontario), over fifty criminal prosecutions for seduction were initiated between 1886 and 1929, in twenty-five
rural and northern counties in the province. The case files vary in
terms of amount of detail, but when combined with local newspaper accounts of the trials they give us a portrait of the social situations which
led to criminal prosecutions. The relatively low numbers of criminal
prosecutions for voluntary sexual relations contrast sharply with cases of
involuntary, forced sexual liaisons. In the same period, in the same regions, there were close to 350 cases of rape, attempted rape, and indecent assault, 100 cases of 'carnal knowledge' (assaults against children),
and 20 cases of incest. On the history of sexual crime in this period see
Karen Dubinsky, 'Improper Advances: Sexual Danger and Pleasure in
Rural and Northern Ontario, 1880–1929' (PhD thesis, Queen's University 1990). For an explanation of the Ontario court system see Margaret
Banks, 'The Evolution of the Ontario Courts 1788–1981,' in David
Flaherty, ed., *Essays in the History of Canadian Law*, vol. 2 (Toronto:
University of Toronto Press 1982), 418–91.

11 John Charlton, 'My Autobiography and Recollections, from 1829 to
1907' (no date, unpublished), 802

12 John Charlton, *Speeches and Addresses: Political, Literary and Religious* (Toronto: Morang and Co 1905), x–xi

13 Canada, House of Commons, *Debates*, 15 March 1883, 220

14 Charlton, *Speeches* 227

15 House of Commons, *Debates*, 1 April 1886, 442

16 The classic Canadian statement of this position is Carol Lee Bacchi, *Liberation Deferred? The Ideas of the English-Canadian Suffragists, 1877–1918*
(Toronto: University of Toronto Press 1983).

17 Mariana Valverde and Lorna Weir, 'The Struggles of the Immoral:
Preliminary Remarks on Moral Regulation,' *Resources for Feminist Re-
search* 17, 3 (Sept. 1988): 31–4. See also Valverde, *The Age of Light,
Soap, and Water: Moral Reform in English Canada, 1885–1925* (Toronto:
McClelland and Stewart 1991).

18 University of Toronto, Thomas Fisher Library, John Charlton, unpublished diary, vol. 5, 1891
19 Charlton, 'Autobiography' 407
20 Charlton, *Speeches*, 281
21 The features of the seduction law are detailed in Constance Backhouse, 'Nineteenth-Century Canadian Rape Law, 1800–92,' in Flaherty, ed., *Essays in the History of Canadian Law*, vol. 2, 200–47; John McLaren, 'Chasing the Social Evil: Moral Fervour and the Evolution of Canada's Prostitution Laws, 1867–1917,' *Canadian Journal of Law and Society* 1 (1986): 125–65, and 'White Slavers: The Reform of Canada's Prostitution Laws and Patterns of Enforcement, 1900–1920,' *Criminal Justice History* 7 (1987): 53–119; Graham Parker, 'The Legal Regulation of Sexual Activity and the Protection of Females,' *Osgoode Hall Law Journal* 21, 2 (June 1983): 187–224; and James Snell, 'The White Life for Two: The Defence of Marriage and Sexual Morality in Canada, 1890–1914,' *Histoire Sociale / Social History* 16, 31 (May 1983): 11–28.
22 House of Commons, *Debates*, 1890, 3166–8 and 3441. See also *Debates* on the bill in 1882 (20 February and 13 March); 1883 (6, 12, 20, and 28 March); 1885 (18 March and 22 June); 1886 (1, 8, and 14 April); and 1887 (25 April and 4 and 6 May).
23 National Archives of Canada (NA), Department of Justice Correspondence, file 63/1894, R.C. Smith to John Thompson, 6 May 1892. On Watt see Parker, 'The Legal Regulation,' and Henry Morgan, ed., *The Canadian Men and Women of the Times* (Toronto: William Briggs 1912), 1149.
24 Joy Parr, *The Gender of Breadwinners: Women, Men, and Change in Two Industrial Towns, 1880–1950* (Toronto: University of Toronto Press 1990), 35
25 Hamilton *Palladium of Labor*, 10 Nov. 1883. On Maria McCabe see NA, RG 13, Capital Case File 174A, vol. 1419, 1883–9. On the gender and sexual politics of the Knights of Labor in Ontario see Gregory S. Kealey and Bryan Palmer, *Dreaming of What Might Be: The Knights of Labor in Ontario, 1880–1900* (Toronto: New Hogtown Press 1987), 316–26, and Karen Dubinsky, 'The Modern Chivalry: Women and the Knights of Labor in Ontario 1880–1891' (MA thesis, Carleton University 1985), 158–201. On women and the Knights in United States see Susan Levine, *Labor's True Woman* (Philadelphia: Temple University Press 1984).

26 Hamilton *Palladium of Labor*, 18 July 1885. The best account of the Maiden Tribute story is Deborah Gorham, 'The Maiden Tribute of Modern Babylon Re-examined: Child Prostitution and the Idea of Childhood in Late Victorian England,' *Victorian Studies* 21, 3 (spring 1978): 353–79.

27 Hamilton *Palladium of Labor*, 18 July 1885

28 On the association of working-class life with sexual immorality in England see Mort, *Dangerous Sexualities*, 42–63. On Canadian working-class views of sexuality see Angus McLaren, 'What Has This To Do With Working-Class Women? Birth Control and the Canadian Left, 1900–1939,' *Histoire Sociale / Social History* 14 (1981): 435–54; Janice Newton, 'From Wage Slave to White Slave,' in Linda Kealey and Joan Sangster, eds., *Beyond the Vote: Canadian Women and Politics* (Toronto: University of Toronto Press 1989), 217–39; and Joan Sangster, *Dreams of Equality: Women on the Canadian Left, 1920–1950* (Toronto: McClelland and Stewart 1989), 38–41 and 157–62.

29 Hamilton *Palladium of Labor*, 10 April 1886, 12 April 1884, 31 July 1886. As well as constructing an alternative discourse of upper-class immorality, the charge was, in this instance, prophetic. One of the most outspoken participants in the discussions of the seduction law in the House of Commons was Malcolm Cameron, MP from Huron. Several years after arguing against the bill in parliament, he was the subject of an enormous scandal in Goderich for allegedly seducing his orphaned servant, who died giving birth.

30 Barbara Taylor, 'The Men Are As Bad As Their Masters ... Socialism, Feminism and Sexual Antagonism in the London Tailoring Trade in the 1830's,' in Judith Newton et al., eds., *Sex and Class in Women's History* (London: Routledge and Kegan Paul 1983), 187–220. An account of how the British labour movement dealt with the class and gender dynamics of sexual assault is Anna Clark, *Women's Silence, Men's Violence: Sexual Assault in England, 1770–1845* (London: Pandora Press 1987), 90–110.

31 Judith Walkowitz, 'Male Vice and Female Virtue: Feminism and the Politics of Prostitution in Nineteenth-Century Britain,' in Snitow et al., eds., *Powers of Desire* 419–38

32 McLaren, 'Chasing the Social Evil,' and 'White Slavers'

33 Backhouse, 'Nineteenth-Century Canadian Rape Law'
34 Parker, 'Legal Regulation'
35 American historian Mary Odem has reached similar conclusions about the operation of the law pertaining to statutory rape, noting that while men were subject to criminal prosecution, women were usually also incarcerated in juvenile detention centres. It does not appear that Canadian women involved in seduction charges were treated similarly; however, women involved in abduction incidents, another charge which usually involved voluntary sexual relations, were often detained in children's shelters. See Odem, 'Statutory Rape Prosecutions in Alameda County, California, 1910–1920,' presented at the Organization of American Historians Annual Meeting, April 1989. Thanks to Christina Simmons for providing me with this paper.
36 Stansell, *City of Women*, 87
37 Ontario Archives (OA), RG 22, Criminal Assize Indictments (CAI), [S], Carleton County, 1891
38 Odem, 'Statutory Rape Prosecutions,' 2. See also Anna Clark, 'Rape or Seduction? A Controversy over Sexual Violence in the Nineteenth Century,' in London Feminist History Group, eds., *The Sexual Dynamics of History* (London: Pluto Press 1983), 13–27.
39 CAI, [J], Parry Sound District, 1897
40 OA, County Court Judges Criminal Court (CCJCC), [C], Ontario County, 1917
41 Cited in Mary Bularzik, 'Sexual Harassment at the Workplace: Historical Notes,' *Radical America* 12 (1978): 35
42 On nineteenth-century workplace sexual harassment see Constance Backhouse and Leah Cohen, *The Secret Oppression: Sexual Harassment of Working Women* (Toronto: Macmillan 1978), 53–72, and Jan Lambertz, 'Sexual Harassment in the Nineteenth Century English Cotton Industry,' *History Workshop Journal* 19 (spring 1985), 29–61.
43 CAI, [D], Elgin County, 1894, and St Thomas *Daily Times*, 9 March 1894
44 CCJCC, [C], Ontario County, 1903
45 CAI, [M], Oxford County, 1895, and Woodstock *Sentinal Review*, 10 Jan 1895 and 22 March 1895
46 John Gillis, 'Servants, Sexual Relations and the Risks of Illegitimacy in London, 1801–1900,' in Newton et al., eds., *Sex and Class*, 114–45. On

illegitimacy in Canada in a later period see Andrée Levesque, 'Deviant Anonymous: Single Mothers at the Hopital de la Miséricorde in Montréal, 1929–1939,' *Historical Papers* 1984, 168–83.

47 Peter Ward, 'Unwed Motherhood in Nineteenth Century English Canada,' *Historical Papers* 1981, 34–56

48 AO, District Count Judges Criminal Court (DCJCC), [L], Algoma Disrict, 1917, and CAI, [L], Algoma District 1922

49 Parker, 'Legal Regulation,' 236

50 CAI, [W] Dufferin County, 1922, and Orangeville *Sun*, 8 June 1922

51 CCJCC, [H], Perth County, 1896

52 CCJCC, [C], Algoma District, 1918

53 CAI, [T], Perth County, 1892, and Stratford *Evening Beacon*, 5 and 6 Oct. 1892

54 CAI, [H], Perth County, 1896

55 CCJCC, [M], Lambton County, 1917. For an account of the importance of character to nineteenth-century working women see Anna Clark, 'Whores and Gossips: Sexual Reputation in London, 1770–1825,' in Arina Angerman et al., eds., *Current Issues in Women's History* (London: Routledge and Kegan Paul 1989), 231–48.

56 Kathy Peiss, 'Charity Girls and City Pleasures: Historical Notes on Working-Class Sexuality, 1880–1920,' in Snitow et al., eds., *Powers of Desire*, 74–87

57 DCJCC, [C], Algoma District, 1896, and CAI, Cook, Dufferin County, 1927

58 CAI, [T], Perth County, 1892, and CAI, [F], Dufferin County, 1896

59 Bryan Palmer, 'Discordant Music: Charivaris and Whitecapping in Nineteenth-Century North America,' *Labour/Le Travailleur* 3 (1978): 59

60 OA, RG 22, Crown Attorney Letterbooks, Ontario County, 1878–82, Letterbook Number 2. On the material and ideological development of the legal system see John Beattie, 'Judicial Records and the Measurement of Crime in Eighteenth Century England,' in Louis Knafla, ed., *Crime and Criminal Justice in Europe and Canada* (Waterloo: Wilfrid Laurier Press 1981), 127–46; Douglas Hay, 'Property, Authority and the Criminal Law,' in Douglas Hay et al., eds., *Albion's Fatal Tree: Crime and Society in Eighteenth Century England* (New York: Pantheon 1975), 17–64; and Alfred Soman, 'Deviance and Criminal Justice in Western Europe, 1300–1800: An Essay in Structure,' *Criminal Justice History* 1 (1980):

1–28. On the state of the legal system in northern Ontario in this pe-
riod see Elizabeth Arthur, 'Beyond Superior: Ontario's New Found
Land,' in Roger Hall et al., eds., *Patterns of the Past: Interpreting Ontario's
History* (Toronto: Dundern 1988), 130–49, and David Tremblay, 'Dimen-
sions of Crime and Punishment at the Lakehead, 1873–1903' (MA thesis,
Lakehead University, 1983).

61 Rosemary J. Coombe, 'The Most Disgusting, Disgraceful and Inequitous
   Proceeding in Our Law: The Action for Breach of Promise of Marriage
   in Nineteenth-Century Ontario,' *University of Toronto Law Journal* 38
   (1988): 64–108

62 Ibid., 80

63 Constance Backhouse, 'The Tort of Seduction: Fathers and Daughters
   in Nineteenth Century Canada,' *Dalhousie Law Journal* 10, 1 (June 1986):
   45–80

64 McLaren, 'Chasing the Social Evil,' 150

65 In criminal courts, people accused of a crime are believed to be innocent. It is up to the state to prove them guilty, beyond a 'reasonable
   doubt.' In civil courts, culpability rests on what is known as a 'balance
   of probability,' which, relative to the criminal courts, tends to skew the
   odds of success in favour of those pressing charges.

66 Backhouse, 'The Tort of Seduction,' 77

67 On courtship in the United States see Beth Bailey, *From Front Porch to
   Back Seat: Courtship in Twentieth Century America* (Baltimore: Johns Hopkins University Press 1988), and Ellen Rothman, *Hands and Hearts: A
   History of Courtship in America* (New York: Basic Books 1984). On Canada
   see Peter Ward, *Courtship, Love and Marriage in Nineteenth-Century English Canada* (Montreal: McGill-Queen's University Press 1990).

68 See, for example, Kathy Peiss, *Cheap Amusements: Working Women and
   Leisure in Turn-of-the-Century New York* (Philadelphia: Temple University
   Press 1986); Joanne Meyerowitz, *Women Adrift: Independent Wage Earners
   in Chicago, 1880–1930* (Chicago: University of Chicago Press 1988); Mar-
   ian Morton, 'Seduced and Abandoned in an American City: Cleveland
   and Its Fallen Women, 1869–1936,' *Journal of Urban History* 11 (Aug.
   1985): 443–69; Stansell, *City of Women*; and, in Canada, Carolyn Strange,
   'From Modern Babylon to a City Upon a Hill: The Toronto Social Survey Commission of 1915 and the Search for Sexual Order in the City,'
   in Hall et al., eds., *Patterns*, 225–78.

69 John Abbott, 'Accomplishing a Man's Task: Rural Women Teachers, Male Culture and the School Inspectorate in Turn-of-the-Century Ontario,' *Ontario History* 78, 4 (Dec. 1986): 313–30

70 Varpu Lindström-Best, *Defiant Sisters: A Social History of Finnish Immigrant Women in Canada* (Toronto: Multicultural History Society of Ontario 1988), 62

71 Simcoe *British Canadian*, 5 May 1880. See also Edward Amey, *Farm Life As It Should Be, and Farm Labourers and Servant Girls Grievances* (Toronto: Ellis and Moore 1885); John MacDougall, *Rural Life in Canada, Its Trends and Tasks* (Toronto: Westminister Co. 1913); and David C. Jones, 'There Is Some Power About Land: The Western Canadian Agrarian Press and Country Life Ideology,' *Journal of Canadian Studies* 17, 3 (1982): 97–108.

72 On rural women's employment in Ontario see Alan Brookes and Catherine Wilson, 'Working away from the Farm: The Young Women of North Huron, 1910–1930,' *Ontario History* 77, 4 (Dec. 1985): 281–300.

73 CAI, [S], Muskoka, 1905

74 Peiss, *Cheap Amusements*, 106; Stansell, *City of Women*, 86

75 CAI, [S], Perth County, 1894, and Stratford *Evening Beacon*, 29 March 1894

76 CAI, [B], Temiskaming District, 1914

77 CAI, [A], Prince Edward County, 1899

78 Strange, 'From Modern Babylon'

79 Lykke de la Cour, ' "Tis Not As It Should Be": The Regulation of Unwed Motherhood in Ontario, 1870's–1920's,' unpublished paper, York University, Jan. 1990. On the regulation of unwed mothers through state welfare policies see Veronica Strong Boag, 'Wages for Housework: Mothers' Allowance and the Beginnings of Social Security in Canada,' *Journal of Canadian Studies* 14, 1 (May 1979): 24–34, and Margaret Hillyard Little, 'Mothers First and Foremost,' paper presented at the Canadian Political Science Association Annual Meeting, Victoria, 1990.

80 Alice Chown, *The Stairway* (1921; Toronto: University of Toronto Press 1988), 108

3 The 'Hallelujah Lasses':
Working-Class Women in the Salvation Army in English Canada, 1882–92
Lynne Marks

HO! EVERYONE

GRAND OPENING
of the
GREAT FREE SALVATION TENT.
Opposite the City Hall. Kingston.

With tremendous Attack on Sin and Satan from
the Market Battery, on Circus Day.

The 5th Canadian Corps of the Salvation Army will hold opening
Donation Service in this grand new tent in the afternoon and
evening of Saturday 21st July A.D. 1883 at 3 p.m. and 7 p.m.,
followed by an

ALL-NIGHT WATCH WITH THE SAVIOUR

On Sabbath, July 22 Hallelujah Knee-Drill at 7 o'clock a.m. ...
Principal Attractions: Superior to any show on earth. Free Salvation. Come and get it. Glorious experiences of Prodigal Sons.
The Silver Band. Magnificent Choruses and Hallelujah Sing Song
by Hallelujah Lasses. Captains Hallelujah Abbie; Happy Nellie,
and Salvation Mary; Capt. Ludgate, Smiling Johnny ... Ingersoll
Maggie, Salvation Billy Shea and Billy the Tinker, the Happy

Shoemaker, Johnny the Drummer, and Jimmy the Bricklayer,
Wright the Printer and many others too numerous to mention.[1]

This advertisement and others like it drew huge crowds to Salvation Army events in the 1880s. Newspapers routinely reported packed halls, with hundreds being turned away at the door.[2] While the Salvation Army deliberately made use of a wide range of tactics to draw crowds, female officers, or 'Hallelujah lasses' as they were popularly known, were clearly a major attraction. The arrival of a new female officer in Kingston led to greater crowds than 'when the Governor General and the Princess were here,' with the hall being 'jammed to the doors.'[3]

Such scenes were repeated across Canada because female preachers, or officers as they were called, were a common feature of the Army. In the 1880s over half of all Salvation Army officers were women, in stark contrast to the religious leadership of all other Canadian denominations, which was exclusively male.[4] The Salvation Army membership followed more familiar patterns, because, as in the mainstream churches, the majority of members, or soldiers as they were known, were also women. Female soldiers, who were also often called Hallelujah lasses, played a more active role in the Army than did their sisters in more established denominations. Like male soldiers, they were expected to stand up in crowded halls, give testimony to their faith in Jesus, and describe the misery of their past lives. They also marched through the streets, beating drums or tambourines to attract attention to the cause.

Salvation Army women, both officers and soldiers, differed in other ways from the female membership of Canada's mainstream churches. Like Salvation Army men, the majority of Salvation Army women were drawn from Canada's emerging working class.[5] The religious experience of this working class, both female and male, has received minimal attention from English-Canadian historians. Historical work on women and religion has focused primarily on female religious associations that provided some autonomy for women, while remaining subordinated to a male church hierarchy.[6] Involvement in such associations is assumed to have been a largely middle-class activity. Labour historians have also neglected the religious dimensions of male and female workers' lives, choosing instead to study workplace experience and union activism.[7] Those few historians who have examined working-class participation in non-workplace activities have focused on leisure rather than religion, and have largely ignored women's experience.[8]

An exploration of women's role in the Salvation Army does not tell us everything about the relationship between Canadian working-class women and religion, but it can illuminate the nature of religious involvement among a significant minority of working-class women. These women's participation in the Army generally reflected deeply felt religious beliefs, but their decision to join this particular religious organization also provides us with an avenue to understanding other facets of their beliefs and experience. An examination of the activities of Salvation Army women can help us both to understand the limitations of working-class women's lives and to recognize that these women were able to make use of opportunities offered by the Army to reorder their lives, and in so doing to challenge the restrictions within which they lived. Since many of these restrictions were linked to prevailing gender-based norms, an exploration of working-class women's responses to such restrictions can provide insights into a significant question within women's history. To what extent did working-class women internalize the prevailing gender ideology, which viewed women as passive, frail, and sexually vulnerable, with higher moral natures and an exclusively domestic mission?[9] Was this vision of fragile true womanhood completely irrelevant to working-class women, who performed arduous labour both in the home and increasingly in the public sphere? Alternatively, did these women refashion this ideal into a specifically working-class femininity that reflected their own experience as well as the most compelling features of the dominant ideology? Answers to such questions are of particular significance within women's history, where working-class women's attitudes and behaviour have often been assumed to mirror those of the middle class, and within labour history, where the limited union involvement of working women is frequently explained with reference to these women's acceptance of dominant norms of feminine passivity and docility.[10]

Sources used for this article include Salvation Army officers' and converts' rolls, handbooks of Army regulations, the *War Cry*, the official Salvation Army paper, and selected secular newspapers from across English Canada.[11] The obvious biases of the two newspaper sources call for particularly careful and critical reading. The *War Cry* is of course primarily concerned with gaining converts and is reluctant to reveal anything negative about the Army. Nonetheless, the paper can provide considerable detail about women's role in the Army – with the ideal role being easily discernible and the reality being pieced together with somewhat more difficulty.

The secular press, which beyond infrequent letters to the editor from female and/or working-class readers is written from a middle-class male perspective, provides equal challenges to efforts to unravel working-class women's experience. What is readily accessible in the secular press is the fundamentally ambivalent middle-class response to the Salvation Army. This response clearly demonstrates that for the middle class, religion was far more than a spiritual phenomenon. Church attendance was an integral part of a middle-class cultural system that valued respectability and was based in patriarchal control. For some, the Salvation Army was tolerated for converting the masses and, more importantly, for bringing them more clearly within the bounds of middle-class values by making them industrious, moral, and family-oriented. Others, however, saw a religious movement that readily adopted aspects of working-class culture in an effort to gain converts and that allowed unprecedented power and freedom to women as a challenge rather than as a bulwark to the dominant social order.

Beginnings: The Salvation Army in England

The Salvation Army began in London, England, in 1878, but emerged from an earlier organization known as the Christian Mission, which was founded in 1865 by William Booth, a former

Methodist preacher. The dominant principle in Booth's life was said to be the need to convert the poorest groups in society, who were generally untouched by the churches.[12] While Booth's earliest efforts were based in traditions of Methodist revivalism, his work soon became distinctive through his willingness to use a variety of unconventional methods to reach the poor. A key method was the adoption of military organization and military trappings. Army structure was firmly hierarchical, with all members expected to obey the orders of superior officers. Supreme power was vested in Booth, who as general commanded an Army which, by the 1880s, had spread around the world. The Army's military trappings included brass bands and uniforms as well as a distinctive vocabulary in which prayer services were called 'knee drills' and saying 'Amen' was known as 'firing a volley.' Those who joined the Salvation Army after conversion were known as soldiers, while preachers were called officers. This militaristic approach was intended to appeal to a jingoistic working class. A Canadian Salvationist provided an equally telling reason for its success. He pointed out that 'it is well known that in many parts of the world – in this country indeed – a strong prejudice exists in the minds of a vast majority of the people against the terms church, cathedral, holy orders, priest, preacher, deacon, elder and such like, and on no account will they have anything to do with them. By calling our body an Army, the places of worship, barracks and the officers, general, major, captain etc., we avoid these prejudices and obtain the attendance of the people.'[13]

Historians of the British Salvation Army have noted the primarily working-class nature of Army members and have suggested that involvement in such a distinctively working-class organization could reflect the emergence of class consciousness.[14] Roland Robertson suggests that for many working-class Salvationists, 'allegiance to the Salvation Army offered an opportunity of maintaining religiosity within the Protestant tradition but in opposition to the middle class identified denominations.'[15] For working-class women, who have generally been considered more religiously observant than working-class men, a class-based religious option may have been particularly welcome.[16] The Salvation Army also offered further opportunities for these women, including greater equality and more access to leadership roles than that available within either the mainstream churches or the labour movement in this period.[17]

Two reasons have been advanced to explain the relative equality of women within the Salvation Army. One was the lack of resources available to the early Christian Mission, which increased the willingness to make use of all potential preachers, regardless of gender.[18] This explanation is inadequate in itself, since other religious movements have faced a shortage of workers but have placed the preservation of patriarchal authority ahead of the saving of souls. This practical need for more workers may, however, have given more force to the arguments of William Booth's wife, Catherine Booth, who has generally been credited with establishing the relative equality of women in the Army.

While the evangelical nature of the Salvation Army led to a focus on spiritual equality that could in itself justify female preaching and had provided some space for female preachers in the early years of Methodism, Catherine Booth went beyond this to provide what was in many ways an explicitly feminist critique of male religious domination.[19] In response to those who cited St Paul as forbidding female preaching, she pointed out that this argument was based solely on male interpretations of the bible. She claimed that once women were able to interpret such passages themselves, the real truth would be forthcoming.[20] For Catherine Booth it was not scriptural authority but male selfishness that relegated women to the private role of visiting the poor and the sick and reserved the honour of the pulpit for men. She argued that 'Our Lord links the joy with the suffering, the glory with the shame.'[21]

Catherine Booth believed that there was nothing inherent in women's nature that made them incapable of preaching. She maintained instead that women had been 'trained to subjection ... imbecile dependence on the judgement of others.'[22] In this she echoed the arguments of many feminists from Mary Wollstonecraft on. However, like most nineteenth-century feminists, Catherine Booth did not believe that all gender differences were socially constructed. Women did have different natures from men, but this did not make women unfit to preach God's word. Booth maintained that rather than unsexing women, preaching 'exalts and refines all the tenderest and most womanly instincts of her nature.'[23]

The Salvation Army's rhetoric regarding women's equality was not always borne out in reality. Men certainly dominated the upper echelons of the Army.[24] Nonetheless, the Army did provide real and unusual opportunities for women. Female soldiers were expected to play an active public role in converting others. Like male soldiers, they were also encouraged to become officers, and thus devote their entire lives to conversion work. As officers, many women gained the rank of captain and were placed in charge of congregations, or corps as they were known.[25] Although Salvation Army captains were not expected to deliver long learned sermons, they did organize and lead the services and delivered short talks and exhortations to the congregations.

The Army in Canada: Methods and Adherents

By the time the Salvation Army entered Canada in 1882 its structure, and women's position within it, had been clearly defined. Neither the nature of the Army, nor the role it offered women, meshed with the religious fabric of Canada in the 1880s. The frontier religious enthusiasm that had dominated Canadian religious life of the 1820s and 1830s was long gone. Most Protestants continued to define themselves as evangelical Christians, but the methods used to bring people to a recognition of their sinfulness and their need to seek salvation through 'the transforming power of faith in Christ' had changed.[26] While certain churches, particularly the Methodist, still held periodic revival meetings, too much 'emotionalism' was shunned.[27] Those attending church were almost as likely to hear learned rebuttals of the latest challenge to religious orthodoxy, be it Darwinism or the Higher Criticism, as they were to be exhorted concerning the state of their souls.[28] Spiritual issues were still important, but the churches had been more fully integrated into the secular world and the concerns of that world. The salvation of souls could no longer justify the flouting of social convention.[29] One casualty of this fading of religious enthusiasm were female preachers, who had been accepted within a few denominations prior to mid-century.[30] Women did play an active role in the churches in the 1880s, but almost exclusively within auxiliary women's associations that raised money for the churches or for foreign missions. The majority of women within these associations appear to have been middle class, as was increasingly the case with the congregations that filled Canada's ever more imposing religious edifices. Church attendance had become one in a constellation of signs that defined middle-class respectability in late nineteenth-century English Canada.

In the eyes of middle-class Canadians, the Salvation Army was completely devoid of the trappings of respectability that were integral to the Christianity of the church-going classes. This certainly did not reduce its popularity for those it sought to attract. The Army, which began in Ontario in 1882, spread rapidly through the province. By 1884 there were Salvation Army corps in seventy-three Ontario towns. Over the next ten years the movement spread throughout Canada, from Victoria to the Maritimes, although the main strength of the Army remained in Ontario.[31] At its height in the mid-1880s the Army had enrolled 25,000 soldiers, although by the 1891 census fewer than 14,000 Canadians claimed membership in the Army.[32] Membership figures exclude most of those who thronged to Army meetings in the early years of the movement. The Army was of particular interest to young people, and many of those temporarily attracted by the novelty of Army meetings were youthful members of mainstream churches.[33] For the majority of the unchurched, the Salvation Army provided entertainment but did not lead to conversion. For many other Canadians, Salvation Army conversion was short-lived, or led to a return to earlier denominational affiliations.[34]

Despite the short-term nature of many conversions, the Army was initially very successful in attracting both working-class women and men to its meetings and in encouraging them to enrol as soldiers. Newspaper reports generally spoke of the Army's ability to attract the 'lower orders' or the 'unchurched masses.' For example, the *Halifax Herald* told its readers that most of those at Army meetings 'belong to what is generally called the lower quarters of the city, and have been regarded as the rougher element.'[35] According to the *Toronto Mail*, Salvation Army soldiers 'are chiefly working people, who give what little leisure they have to helping the cause.'[36] The few surviving converts' rolls also suggest that even in smaller communities those attracted to the Army were almost exclusively working class (see table 1).[37]

Salvationists were primarily white, but black Canadians also became involved in the Army. A 1882 editorial in the Toronto *World* characterized the Army as being 'nearly all imported stock from England with a sprinkling of Irish, Scotch and Africans.'[38] In Chatham, a major area of black settlement, it was reported that 'a great number of coloured people have joined the Army.'[39] Spiritual equality was thus taken seriously in terms of race as well as gender, in a period when blacks were discouraged from joining mainstream churches or were segregated in church galleries.[40]

Newspaper reports also make it clear that women made up the majority of Salvation Army soldiers (see table 2).[41] In response to 'very hard pleading for converts' at a Kingston meeting, only women came forward, while in Fredericton 'fully three-fourths of those who took part in [an Army] parade were females.'[42] In the Fredericton parade, as in other places, reporters noted that a high proportion of female Salvationists were domestic servants.[43] Servants composed more than half of all female converts within each of the three corps for which converts' rolls have survived (see table 1).

While part of the Salvation Army's appeal to working-class audiences was its old-fashioned revivalism, which owed much to its Methodist roots, the Army made use of a variety of tactics to attract crowds. Officers were told that meetings must be interesting and lively, and were encouraged to use innovative methods. They were informed that 'the respectabilities and proprieties will some of them pay to be put to sleep, but the unwashed and unshaven will quickly make off and come there no more until

TABLE 1
Occupation of Salvation Army Converts in Selected Corps, by Sex, 1887–1900

	Corps					
	Petrolia		Listowel		Feversham	
Occupation	Number	Per cent	Number	Per cent	Number	Per cent
Women						
At home[a]	39	39	22	31	24	48
Dressmaker	4	4	1	1		
Servant	52	52	38	53	26	52
Other	5	5	11	15		
Total	100	100	72	100	50	100
Men						
Clerk	3	2	1	1		
Skilled worker	24	18	14	16	1	2
Semiskilled	12	9	1	1		
Labourer[b]	83	60	51	59	23	41
Farmer	9	7	16	18	31	55
Other	6	4	4	5	1	2
Total	137	100	87	100	56	100

Source: Corps Records, Salvation Army Archives, Toronto
Notes: These are the only corps for which converts' rolls appear to have survived for this period. This table does not include those converts for whom occupation was not reported.
[a] Term used in roll
[b] Including farm labourers (only in Feversham was this a significant group)

assured of an entire change in the performance.'[44] Methods included open-air meetings and parades, with colourful banners, the music of tambourines, triangles, and drums, the singing of hymns to the tunes of popular songs, and a variety of events, many of which were intended to provide a religious alternative to popular amusements. A clear example is seen in the opening quotation, in which a Kingston Army service ('superior to any show on earth') is advertised as a counter-attraction to the visiting circus. Other such events included Hallelujah Sprees, Popular Matinées, Hallelujah Picnics, Free and Easy Meetings, and Grand Tea Fights.

Some Army events were of particular interest to women. This was certainly true of 'Hallelujah weddings,' as the marriages of

TABLE 2
Sex of Salvation Army Converts in Selected Corps, 1887–1900

	Petrolia		Listowel		Feversham	
Sex	Number	Per cent	Number	Per cent	Number	Per cent
Male	236	46	129	47	65	44
Female	274	54	144	53	84	56
Total	510	100	273	100	149	100

Source: Corps Records, Salvation Army Archives, Toronto
Note: These are the only corps for which converts' rolls appear to have survived for this period.

officers were popularly known. A typical Hallelujah wedding, which occurred in Hamilton in the summer of 1884, attracted over 1500 people, who had to pay fifteen cents each to get in. The *Hamilton Spectator* claimed that the event was 'the biggest display ever seen at a wedding in Hamilton.'[45] The couple paraded the streets in a carriage 'decked out with many coloured ribbons,' while banners, tambourines, and choruses of hallelujahs helped keep excitement at fever pitch during the ceremony. Apparently women made up the majority, and certainly the most interested portion of the crowd. The *Hamilton Spectator* claimed that 'the ambition of the majority of hallelujah lasses is to have a hallelujah wedding,' and quoted one 'hallelujah lass' as saying to another at the end of the ceremony: 'That's the way I'm going to get married ... What do you say Nellie? Isn't it just scrumptious?'[46]

Female Soldiers and Adherents

Such weddings were clearly intended to appeal to what were assumed to be the conventional feminine interests of female soldiers and potential soldiers. The Salvation Army also appealed to traditional female roles and responsibilities through its use of familial rhetoric. In a variety of other ways, however, the Army either required or provided the space for female soldiers and potential adherents to behave in a manner that ran counter to conventional female roles of docility, passivity, and domesticity. An exploration of the response of female Salvation Army soldiers to the unusual opportunities available to them in the Army provides insights into the nature of working-class women's lives and can help to illuminate the distinct nature of working-class femininity.

The Salvation Army and the Dominant Family Ideology
A 1885 Army report out of Ingersoll gloried in the fact that 'lots of families who used to be in sin, drunkeness, and misery ... now have homes like little Heavens,' while a saved drunkard's wife from Palmerston testified that 'she thanked God for the Army, as it had picked her husband up. She said it was the happiest Xmas she had spent for nine years.'[47] The Salvation Army took considerable credit, which the secular press was also willing to grant them, for having dramatically increased domestic felicity by reducing male drunkeness. The *War Cry* was full of images of reunited families and of homes made into 'little Heavens.' Such rhetoric reinforced the dominant family ideology, which saw the home as a warm haven from the outside world. Ideal gender roles, with women as patient moral nurturers and men as reliable breadwinners, were also featured in Army descriptions of families rescued from drunkenness.[48]

This rhetoric may be viewed as symptomatic of Army efforts to impose the dominant family ideology on the working class. It should also be recognized that images of Army-induced domestic bliss reflected a certain reality for at least some working-class families. Husbands were the primary wage-earners in most working-class families, which meant that male alcoholism exacerbated the poverty of these families.[49] Male drunkenness also frequently led to wife abuse. The statement by one female Salvationist that 'I'd rather have my husband beat the Salvation Army drum than beat me' may be apocryphal, but it probably reflected the feelings of many working-class wives.[50] These women would indeed have reason to be thankful for the conversion of their husbands, and to regret the transient nature of many such conversions.

The Salvation Army may have seen itself as shoring up the

ideal Victorian family, but it also undermined the patriarchal nature of the family by requiring female soldiers and adherents to play active public roles within the organization. As well as performing their secular responsibilities in the home or in the workplace, female soldiers were expected to spend weary hours going door to door selling the *War Cry* and trying to bring other townspeople to Christ. They also took part in the frequent noisy and flamboyant street parades of the Army. One such parade in London involved 'the backward jumping of the leading officers and the waving and swinging of the kerchiefs and streamers ...' the drums and chorus [going] at their full beat.' At this parade an elderly lady observed that 'there's a brave lot of lasses in the ranks, and they walk just as bravely as the men, and just take as big a step.'[51] The fragility and timidity of ideal Victorian ladyhood was not much in evidence here.

Female Salvationists were also expected to speak up in meetings to tell of their faith in God and to describe their past experiences. Women were not accustomed to speaking in public. Those who had internalized dominant gender roles may have been particularly reluctant to expose their private lives and spiritual beliefs to public scrutiny. It is therefore not surprising that, although women made up the majority of those attending Army meetings, men appear to have predominated among those giving testimony. Women who did testify were sometimes inaudible. Because testifying to the impact God had had on their lives was considered a religious responsibility, women who felt the urge to give testimony but failed to do so were seen as disobeying God's will.[52] At least in certain corps, every effort was made to encourage women to testify. Some corps had 'sisters meetings,' where only women gave testimony.[53] In other cases officers, particularly female officers, made a particular point of encouraging women to testify and to pray publicly.[54]

Many women were not at all reluctant to testify. Outraged middle-class observers witnessed women who testified loudly and joyfully, sometimes shouting, jumping up and down, and going into trances.[55] Ecstatic faith in God could overcome many inhibitions, and certainly had been known to do so in earlier revivals.[56] However, by this period even appeals to God's spiritual power could not justify such behaviour for most Canadians.[57] Female piety was valued, but only in the context of sedate, lady-like church attendance. The behaviour of Salvation Army women therefore hints at the possibility that middle-class conventions of passive, pious femininity had little relevance to the lives of many working-class women. The Salvation Army provided such women with the opportunity to play a more public role, and encouraged women who were more constrained by traditional gender roles to greater confidence in public forums.

Women's responsibility to testify to God's love was assumed to supersede their responsibility to obey temporal authorities, such as husbands and fathers. In the London barracks, when a husband tried physically to stop his wife from kneeling at the penitent form and from testifying, he was prevented from doing so by 'members of the Army, especially the females.' He was told that his wife was 'God's property now.'[58] For other married women the Salvation Army could justify a rejection of traditional roles and responsibilities, despite the opposition of husbands. One husband complained his wife kept him awake at night by holding 'knee-drills' at all hours, while the Toronto *World* reported a more extreme case of a husband who allegedly tried to commit suicide because 'his wife, who joined the Salvation Army last March ... has not been home, so he says, an evening since.'[59]

Men might have felt abandoned, but women believed that conversion gave them the responsibility to be more than domestic drudges. 'Drum Major Annie' of Petrolia provides us with what appears to be the authentic voice of one such woman. In responding to a satirical attack on the Army she commented: 'Give us credit for the energy displayed in beating a drum, in playing a tambourine, in marching weary miles daily after attending to our domestic duties, the daily part of our unending toil, for while man's work is from sun to sun, women's work is never done ... we have willingly added to a toilsome, weary life much more of toil, and of weariness, of sorrow, of strivings, physical and spiritual, of anxious pleadings, of earnest exhortations, of willing self-sacrifice, that he and kindred wretches might be saved from the punishment they so richly deserve.'[60] Attempting to save the souls of these wretches may have added to women's traditional burdens, but it also offered a sense of mission and significance to the otherwise narrow and undervalued lives of working-class wives, as well as providing a justification for moving beyond the domestic sphere.

For unmarried female soldiers, the Army provided a similar rationale for moving beyond parental authority. Concerns were expressed that young people were disobeying their parents by attending Army meetings far into the night.[61] For many working women, involvement with the Army also justified defying employers. This appears to have been particularly true of servants. A number of newspapers echoed the complaint of Barrie's *Northern Advance* that 'a large number of the soldiers are domestics who should be at home at 10 o'clock at the outside, but who are often out until after midnight. It is impossible for them to attend to their duties property the next day.'[62] The *New Brunswick Reporter* chronicled the sad stories of several employers of Salvationist domestic servants, including that of a businessman who complained that he 'sat up until a quarter past twelve waiting for the girl to come home [from the Army meeting] and in the morning had to light the fires and get his own breakfast.[63]

Sexuality and Salvation

While the evangelical emphasis of the Army could directly justify the defiance of husbands, parents, and employers in the name of salvation, the Army could also inadvertently provide space for those who sought to defy other social conventions that were strongly upheld by the Army. The Army went to considerable effort to ensure that their meetings would be exclusively religious and would not be used as an excuse for any kind of sexual involvement. The Salvation Army in Kingston forbade young men from walking young women home from meetings, although this was a common practice within the churches.[64] In other towns, Salvation officers vigilantly tried to prevent the exchange of flirtatious looks or comments during religious meetings.[65] Despite this precaution, Army meetings did provide an opportunity for young women and men, both soldiers and those who attended on a more casual basis, to meet and become involved.

The late hours of Salvation Army meetings were justified by the need to struggle with those on the verge of a conversion experience. Many middle-class commentators, however, echoed the Anglican cleric who argued that 'excited meetings held up to late hours have led to licentiousness.'[66] These commentators were also horrified to report that at these meetings female officers kissed other women and hugged men in their efforts to bring them to salvation.[67] If we strip away the shocked moralism here, it does appear likely that the late hours and emotionalism of Salvation Army meetings could provide both the atmosphere and the opportunity for sexual contact among the many young people attending them. Army meetings also cast young women and men in an unaccustomed public light, which could increase their attraction to potential partners. A Salvation Army handbook cautioned: 'In selecting an individual for so important a relation as marriage, let no one be carried away with the mere appearance of a person in uniform, or their ability to speak or solo. A person who is all that can be desired on the platform may be entirely unsuitable as husband or wife.'[68]

There are also hints that claims of attendance at Army meetings were sometimes used as an acceptable excuse for late hours and more appealing activities. When asked by a Halifax reporter why the Army kept young girls at meetings so late at night, the captain responded: 'Few girls stay to the after meetings. People should not allow themselves to be deceived by girls simply saying they have been to the Army meetings.'[69]

Stories in the popular press suggest that male Salvationists made use of the Army to 'take advantage of' young women, but the nature of many of these relationships remains unclear. Some itinerant officers do appear to have exploited their public role to gain sexual access to women in the various corps where they were stationed. This was clearly the case with 'Happy Bob,' who kept a photograph album titled 'The conquests of Happy Bob of Canada ... The name and the age of some of my mashes while in the Salvation Army.'[70] The officers' responsibility for visiting converts and potential converts certainly gave them considerable opportunity for sexual adventure. However, women were not always simply the passive victims here. For some courting couples, drives home from Salvation Army meetings provided the opportunity for more consensual sexual relationships.[71] The frequent accusations in the press of general sexual looseness within the Salvation Army suggest that at the local level the Army may have provided both women and men with a less constrained space for traditional courtship, a space that had at least a certain sanction of religious legitimacy.[72]

Army meetings may also have given young people a chance to meet potential partners with whom they might not otherwise have contact, as is suggested by a disapproving reference in a London paper to a marriage between a 'coloured' male Salvationist and a white woman.[73]

While many who used Salvation Army meetings as an opportunity for courtship were not Salvation Army members, it is clear that many Salvation soldiers did deviate considerably from official Army policy. This is also evident in a running battle over the wearing of uniforms found in the pages of the *War Cry*. By the mid 1880s all Salvationists were expected to wear a common official uniform. This plain navy-blue uniform was to set them apart from the fashionable secular world and to proclaim their dedication to salvation. While the *War Cry* denounced the many Salvation soldiers of both sexes who did not wear the uniform, most articles on this topic were aimed at women, who would often subvert the uniform's purpose by adding lace, ribbons, or silk, or by wearing jewellery.[74] These women may have had a religious commitment to the Army but were clearly not willing to renounce the world, as was expected of Salvation soldiers. They defined for themselves the nature of their involvement, which did not preclude participation in the contemporary young women's culture, with its emphasis on fashion and personal appearance.[75]

For the majority of young women who never became Salvation soldiers, attendance at Army meetings did not require any compromise with contemporary feminine interests. For these women, many of whom were also involved in other churches, the Salvation Army provided excitement and entertainment, especially in smaller towns which offered few other options.[76] In some cases these women attended Army services to laugh, heckle, and disrupt. Although such behaviour was far more common among young men, the 'giddy girls' reported in such incidents seem as far removed from the dominant feminine ideal as the women leading the services.[77]

Female Officers

The women who preached to the crowds that flocked to Army meetings to heckle, to court, and to get salvation did pose a major challenge to traditional gender roles. Within English Canada, over 850 women took up this challenge by becoming officers between 1882 and 1890. These Hallelujah lasses made up 56 per cent of all English-Canadian officers.[78] They were recruited from among Salvation soldiers but, unlike soldiers and adherents, they were expected to dedicate their entire lives to the salvation of others. Almost all female officers were involved in field work, which meant they worked with local corps. Two or three officers – a captain, a lieutenant, and sometimes a cadet – would be posted at each corps. They were expected to follow the directives issued by headquarters in Toronto, and were subject to transfer at any time. Their work required considerable initiative and effort, however, since field officers were responsible for all the tasks necessary to keep a local corps going. They had to organize and preach at a variety of services every night of the week, as well as on Sunday. They were also responsible for financial management of the corps, which involved organizing collections, paying local bills, and reporting on their financial situation to Headquarters. During the day they were expected to visit both the converted and the unconverted, and to sell the *War Cry* in the streets and encourage soldiers to do likewise. Officers also organized and led frequent street parades and were expected to plan innovative methods of drawing crowds.

In the early- to mid-1880s many female officers were sent to 'pioneer' the work in new towns. They faced particularly daunting tasks, often preaching in the streets until they raised enough money to rent a hall. In order to gain an audience, these women had to be particularly imaginative. Before the development of standard Army uniforms, many deliberately exploited the particular interest shown in female preachers by wearing outfits designed to attract further attention to themselves and their cause. 'The three lassie officers who pioneered the work in Paris, Ontario,' for example, 'appeared in long red silk dresses reaching to within four inches of the ground. Six inches from the hem, in deep red letters, was the word "Hallelujah," and across the breast was boldly inscribed "The Salvation Army." Others wore red basques and blue shirts, red blouses or guernseys generously labelled with texts and declarations of faith. Immense straw hats draped with red bandana handkerchiefs were not uncommon.'[79] Catherine Booth may have argued that preaching would only exalt female officers' most womanly instincts, but the role of Salvation Army officer would appear to violate almost every facet of the dominant feminine ideal. Ladies were not expected to call attention to themselves, certainly not by marching in the streets in bizarre outfits. They were not supposed to abandon the domestic sphere for the public platform, let alone usurp the patriarchal role of religious leader.

What women would choose to take on this role, and why would they be attracted to it? To begin to answer these questions we will examine the backgrounds of early female officers. Such an exploration of the reasons these women chose to enter the Army will also provide further insights into the backgrounds and motivations of the far larger number of 'Hallelujah lasses' who made the lesser commitment of becoming Salvation Army soldiers.

Who Were the Officers?

Most female officers were working class, reflecting the class makeup of Salvation Army congregations. They were primarily young and unmarried and had generally been employed prior to becoming officers. The majority were also white and Canadian born. The following analysis will focus on officers who joined the Army within English Canada between 1882 and 1890.[80]

Female officers tended to be slightly younger than male officers, with 14 per cent of women being under eighteen on becoming officers, as compared with less than 9 per cent of men. Most officers of both sexes were relatively young, however, with 80 per cent being under twenty-five (see table 3).

The vast majority (96 per cent) of these women were unmarried.[81] Almost three-quarters had been engaged in a wage-earning occupation on becoming candidates (see table 4). Although in this period unmarried women were far more likely to be employed than married women, Salvation Army officers revealed much higher labour-force participation rates than the average unmarried Canadian woman.[82] Female officers were employed in traditional female occupations such as domestic service, dressmaking, nursing, and teaching (see table 4). They were more likely to be employed as domestic servants than the average Canadian woman worker, and were less likely to be involved in the somewhat more middle-class female occupations of teaching, nursing, and clerical work.[83] It is not possible to provide definitive answers regarding the class backgrounds of the 23 per cent of female officers who entered the Army directly from home. Given the largely rural nature of Canada in this period and the fact that 20 per cent of male officers had previously been farmers, it seems likely that many of these women were from farm families. The predominance of skilled workers among male Salvation Army officers suggests that many female officers may also have come from such backgrounds (see table 4).

Little evidence is available regarding the racial or ethnic background of officers. Although the first Army officers were primarily English immigrants, most thereafter appear to have been Canadian born.[84] The vast majority of these recruits were white. There are, however, infrequent references in both the *War Cry* and the secular press to 'coloured' officers, suggesting that some black soldiers did became officers. It is not clear, however, how many black women became officers or if they were able to com-

TABLE 3
Ages of Female and Male Salvationists on Becoming Officers, 1882–90

Age	Women		Men	
	Number	Per cent	Number	Per cent
Less than 16	4	1.0	2	0.5
16–17	83	13.0	39	8.0
18–19	134	20.0	103	20.0
20–24	302	46.0	266	52.0
25–30	110	17.0	79	15.0
31–40	24	4.0	24	5.0
Over 40	3	0.5	4	1.0
Total	660	100	517	100

Source: Officers' Rolls, Salvation Army Archives, Toronto
Note: 'C' Roll was the major source of data for the background and careers of officers. This roll apparently lists all, or almost all officers who entered the Canadian
Army in this period. This table does not include information for officers transferred
from England, or those who enlisted in Quebec or Newfoundland.

mand corps, which was the highest Army position attained by
most white women.[85]

Why Become an Officer?
The relative youth of most Salvation Army officers, both male
and female, can be explained in a number of ways. It can certainly
be linked to the youthful nature of the Army congregations from
which officers were drawn. Younger people would also be less
burdened with family responsibilities and, as a result, more willing to take up the itinerant role of Salvation Army officer. Army
officers were generally transferred from place to place every three
to six months, and for many young people the opportunity to
travel, and perhaps the excitement of moving from small towns
to larger cities, may have been appealing.[86]

In the nineteenth century, youth was also a period of spiritual
introspection. For those brought up in the evangelical tradition,
this was generally the time when one was expected to have a
conversion experience. Such an experience involved being
brought to a recognition of one's sinful nature, and then being

TABLE 4
Occupations of Salvation Army Officers upon Becoming Officers, by Sex, 1882–90

	Number	Per cent
Women		
At home	179	28
Clerks	12	2
Nurses	10	2
Teachers	26	4
Dressmakers/tailoresses/milliners[a]	122	19
Factory workers	42	7
Servants	240	38
Other	5	1
Total	636	100
Men		
At home	9	2
Businessmen/professionals	19	4
Clerks	40	8
Teachers	6	1
Farmers	102	20
Skilled workers/artisans[b]	225	44
Semiskilled workers	32	6
Factory workers	36	7
Labourers/unskilled	46	9
Servants	6	1
Total	512	100

Source: Officers' Rolls, Salvation Army Archives, Toronto
Note: See table 3.
[a] Some of these women probably worked in factories, but this is impossible to determine.
[b] Some of these men may have been self-employed, or even small masters, while many probably worked in factories. The roll only provided occupational titles.

spiritually 'born again' and dedicated to a more holy, Christian life. Autobiographies of female officers make it clear that many had been brought up in Methodist homes, where the conversion experience was of major importance and, according to certain historians, 'was closely associated with the passage into adulthood.'[87] For such women, becoming an officer, which required not only conversion but also a complete rejection of the secular world and a commitment to assist in the conversion of others, was congruent with the religious values they had learned in childhood. In fact, the Salvation Army offered these women a more active role than their own church in the spiritual work of salvation that Methodists claimed to value most highly.[88]

The weakening of the evangelical tradition within mainstream churches is demonstrated by the fact that Methodist parents were as opposed as other parents to their daughters' decision to dedicate their lives to the salvation of others as officers in the Salvation Army. The high proportion of female officers who were employed may be explained in part by the fact that such women would be less constrained by family opposition to their joining the Army. This would be particularly true for servants, who did not live with their own families. Many other working women did live with their parents, but may have found that wage earning provided them with some margin of independence in opposing their parents' wishes. According to autobiographies published in the *War Cry*, many officers shared the experience of Captain Abbie Thompson of Kingston who, on entering the Army, 'left home, disowned and rejected.'[89] Some parents' opposition was based on a rejection of their daughters' religious beliefs, while for others their daughters' religious commitment could not justify what was clearly viewed as a less than respectable way of life.

While religious commitment did not mollify outraged parents, it did provide a justification for challenging parental authority. One woman whose parents would not allow her to become an officer 'threw [herself] at His feet and gave Him my life and my all ... After promising the Lord, I told my parents what I had done, and now that I must go without their consent if they would not grant it.'[90] Like other evangelical sects, the Salvation Army's primary emphasis on the salvation of souls left more space for challenging traditional authority structures than did more mainstream churches.[91] Religious commitment, while sincere, could thus be used to carve out some autonomy for young women and could justify escaping oppressive family situations. Such commitment could justify leaving not just family but also native land, as the case with the early English officers.

For some women, escaping from parental supervision also provided more freedom to meet potential marriage partners. One case demonstrates how some women could use the Army for both purposes: 'Shouting Nelly, the Hallelujah lass from Toronto whose mother was recently compelled to invoke the authority of the police to compel her to remain at home, has returned to the city and has most effectually prevented the old lady from interfering with her liberty in the future by marrying one of the Army boys.'[92] Male and female officers, most of whom were single, had frequent contact and would sometimes work together. The Army clearly provided them with even more opportunity for courting than it did for soldiers. The following excerpt from the *War Cry* suggests that the Army was aware that a search for romance played a role in many enlistment decisions. 'Men become officers to get wives? Girls come into the Army to find a man, get married and settled down? Perhaps some do ... The cap may fit some readers. Well, don't ask others to wear it.'[93] The fact that the manual stated that courting was forbidden during an officer's first twelve months and that flirting would result in dismissal is also telling.[94] The predominance of servants among both female officers and soldiers may in part be explained by the opportunities for contact with men available in the Army. Such opportunities were generally denied servants through the conditions of their work, since they had only one evening off a week and were unable to receive 'gentlemen callers.'[95]

Although both senior Army officials and the popular press were most concerned about heterosexual involvement among officers, the Salvation Army provided female officers with a variety of social relationships. It appears that, within the Army, many female officers developed the close relationships with other women that were apparently common among nineteenth-century middle-class women.[96] Newspapers frequently commented on the warm friendships among female Salvation Army officers. For example, when Captain Nellie Ryerson, who had been working in Kingston with Captain Abbie Thompson, was to be sent to a new post, the two women 'were the objects of much attention as they walked about the waiting room with their arms around each others waists like two happy school girls, and this evidence of their affection for each other was supplemented by a hearty kiss.'[97] The Salvation Army Training Home for Women also provided an opportunity for young working-class women to live, work, and study together in a manner generally only available to middle-class women who attended boarding school or university.[98] It appears likely that the shared religious mission of Training Home women would have fostered particularly close ties between them.[99] Relationships among these women may also have been encouraged by the Army rule that single women must work in couples, to avoid endangering their reputations. Thus two or three women often ventured alone into a new town to set up a corps, sometimes facing hostility and persecution, conditions that were likely to develop close bonds among those involved. These relationships might be particularly sought by servants, whose working conditions provided as little opportunity for socializing with peers as they did for meeting potential marriage partners.

The community and comradeship found among Salvation Army officers may have been particularly appealing in a time of social and economic change. By the 1880s industrialization had taken off across Ontario. Factories were common not just in the manufacturing centres of Toronto and Hamilton, but in smaller industrial towns and villages throughout the province. Although we as yet know little about how industrialization affected traditional values and family relationships, it seems likely that many working people, finding themselves in new environments often far from home, might seek out alternative forms of community.[100] The Salvation Army may have been particularly appealing, since it took on the familiar forms of popular culture, and also spoke in what to many workers were the equally familiar tones of evangelical Christianity. As Herbert Gutman has demonstrated, most nineteenth-century workers continued to acknowledge the legitimacy of Christian beliefs and values, although often rejecting the churches as middle-class institutions.[101] The Army may therefore have provided both officers and soldiers with a moral certainty and sense of mission that was congruent with their own value systems and was particularly welcome in a rapidly changing world, but which was distinct from the mainstream churches in which they no longer felt comfortable.

Some secular newspapers of the period put forward another, far more material explanation for the motivations of Salvation Army officers. The Toronto *World* suggested that the Salvation Army 'offers "light" work, along with good clothes, good board, and a good time generally. What wonder then, that "Captain Jacks" and "Hallelujah Lasses" abound? They are simply trying to earn their living in this way, because situations in stores are difficult to obtain and they will not go on the farm ... The "lass" ... wants to escape the drudgery of the kitchen, or the factory. More than that, it may be that opportunities for entering upon such drudgery may not very easily be found, to suit her. The "hallelujah" door is open, and she goes in. Employment, wages and living make the main motive.'[102]

The *World* was generally hostile to the Salvation Army, and the above passage has a clear class bias. Nonetheless, it is possible that it also reflects a reality for at least some potential officers. Army officials were aware of this, and in their fervent appeal for candidates they state that 'people who have anything in a material sense to gain by volunteering are not required.'[103] Salvation Army wages were not high. Single male field officers appear to have received $6 a week, single women $5 a week, and married men $10.[104] Since wages were generally taken out of local collections, officers with little local support earned much less. Nonetheless, for most women wages in the Army were at least equal to those they could receive in other employment.[105] This does not suggest that women were joining the Army just to make a living, although this may have been true for some, especially those facing unemployment. It does suggest that material conditions did not discourage women from entering the Army. If facing the choice between drudgery in a factory or in someone else's kitchen or the life of a Salvation Army officer with its sense of high spiritual calling, relative freedom, and male and female companionship, it is not surprising that many women chose to become officers.

Hallelujah Lasses, Working-Class Women, and the Feminine Ideal

The public role offered by the Salvation Army appears to have provided a further attraction for potential candidates. In no other sphere of life did women, particularly working-class women, play such an active, powerful public role. The official appeals for candidates reflect an awareness by Army officials that the public nature of this role could draw both women and men. They point out to potential female candidates that 'the little lassie whom nobody knew when she was a servant at Mr. Grocer's, is welcomed by streets full of people.'[106]

How can we understand this apparent willingness to flout traditional gender roles among a significant number of Canadian working women? Does this suggest that working-class women's material experience was so different from that of middle-class women that they simply did not accept the dominant definitions of femininity? Canadian labour historians provide mixed answers to this question. Some echo a contemporary working woman quoted by a female correspondent to a labour paper, *The Palladium of Labor*: ' "Organization," ' she said, ' "was all very well, but how were girls to accomplish it; were they to advertise mass meetings, mount platforms and make speeches? If so, the Canadian girls, at least, would never organize." '[107] These historians argue that working women had internalized the dominant gender ideology, and as such were too timid and modest to get involved in union organizing. Others argue instead that a variety of structural factors, as well as male union indifference or hostility, explain the apparent passivity of working women. These historians point out that working-class women who overcame such barriers and did unionize and strike displayed considerable militance.[108] While this is true, there is some evidence to suggest that some working women did internalize certain aspects of the dominant gender ideology. Leonora Barry, general investigator of women's work and wages for the Knights of Labor, cited 'natural pride, timidity and the restrictions of social custom' as among the many barriers to women's organization.[109] It is also interesting to note that while Katie McVicar, a Hamilton working woman, was eager to unionize her co-workers, she was reluctant that 'any particular one of us appear as the moving spirit,' so that none of them be seen by their co-workers to be 'angling for notoriety.'[110]

Why, then, were Salvation Army officers so willing to court notoriety, and so ready 'to advertise mass meetings, mount platforms and make speeches'? One possibility is that the activities of the 'Hallelujah lasses' simply undermine historians' arguments regarding the passivity of working-class women and suggest that these women did not internalize middle-class conceptions of femininity. If true, the poor record of women's labour organizing could then be attributed exclusively to structural factors and male hostility. However, there is another issue that must be addressed here. Unlike union women, Salvation Army officers were not mounting platforms and making speeches to improve their own lives and their own working conditions. As the *War Cry* continually reminded them, by becoming Salvation Army officers they had abandoned all self-interest and dedicated their entire lives to Christ. In their autobiographies, many women spoke of the complete self-sacrifice and the perfect obedience they were willing to give to God.[111] Such self-sacrifice and submission, while expected of all officers, may have been particularly attractive to women, since it fit so clearly with the contemporary feminine ideal.[112] For some women the public behaviour required of them as officers may have been justified as part of a most feminine and Christian submission to God's will. This was clearly the official Salvation Army position, as illustrated by a story in the *War Cry* of an officer's wife whose refusal to preach and testify publicly is presented as evidence of disobedience to God's will and a refusal to give herself completely to God.[113]

The question remains, however, whether female Salvation Army officers flouted dominant gender roles reluctantly, as part of a submission to God's will; whether they consciously rejected these roles, while clothing this rejection in the conventional rhetoric of feminine passivity; or whether such roles were simply not relevant to their own experience as working-class women. An

examination of women's role in Salvation Army rescue work provides some clues here.

In 1886 the Canadian Salvation Army followed the lead of the
English Army by entering into social service work. The first Canadian effort in this direction was the founding of a rescue home
for prostitutes in Toronto. In 1890 further rescue homes were
opened in a number of cities, as was a children's shelter and two
homes for discharged prisoners. Social service work fit the contemporary feminine ideal far more closely than did preaching
before crowds. Appeals for volunteers for the social service division relied heavily on contemporary conceptions of femininity.
The *War Cry* called for 'whole-hearted devoted women ... charged
with a deep compassion for the lost' whose 'highest joy is self-
sacrifice.'[114] It appears that the response to this appeal to wom-
en's feminine nature was less than expected. In 1888 the *War Cry*
called on 'officers and soldiers ... girls and women ... who from
diffidence and possible lack of knowledge of the need have re-
frained from offering for service in this direction.'[115] Since the
rescue work was continually highlighted in the *War Cry* over the
next two years, ignorance of the work could not explain why in
1890 Army leaders were still calling almost desperately for volunteers.[116]

In an article entitled 'How she became a Rescue Officer,' the
subject provides a candid confession of her reluctance to leave
preaching for rescue work. Other autobiographies of rescue officers express a similar reluctance to enter the work, although
once involved they claim to come to love it.[117] Many women did
not come to love this work, as is demonstrated by the fact that
of all women who were posted to rescue work, half left the Army
immediately after this posting.[118] Most female officers clearly
preferred active public roles as preachers to more private, self-
denying, suitably feminine roles as angels of mercy. This implies
a certain rejection of or indifference towards middle-class norms
of femininity among Army officers. However, the reluctance to
enter social service work reflected not just an unwillingness to
give up preaching, but also a refusal to work with 'fallen' women

and female drunkards.[119] This suggests that most female officers shared certain contemporary attitudes concerning such women. Neither self-denying religious commitment nor sisterhood could overcome both a distaste for the 'fallen' and a fear of moral contagion instilled by the mores of the dominant culture.

Why Leave the Army?

While women who entered social service work were most likely to leave the Salvation Army, turnover rates were quite high among all officers. The Army was rarely a lifetime commitment. For most young women the role of Hallelujah lass represented a relatively brief phase in their life cycle. Over a third (34 per cent) of female officers remained in the Army for no more than a year, while more than 60 per cent remained for three years or less. Male officers had an even higher turnover rates, with 39 per cent remaining in the Army for no more than a year (see table 5). The Army was certainly aware that high turnover was a problem, and poured bitter scorn on those who 'turn traitor and betray [their] divine trust ... Hundreds of dear young men and women in the Dominion today weep bitter, hot scalding tears of sorrow and remorse over their backslidden state. Once they testified, once they marched, once they prayed, once they were commissioned as officers, once their lives were full of joy without alloy.'[120] Potential candidates were told that 'the dying world demands *your whole life*. God is not pleased with those who, because of little difficulties, run away from the foe.'[121]

The relatively brief careers of most officers, as well as the rapid falling away of many soldiers, can be explained in part by the highly evangelical nature of the Army. Most emotional revivalistic religious movements that focus particularly on conversion have similar difficulty in retaining members over the long term.

The 'little difficulties' facing Salvation Army officers also help to explain high turnover rates. One of these difficulties was material hardship. As mentioned earlier, officers took their salaries from local collections, so if there was little or no local interest in the Army they could face major financial problems. The *War Cry* was full of stories of how officers who were unlucky enough to

TABLE 5
Length of Service of Female and Male Salvation Army Officers Who Entered Army Service between 1882 and 1890

Length of service	Women		Men	
	Number	Per cent	Number	Per cent
One year or less	300	34	275	39
Over one year, up to three years	249	28	184	26
Over three years, up to five years	142	16	90	13
Over five years, up to ten years	115	13	69	10
Over ten years[a]	71	8	82	12
Total	877	100	700	100

Source: Officers' Rolls, Salvation Army Archives, Toronto
Note: See table 3.
[a] This includes those who were transferred to England or the United States, so it is not possible to have an exact idea of how long they remained in the Army. However, most of these officers had already had considerable experience in Canada, and the transfer suggests that they were considered 'career officers.'

find themselves in a unfriendly environment readily slept on the floor and lived on bread and water in their efforts to bring people to God.[122] Almost all of these stories feature female officers. It is quite likely that this reflects the reality, since women might be more likely to accept such hardships as part of a feminine spirit of self-sacrifice and submission to God's will. Women also had fewer other options available to them. Male officers, almost half of whom had been skilled workers prior to entering the Army, could expect far higher wages outside the Army than within it. This was much less true for women. Several married male officers appear to have left the Army in order to provide adequately for their families.[123] They were unlikely to have been satisfied with the response given to a male officer, who wrote to enquire about what would happen to his family after his death and was told not to concern himself with material things since 'officers, old and young are "kept by the power of God unto Salvation."'[124]

Men might also have been less ready to accept the strict discipline and hierarchical nature of the Army than women, who may have been willing to accept what was to them a familiar patriarchal structure, but one which provided more opportunities than most other options open to working-class women. One of these opportunities was the chance to have authority over both male and female subordinate officers and soldiers. This reversal of contemporary gender roles was clearly very difficult for Army men to accept. Both of the major revolts that occurred at local corps in the early years of the Army involved female commanding officers and male subordinates.[125]

Another 'little difficulty' which may have discouraged many officers from remaining in the Army was the harassment and persecution they often faced. The large crowds attracted by the Army frequently included groups of local young men who subjected the officers to verbal and sometimes physical abuse.[126] In several towns officers also faced persecution from local town councils, which passed by-laws to prevent public marching and drum-playing. In London, six Hallelujah lasses were jailed for defying a by-law which prohibited drum-playing.[127] While such arrests generated considerable public sympathy, particularly for female officers, and could also provide a satisfying sense of martyrdom, a life of persecution and harassment could soon lose its appeal.[128]

Articles in the *War Cry* denouncing marriage to non-Salvationists suggest that such marriages, which were forbidden to officers, may also explain the relatively high turnover rates.[129] While the Army stressed that officers, who had committed their lives to God, could live happy, holy, and useful lives if they remained unmarried, dominant values, which viewed unmarried women as failures, were not so readily disregarded.[130] Among the minority of female officers who made a commitment of over ten years to the Army, almost half had married fellow officers within the first five years of their officerships.[131]

Middle-Class Response

The unconventional nature of women's role in the Salvation Army is crucial in understanding the profoundly ambivalent response of middle-class Canadians to the Army. Middle-class reactions reveal the intersections and contradictions of gender- and class-based anxieties in a period of rapid social and economic change.

Although the Salvation Army's mission was ostensibly identical to that of the churches – to bring souls within the fold of Christianity – spiritual commonalities did not reconcile middle-class observers to the unique approach taken by the Army to gain this end. For many of these observers, the respectable trappings of the mainstream churches were integral to Christianity as they defined it. The Army was frequently accused of treating Christianity with vulgarity, levity, and frivolity, and Army activities were disparagingly compared to working-class entertainments.[132] A common and telling comparison identified the Army as being worse than 'a negro minstrel show.'[133] The adoption of the cultural forms of the marginal and the devalued, whether by class or by race, placed the Army beyond the pale of true Christianity, which in the dominant discourse of the period was inextricably linked with respectable middle-class culture.

Patriarchal authority was integral to this vision of Christianity. For critics like the Rev. A. Wilson of Kingston, 'female preaching and fantastic dressing, the outrageous talk and singing of doggerel hymns' combined to render the Army completely unacceptable.[134] Some of the opposition to female preaching focused exclusively on St Paul and other biblical sources. Others, however, defined the patriarchal nature of the mainstream churches more explicitly by denouncing men who, 'weak-minded, ignorant, wilfully ... placed themselves under the government and control and teaching of a woman.'[135] Ministers generally led the attack on female preaching, which is not surprising, since both the basis of their authority and the loyalty of their congregations were most directly threatened by the Hallelujah lasses.[136] Some secular critics were equally hostile to 'petty coats in the pulpit,' although others were more bemused than horrified to see 'a mere girl' keep order over large crowds.[137]

What is most surprising about the opposition to female preaching in the Salvation Army is that there was not more of it. In some towns the practice was denounced by a minister or two upon the arrival of the Army, while in others even those hostile to the Army did not mention it. The absence of sustained outrage is particularly perplexing since the early years of the Army did not witness a ready acceptance of women's entrance into the public sphere. In the 1880s major battles took place at Ontario universities over the admission of women, and the few women bold enough to demand female suffrage received a chilly reception.[138] Female preaching, which strikes at the heart of patriarchal authority, would seem a more radical measure than either female education or suffrage.

The muted opposition to female preaching in the Salvation Army may be explained by the working-class nature of the movement. For middle-class observers, female preaching might have been just one more bizarre element within a religious movement that was already divorced from respectable mainstream Christianity. Working-class women who preached primarily to other working-class people may have presented less of a challenge than those middle-class women who sought to enter the public spheres of power and authority viewed by middle-class men as their exclusive preserve. While working-class women's self-perception requires further study, women who toiled in factory or kitchen were, on the basis of middle-class perceptions, at least partially excluded from the cult of true womanhood. Such women, who were not expected to display the frailty of middle-class women and who were increasingly entering the public sphere of paid work, might have appeared less anomalous on a public platform than middle-class 'angels in the home,' as long as they were preaching only to those of their own class.

While uneasiness about female preaching was more limited than expected, middle-class concern over the relative autonomy of women in the Army was expressed in other ways. As previously mentioned, newspapers were quick to report how involvement in the Army could lead women to defy the authority of husbands, parents, and employers. The Army's threat to authority relations, particularly within the family, removed it further from the mainstream churches, which saw the reinforcement of dominant social and economic structures as an integral part of their role.[139]

While such attacks on authority relations were a concern, the secular press was more preoccupied with the issue of sexuality, which for many posed a more subtle but pervasive threat to the social order. The papers were full of stories of elopements of Salvationists, male Salvationists found in the rooms of female Salvationists, as well as general accusations of licentiousness and immodesty at Army meetings. As discussed earlier, the Army may have provided slightly more space than that generally available for young people to meet and court, but this does not explain the near hysterical concern of certain commentators. This may have been a straightforward attempt to discredit the Army – to make a movement which did not fit within the respectable mainstream of the churches appear still less respectable. The focus on sexuality may also be linked to concerns that former prostitutes had been converted by the Army. These women are mentioned in a few reports, but they are not the primary focus.[140] The relative autonomy and public role of women within the Army and the class nature of the movement appear to have combined to fuel sexual fears. The fact that the Army provided working-class women, whose purity in middle-class eyes was sullied by their relative autonomy and by their working-class status, with the opportunity to associate relatively freely with working-class men under the disreputable conditions of Army meetings, encouraged middle-class fears over sexuality to run rampant.

This middle-class response may also have been part of what Jeffrey Weeks has termed a 'moral panic,' in which sexual behaviour is used as a scapegoat in dealing with broader concerns about social change.[141] In the 1880s rapid industrialization and urbanization and the accompanying emergence of an increasingly separate working class brought with it fears of crime, disorder, and loss of middle-class control.[142] Hysteria over uncontrolled working-class sexuality may thus have been symptomatic of deeper fears of social disorder.

The letters and editorials condemning the vulgarity, frivolity, disorder, and unbridled sexuality of the Army do not, however, reflect a monolithic opposition to the new religious movement. Such opposition was met in the secular press by many who wrote to support the Army. While some of those writing were Army members, the Army also had an increasing number of middle-class supporters who looked beyond the disreputable trappings of the movement and focused on its potential to serve middle-class interests. The Army was frequently praised for its ability to bring Christianity to those who would never enter the main-stream churches.[143] Middle-class observers were no doubt gen-uinely pleased by the Army's ability to save the souls of 'the perishing masses.' However, for these middle-class supporters, 'getting religion' meant considerably more than accepting Jesus Christ. Those who saw the Army as a threat to patriarchal au-thority were increasingly drowned out by those who pointed out how the Army's attack on drunkenness could restore domestic harmony, and thus conventional family structures, among the working class.[144] The testimony of businessmen who pointed to the increased industriousness of their Salvationist workmen, overshadowed reports of servant girls staying out too late at meet-ings.[145] Concerns over sexuality and disorder were met with sta-tistics that pointed to major reductions in crime following the advent of the Army.[146] Observers increasingly came to recognize that despite its appearance, the Army's evangelical message of salvation and the rejection of sin was a familiar one, and one that brought the working class more firmly within the orbit of the dominant value system.

The limited opposition to female preaching may best be under-stood within this context. Attacks on the Hallelujah lasses were frequently countered by arguments that these women were able to transform the 'rougher elements' into moral, sober, orderly, and industrious workers. Like middle-class 'angels in the home,' female preachers were using their moral, feminine natures to tame men. The fact that they were doing so from public platforms rather than within the domestic sphere was troubling. Maternal feminist arguments that women's higher morality was needed in the public arena were gaining some currency, but did not yet justify major intrusions into male bastions of power.[147] Unlike maternal feminists, however, the Hallelujah lasses were not mid-dle class. They might be endowed by middle-class observers with feminine morality, but not with those more class specific feminine qualities of frailty and gentility that could preclude involvement in the public world. The crucial nature of their mission also overcame many misgivings. The relative significance of class and gender has been endlessly debated. In this particular historical instance it appears that the enforcement of dominant gender roles was both mediated by class specific definitions of such roles and subordinated to class-based fears.

Conclusion

This study of women's role in the early years of the Salvation Army is a first step in the development of our understanding of the nature of working-class women's involvement in English-Canadian religious life. The Salvation Army was not, however, typical of the religious options available to these women in nineteenth-century Canada. The unique opportunities made available to working-class women through the Army provide the historian with a window through which to view the interplay of class and gender both in the lives of those women who chose to join the Army and in the attitudes of middle-class Canadians.

The Salvation Army was a male-dominated hierarchical organization that preached submission to God's will and idealized the dominant form of the family. Despite this focus, working-class women, whose lives were restricted by both patriarchal authority and material constraints, were able to use the Army to carve out more space for themselves. For many, the Army provided the justification to defy parents, husbands, and employers, the opportunity to create their own community, and increased freedom to meet potential marriage partners within this community. The Salvation Army also provided working-class women with an unprecedented public voice. These women were certainly not speaking out for their own liberation. However, by testifying in public, or preaching before crowds, Salvationist women were far more audible and visible than the constraints of their lives usually permitted.

The fact that many women took up the opportunities made

available by the Army suggests that the dominant ideal of passive, silent femininity may have had little reality for most working-class women. Its continued relevance, in at least some form, is seen, however, in the reluctance of many women to speak out in public, and in the fact that those who did so justified their behaviour in terms of a most feminine submission to God's will. The relatively limited significance of the Salvation Army experience in the overall life cycle of most Hallelujah lasses demonstrates most clearly the continued value placed on conventional female roles, as well as the hardships and limitations of Army life. The opportunities made available through the Army were real, but for most women, particularly officers, they were taken up only briefly in the years prior to marriage.

Middle-class response to the Army was equally complex. While the flouting of dominant gender roles and of class-defined conceptions of proper Christian decorum were condemned, recognition of the value of the Army's message soon overshadowed concerns over the methods adopted to convey it. The Army gradually came to be perceived as a bulwark against other working-class movements, movements that offered the working class not individual salvation in heaven but collective salvation on Earth.

This study demonstrates the importance of looking beyond home and workplace to come to a fuller understanding of the lives of working-class women, and indeed of the entire working class. For women's historians it also demonstrates the limitations of an exclusive focus on middle-class experience. Women's historians have spent considerable effort studying women like Elizabeth Smith, one of Canada's first medical graduates. They have, however, ignored women like the enormously popular Captain Abbie Thompson who, as Smith studied her medical texts in a Kingston boarding house in the spring of 1883, was leading the Army's assault on that city.[148] As middle-class women were taking their first tentative steps beyond a restrictive women's sphere, Hallelujah lasses were standing on platforms and leading parades, demonstrating a clear divergence between middle- and working-class definitions of this sphere.

NOTES

I would like to thank Salvation Army archivist Johanne Pelletier for all her help. I would also like to thank John Blakely, Dan Hawthorne, Craig Heron, Susan Houston, Meg Luxton, Lara Marks, Sylvia Van Kirk, the other contributors to this volume, and the Labour Studies Group for their comments on various drafts of this paper. I am grateful to the Imperial Order Daughters of the Empire (IODE) for its financial support through a War Memorial Scholarship, and to the Canadian Research Institute for the Advancement of Women (CRIAW) for its assistance with research costs through the Marta Danylewycz Memorial Award.

1 Kingston *Daily British Whig*, 14 July 1883
2 Ibid., 26 March 1883; *London Advertiser*, 27 March 1883; *Newmarket Era*, 13 June 1884; Barrie *Northern Advance*, 22 Nov. 1883; *Fredericton Evening Capital*, 20 Oct. 1885; *Halifax Herald*, 28 Oct. 1885
3 *Daily British Whig*, 1 Oct. 1883
4 With the move towards a more educated ministry in the 1840s and 1850s, female preaching, which had been tolerated in certain evangelical denominations, gradually died out. See John Webster Grant, *A Profusion of Spires: Religion in Nineteenth-Century Ontario* (Toronto: University of Toronto Press 1988), 111 and 168.
5 In Canada in the 1880s, class is not always readily defined. By this period the majority of Canadian town dwellers were working class in an objective sense, in that as skilled and as unskilled workers they directly sold their labour power for a wage in order to survive, or were part of families whose members did so. While working-class consciousness, or the sense of oneself as belonging to a working class, may have been stronger in cities, which had more clearly defined class divisions, the strength of the Knights of Labor in this decade in towns and cities across Ontario suggests that such consciousness was not confined to workers in larger centers. See Gregory S. Kealey and Bryan D. Palmer, *Dreaming of What Might Be: The Knights of Labor in Ontario, 1880–1900* (Toronto: New Hogtown Press 1982).
6 Wendy Mitchinson, 'Canadian Women and Church Missionary Societies in the Nineteenth Century: A Step towards Independence,' *Atlantis* 2, 2,

part 2 (spring 1977). Canadian women's historians have also explored women's roles within the churches as deaconesses and missionaries. See John D. Thomas 'Servants of the Church: Canadian Methodist Deaconess Work, 1890–1926,' *Canadian Historical Review* 65, 3 (1984), and Ruth Compton Brouwer, 'Women as Foreign Missionaries in Central Canadian Presbyterianism, 1876–1896: Context and Personal Background' (doctoral paper, York University 1981). Quebec historians have also examined the extent to which the convent provided women with alternative options. See Marta Danylewycz, *Taking the Veil: An Alternative to Marriage, Motherhood, and Spinsterhood in Quebec, 1840–1920* (Toronto: McClelland and Stewart 1987).

7 See, for example, Craig Heron and Robert Storey, eds., *On the Job: Confronting the Labour Process in Canada* (Kingston and Montreal: McGill-Queen's University Press 1986); Ian Radforth, *Bushworkers and Bosses: Logging in Northern Ontario, 1900–1980* (Toronto: University of Toronto Press 1987); Craig Heron, *Working in Steel: The Early Years in Canada, 1883–1935* (Toronto: McClelland and Stewart 1988); and Ruth Frager, 'No Proper Deal: Women Workers and The Canadian Labour Movement, 1870–1940,' in Linda Briskin and Lynda Yanz, eds., *Union Sisters: Women in the Labour Movement* (Toronto: Women's Press 1983). Studies of the household economy, which focus on the household as women's primary workplace, could be included here. See, for example, Bettina Bradbury, 'The Family Economy and Work in an Industrializing City: Montreal in the 1870s,' Canadian Historical Association, *Historical Papers* (1979), and Bradbury, 'Pigs, Cows and Boarders: Non-Wage Forms of Survival among Montreal Families, 1861–1891,' *Labour/Le Travail*, 14 (1984).

8 See Bryan Palmer, *A Culture in Conflict: Skilled Workers and Industrial Capitalism in Hamilton, Ontario, 1860–1914* (Montreal: McGill-Queen's University Press 1979). American historians who examine working-class leisure do not completely ignore religion, although it generally merits only a brief discussion. See, for example, Roy Rosenzweig, *Eight Hours for What We Will: Workers and Leisure in an Industrial City, 1870–1920* (Cambridge: Cambridge University Press 1983); Francis G. Couvares, *The Remaking of Pittsburgh: Class and Culture in an Industrializing City 1877–1919* (Albany: State University of New York Press 1984); and Ste-

ven J. Ross, *Workers on the Edge: Work, Leisure and Politics in Industrializing Cincinnati, 1788–1890*, (New York: Columbia University Press 1985).

9 For a description of the feminine ideal see Barbara Welter, 'The Cult of True Womanhood: 1820–1860,' *American Quarterly* 18, 2, part I (summer 1966): 151–74.

10 For a critique of the concept of a cross-class women's culture see Sarah Eisenstein, *Give Us Bread But Give Us Roses: Working Women's Consciousness in the United States, 1890 to the First World War* (London: Routledge and Kegan Paul 1983), and Nancy Hewitt, 'Beyond the Search for Sisterhood: American Women's History in the 1980s,' *Social History* 10, 3 (Oct. 1985): 299–321. Bettina Bradbury notes the existence of a distinct working-class definition of femininity in 'Women's History and Working Class History,' *Labour/Le Travail* 19 (spring 1987): 35. For a critique of the argument that working-class women's passivity can be explained primarily as an acceptance of dominant norms of femininity see Wayne Roberts, *Honest Womanhood: Feminism, Femininity and Class Consciousness among Toronto Working Women, 1893 to 1914* (Toronto: New Hogtown Press 1986), and Frager, 'No Proper Deal.'

11 A Salvation Army officer has gone through over thirty Canadian newspapers for the first few years of the Army's presence in each town and has copied out all references to the Army in the local papers. This was the source used in most references to the secular press.

12 R.G. Moyles, *The Blood and Fire in Canada: A History of the Salvation Army in the Dominion, 1882–1976* (Toronto: Peter Martin Associates 1977), 5

13 Woodstock *Sentinel Review*, 6 June 1884

14 Victor Bailey, ' "In Darkest England and the Way Out": The Salvation Army, Social Reform and the Labour Movement, 1885–1910," ' *International Review of Social History* 29, 2 (1984): 141

15 Roland Robertson, 'The Salvation Army: The Persistance of Sectarianism,' in Bryan Wilson, *Patterns of Sectarianism* (London: Heinemann 1967), 94

16 For the British context see Hugh McLeod, *Class and Religion in the Late Victorian City* (London: Croom Helm 1974), 62. For Canada see Lynne Marks, 'Religion, Class and Gender in an Ontario Mill Town: Participation in the Protestant Churches of Campbellford, Ontario, 1888–1894' (doctoral paper, York University 1987).

17 Bailey, 'In Darkest England,' 142. This was less true of the Knights of Labor, but, despite their stated commitment to women's equality, their position was in fact somewhat contradictory. For a discussion of women in the Knights of Labor see Kealey and Palmer, *Dreaming of What Might Be,* and Karen Dubinsky, ' "The Modern Chivalry": Women and the Knights of Labor in Ontario, 1880–1891' (MA thesis, Carleton University 1985).

18 Bramwell Booth, 'The Call and Ministry of Women,' in John Waldron, eds., *Women in the Salvation Army* (Oakville, Ont.: Triumph Press 1983), 89

19 On female preachers in early Methodism see Anna Clark, 'The Sexual Crisis and Popular Religion in London, 1770–1820,' in *International Labor and Working-Class History* 34 (fall 1988): 56–69. Also see Gail Malmgreen, 'Domestic Discords: Women and the Family in East Cheshire Methodism, 1750–1830,' in Jim Obelkevich, Lyndal Roper, and Raphael Samuel, eds., *Disciplines of Faith: Studies in Religion, Politics and Patriarachy* (London: Routledge and Kegan Paul 1987), and, for a study of female preachers among Primitive Methodists, see Deborah Valenze, *Prophetic Sons and Daughters: Female Preaching and Popular Religion in Industrial England* (Princeton: Princeton University Press 1985).

20 Catherine Booth, 'Female Ministry,' in *Papers on Practical Religion* (London: S.W. Partridge 1890), 160

21 Ibid., 152

22 Catherine Bramwell-Booth, *Catherine Booth: The Story of Her Loves* (London: Hodder and Stoughton 1971), 395

23 Catherine Booth, 'Female Ministry,' 135

24 By the 1890s it was also clear that although official Army policy insisted on the autonomy of women within marriage and recognized both partners as officers, in practice the couple went where the husband was sent. Female officers with children had little opportunity to move beyond the home. See, for example, *The Officer,* Nov. 1902.

25 Despite their rhetoric of equality, there was initial reluctance to place women in command of men in this way. See Bramwell Booth, 'The Call and Ministry of Women,' 92.

26 The definition of evangelical is taken from Grant, *A Profusion of Spires,* ix.

27 See William Westfall, *Two Worlds: The Protestant Culture of Nineteenth-Cen-*

tury Ontario (Kingston and Montreal: McGill-Queen's University Press 1989), 67 and 193.

28 See Ramsay Cook, *The Regenerators: Social Criticism in Late Victorian English Canada* (Toronto: University of Toronto Press 1985).

29 See, for example, S.D. Clark, *Church and Sect in Canada* (Toronto: University of Toronto Press 1948), and Neil Semple, 'The Impact of Urbanization on the Methodist Church of Canada, 1854–1884,' Canadian Society of Church History, *Papers* (1976).

30 Grant, *A Profusion of Spires*, 111. Female preachers had been particularly common among Bible Christians and Primitive Methodists. By 1884 Salvation Army competition provided an impetus for Canadian Methodists to permit a small number of women to act as travelling evangelists. See Marilyn Fardig Whiteley, 'Modest, Unaffected and Fully Consecrated: Lady Evangelists in Canadian Methodism, 1884–1900,' Canadian Methodist Historical Society, *Papers* 6 (1987).

31 Moyles, *The Blood and Fire in Canada*, 9 and 11. By 1892 there were corps in 264 towns across Canada.

32 Figures on Army membership for the 1880s are hard to find. The figure of 25,000 is cited by A. Sumner in *The New Papacy: Behind the Scenes in the Salvation Army by an ex-Staff Officer* (Toronto: Albert Britnell 1889), 7. Sumner, who denounced the Army in this pamphlet, would have insider knowledge of Army figures, as well as no reason to make the Army look good. The 1891 census figures would also include children of active Salvationists. Canada, *Census of Canada 1891* vol. 1, table IV.

33 See, for example, Barrie *Northern Advance*, 22 Nov. 1883, and Toronto *Globe*, 26 March 1884.

34 It appears to have been a common practice to be converted by the Army but to return to one's own denomination, rather than being enrolled as a Salvation Army soldier.

35 *Halifax Herald*, 28 Oct. 1885

36 *Toronto Mail*, 17 July 1882. In a few towns both middle- and working-class people appear to have been attracted to the Army; see, for example, Kingston's *Daily British Whig*, 17 July 1883.

37 Workers clearly predominate within the Army in Petrolia and Listowel. Both towns had populations under 5000. The relative predominance of farmers in Feversham can be explained by the fact that this was a largely rural community.

38 Toronto *World*, 12 Sept. 1882

39 *London Advertiser*, 8 Jan. 1883

40 See Robin W. Winks, *The Blacks in Canada: A History* (Montreal: McGill-Queen's University Press 1971), 338, and Grant, *A Profusion of Spires*, 156.

41 This impression is reinforced through surviving Army records. For example, soldiers' rolls for Listowel and Petrolia for the 1886–1900 period show that women made up at least 58 per cent of all soldiers. Corps Records, Salvation Army Archives, Toronto

42 *Daily British Whig*, 31 Jan. 1883, and *Fredericton Evening Capital*, 4 Dec. 1886

43 *Fredericton Evening Capital*, 20 Oct. 1885; *Northern Advance*, 13 Oct. 1883

44 General Booth, *The Doctrines and Discipline of the Salvation Army*, prepared for the Training Home (Toronto 1885), 103

45 *Hamilton Spectator*, 15 July 1884

46 Ibid.

47 *War Cry*, 10 and 24 Jan. 1885

48 Ibid., 25 Dec. 1884

49 Children's wages were usually necessary to supplement male wages in the working-class household, but men's wages were of major importance to the family economy. See Bradbury, 'The Family Economy and Work.'

50 *War Cry*, 2 Aug. 1890

51 *London Advertiser*, 18 April 1884

52 *War Cry*, 1 Dec. 1888

53 *Hamilton Spectator*, 27 June 1884

54 *War Cry*, 11 May 1889

55 *Sentinel Review*, 14 Dec. 1883, and *World*, 4 Jan. 1883

56 See, for example, Westfall, *Two Worlds*, 60–3; Clarke, *Church and Sect in Canada*; and Anna Clark, 'The Sexual Crisis and Popular Religion.'

57 See Westfall, *Two Worlds*.

58 *London Advertiser*, 3 March 1884

59 Ibid., 30 March 1883, and *World*, 3 Feb. 1885

60 *Petrolia Advertiser*, 8 Aug. 1884

61 *Daily British Whig*, 28 Sept. 1883, and *Halifax Herald*, 28 Oct. 1885

62 *Northern Advance*, 18 Oct. 1883; *Hamilton Spectator*, 26 March 1884

63 *New Brunswick Reporter and Fredericton Advertiser*, 20 Jan. 1886

64 *Daily British Whig*, 20 March 1883

65 See, for example, *Wiarton Echo*, 12 Dec. 1884

66 *Dominion Churchman*, 10 May 1883

67 *Petrolia Advertiser*, 23 May 1884

68 *Orders and Regulations for Soldiers of the Salvation Army*, by the General (London 1889)

69 *Halifax Herald*, 28 Oct. 1885

70 This was revealed when he was on trial for murder in New York State. *Thorold Post*, 25 Feb. 1887

71 See Karen Dubinsky, ' "Maidenly Girls" ' or "Designing Women"? The Crime of Seduction in Turn-of-the-Century Ontario,' in this volume for an example of how drives home from Army meetings could provide the opportunity for sexual relations.

72 It is also possible that there was not so much emphasis on the seduction of young women because these were working-class women. For stories regarding sexuality and seduction within the Salvation Army see, for example, *Orillia Times*, 21 Aug. 1884; *St Thomas Times*, 6 Aug. 1883; *Stratford Times*, 13 Aug. 1884; *Newmarket Era*, 13 June 1884; *Renfrew Mercury*, 8 April 1887; and *Thorold Post*, 11 April and 20 June 1884.

73 *London Advertiser*, 27 Feb. 1884

74 *War Cry*, 13 Dec. 1884, 1 Aug. 1885, 12 Nov. and 24 Dec. 1887, and 25 May 1889

75 See Kathy Peiss, *Cheap Amusements: Working Women and Leisure in Turn-of-the-Century New York* (Philadelphia: Temple University Press 1986), 63–6, for a discussion of the role of fashion within the contemporary young women's culture of New York working-class women.

76 Several papers reported that young church members attended Salvation Army services. See, for example, *Northern Advance*, 22 Nov. 1883; *The Globe*, 26 March 1884.

77 *Ottawa Free Press*, 4 April 1885

78 The names of 855 female officers and 669 male officers who were recruited within English Canada were found on the 'C' Roll, Officers' Rolls, Salvation Army Archives, Toronto. This roll apparently includes the names of all, or almost all officers for this period. Many more soldiers applied to be officers than were accepted. By the later 1880s almost half of all applicants were rejected. *War Cry*, 9 Aug. 1890

79 Moyles, *The Blood and Fire in Canada*, 16

80 'c' Roll, Officers' Rolls. For long-serving officers, rolls 'A' and 's' were occasionally consulted for career information.

81 Only 5 per cent of men appear to have been married when they became officers. Except in the very early years, both partners had to be Army officers.

82 In 1891 less than 11 per cent of the female population of Canada engaged in paid employment. Most of those who were employed were unmarried. However, although the 1891 census does not provide a breakdown of female employment by marital status, we can be relatively certain that less that half of the unmarried female population was employed in this period. In 1921, when over 15 per cent of the female population was gainfully employed, only 49 per cent of unmarried women between the ages of fifteen and thirty-four were employed. Canada, Dominion Bureau of Statistics, *Census of Canada, 1921*. Canada, Dominion Bureau of Statistics, *Occupational Trends in Canada, 1891–1931* (Ottawa 1939)

83 Of the gainfully employed Canadian women in 1891, 41 per cent were servants, while 53 per cent of female officers who had previously been employed had worked as servants. Army officers were somewhat more likely to have been involved in manufacturing (including dressmakers/milliners) than the average Canadian woman worker (36 per cent of previously employed Army officers as compared with 31 per cent of all women workers). Out of all previously employed female officers, only 11 per cent had been teachers, nurses, or clerks, while women in these occupations (professional service and clerical) made up 14 per cent of the female labour force in 1891. See *Occupational Trends in Canada, 1891–1931*. While teaching might be seen as a middle-class occupation, large numbers of women from working-class backgrounds were becoming teachers. Nursing remained primarily a working-class occupation in this period. See Marta Danylewycz and Alison Prentice, 'Teachers, Gender and Bureaucratizing School Systems in Nineteenth Century Montreal and Toronto,' *History of Education Quarterly* 24, 1 (spring 1984): 75–100, and Judi Coburn, ' "I See and am Silent" ': A Short History of Nursing in Ontario,' in *Women at Work, Ontario 1850–1930* (Toronto: Canadian Women's Educational Press 1974), 127–64.

84 The Saint John *Daily Sun*, 16 Feb. 1886, reported that the Army claimed that 450 out of 500 officers were native-born Canadians. Also

see Stephen M. Ashley, 'The Salvation Army in Toronto, 1882–1896' (MA thesis, University of Guelph 1969), 24. Ashley suggests that after 1886 the Army started to import some English officers again.

85 The fact that the ethnic background of officers was generally mentioned in the *War Cry*, more explicitly than was gender, might suggest that ethnic divisions remained a significant issue in the Army.

86 Geographical mobility was high in the nineteenth century. See, for example, Michael Katz, *The People of Hamilton, Canada West* (Cambridge, Mass: Harvard University Press 1975), and David Gagan, *Hopeful Travellers: Family, Land and Social Change in Mid-Victorian Peel County, Canada West* (Toronto: University of Toronto Press 1981). However, the Army may have provided unusual opportunities for mobility for young women, since such mobility took place outside family networks and beyond family supervision.

87 Malmgreen, 'Domestic Discords,' 59

88 Although by this point even the Methodist church was as concerned with respectability as with salvation. See, for example, Clark, *Church and Sect in Canada*, and Neil Semple, 'The Impact of Urbanization on the Methodist Church of Canada, 1854–1884,' Canadian Society of Church History, *Papers* (1976).

89 *Daily British Whig*, 29 Jan. 1883

90 *War Cry*, 1 Aug. 1885

91 For a discussion of how early Methodism could provide such opportunities see Henry Abelove, 'The Sexual Politics of Early Wesleyan Methodism,' in Obelkevich et al., eds., *Disciplines of Faith*.

92 *The World*, 17 May 1884

93 *War Cry*, 19 July 1890

94 Booth, *The Doctrines and Discipline of the Salvation Army*, 111

95 Katie McVicar, a Knights of Labor activist, comments in the *Palladium of Labor* on the lack of opportunities for domestic servants to meet potential marriage partners, as cited in Dubinsky, 'The Modern Chivalry,' 48. Also see Genevieve Leslie, 'Domestic Service in Canada, 1880–1920,' in *Women at Work, Ontario, 1850–1930*.

96 See, for example, Caroll Smith-Rosenberg, 'The Female World of Love and Ritual: Relations between Women in Nineteenth-Century America,' in her *Disorderly Conduct: Visions of Gender in Victorian America* (New York: Oxford University Press 1985).

97 *Daily British Whig*, 22 Oct. 1883

98 Salvation Army women spent a briefer time at the Training Home than middle-class women spent at boarding school or university, with Army training in this period ranging from three weeks to three months. Moyles, *The Blood and Fire in Canada*, 283–5

99 References to the sadness of having to 'break up our family' at the end of the Training Home course reinforce a sense of the closeness among women there. *War Cry*, 7 May 1887

100 In *Church and Sect in Canada*, 433, Clark suggests that the basis of the Salvation Army's appeal was its ability to provide a sense of 'social solidarity' to the 'rootless social masses'. While Clark's approach is overly functionalist, his insight should not be completely discarded. For a discussion of the importance of a sense of community within revivalistic sects see also Malmgreen, 'Domestic Discords,' 59.

101 Herbert Gutman, 'Protestantism and the American Labor Movement,' *Work, Culture and Society in Industrializing America* (New York: Random House 1966). Also see Lynne Marks, 'The Knights of Labor and the Salvation Army: Religion and Working Class Culture in Ontario, 1882–1890,' paper presented at the Canadian Historical Association, Victoria, May 1990.

102 *World*, 3 July 1884

103 *War Cry*, 19 Nov. 1887

104 See Sumner, *The New Papacy*, 61. Although married women were also considered officers, wages were paid to the husband.

105 Working-class women's weekly wages seem to have ranged from $1.50 up to $7.00 or $8.00. The average appears to have been less than $5.00 a week. See, for example, Dubinsky, 'The Modern Chivalry,' 25, and *Women at Work*, 48.

106 *War Cry*, 25 May 1889. Also see Sumner, *The New Papacy*. Sumner argues that many officers were attracted to the Army because it allowed individuals in 'humble circumstances' to gain public positions of influence and respect (53).

107 In a letter to the *Palladium of Labor*, 13 Oct. 1883, Katie McVicar quotes a co-worker as making this comment. Dubinsky, 'The Modern Chivalry,' 32

108 See, for example, Frager, 'No Proper Deal,' and Alice Kessler-Harris,

Out to Work: A History of Wage-Earning Women in the United States (Oxford: Oxford University Press 1982).

109 Dubinsky, 'The Modern Chivalry,' 141. Barry also cites the selfishness and injustice of men as explaining the inequality of women in the workplace.

110 *Palladium of Labor*, 10 Nov. 1883, quoted in Dubinsky, 'The Modern Chivalry,' 53.

111 See, for example, *War Cry*, 4 Dec. 1886, 5 Feb. 1887, and 12 July 1890.

112 In 'The Cross and the Pedestal: Women, Anti-Ritualism and the Emergence of the American Bourgeoisie,' Carroll Smith Rosenberg argues that concepts of Christian self-sacrifice and submission, common to evangelical revivalism, had a particular appeal to women. See her *Disorderly Conduct: Visions of Gender in Victorian America*, 154.

113 *War Cry*, 1 Dec. 1888

114 Ibid., 27 Sept. and 2 Aug. 1890

115 Ibid., 24 Nov. 1888

116 Ibid., 27 Sept. 1890

117 Ibid., 2 Aug. 1890. The bias in such claims is obvious, since these articles were used to recruit potential rescue officers.

118 Of the thirty-six women who entered the Army between 1882 and 1890 and were involved in rescue work, eighteen left the Army after their first posting to rescue work. Most of these women had previously had several postings as field officers (preachers). Half of the thirteen men who were involved in rescue work in this period also left the Army after their first posting to this work. 'c' Roll, Officers' Rolls. In 'The Salvation Army in Toronto,' 90, Ashley also argues that Army officers were reluctant to enter social service work.

119 See, for example, *War Cry*, 2 Aug. 1890

120 Ibid., 19 July 1890

121 Ibid.

122 Ibid., 9 July 1887 and 22 Aug. 1885. In *The New Papacy*, 37, Sumner claimed that by the late 1880s collections were so low that in 60 per cent of corps, officers received no cash wages and survived on food and accommodation provided by local Army soldiers.

123 *War Cry*, 7 May 1887

124 Ibid., 24 Dec. 1887. Despite such rhetoric, some material efforts were

made to assist worn-out and sick officers through the founding of a rest home.

125 It is interesting to note that in the Kingston revolts one of the charges against Captain Abby Thompson was that she was spending Army money on frivolous feminine pleasures such as silk dresses. *Daily British Whig*, 25 Oct. 1883. See also *Hamilton Spectator*, 10 Sept. 1884.

126 See, for example, *London Advertiser*, 15 July 1884.

127 Ibid., 19 and 20 June 1884

128 Ibid., 14 July 1884

129 *War Cry*, 25 Dec. 1886, 25 June 1887, and 25 May 1889. Although only 9 per cent of women (as compared to 1 per cent of men) officially resigned their officerships to marry, many officers who provided no reason for their resignations and withdrawals may also have had matrimonial plans.

130 Ibid., 1 May 1897

131 The twenty-three (out of forty) long-serving female officers who do not appear to have married were in most cases transferred to other countries, where some may have married. The Army may also have provided some of these women with a welcome alternative to marriage, since such alternatives were extremely limited for working-class women.

132 For comments regarding the Army's levity and vulgarity see, for example, *Daily British Whig*, 30 April 1883; *London Advertiser*, 7 April 1884; and *Sarnia Observer*, 16 May 1884.

133 *Fredericton Evening Capital*, 7 Nov. 1885; *St Thomas Times*, 17 Aug. 1883; and *World*, 5 Sept. 1884

134 *Daily British Whig*, 31 Aug. 1883

135 Ibid., 30 April 1883

136 Regarding the loss of church members to the Salvation Army see, for example, *London Advertiser*, 30 May 1884; *Belleville Daily Intelligencer*; 26 Nov. 1883; *Sarnia Observer*, 4 July 1884; and *Globe*, 26 March 1884.

137 Westminster *Mainland Guardian*, 29 Feb. 1888; *Halifax Herald*, 28 Oct. 1885

138 A.A. Travill, 'Early Medical Co-education and Women's Medical College, Kingston, Ontario, 1880–1894,' *Historic Kingston* 30 (Jan. 1982): 68–89; Veronica Strong-Boag, 'Canada's Women Doctors: Feminism Constrained,' in Linda Kealey, ed., *A Not Unreasonable Claim: Women and Reform in Canada, 1880s–1920s* (Toronto: Women's Press 1979), 109–29;

Catherine Cleverdon, *The Woman Suffrage Movement in Canada* (Toronto: University of Toronto Press 1974); and Alison Prentice et al., *Canadian Women: A History* (Toronto: Harcourt Brace Jonanovich 1988).

139 In 'The Impact of Urbanization on the Methodist Church,' 52, Semple argues that by the 1850s the churches saw one of their roles as being the reinforcement of the legitimacy of wealth.

140 For attacks on the Army for attracting prostitutes see *London Advertiser*, 7 April 1884, and *St Thomas Times*, 4 April 1883.

141 Jeffrey Weeks, *Sex, Politics and Society: The Regulation of Sexuality since 1800* (London: Longman 1981), 14 and 92

142 For a discussion of middle-class efforts to control working-class behaviour in this period see, for example, Graeme Decarie, 'Something Old, Something New ... Aspects of Prohibitionism in Ontario in the 1890s,' in D. Swainson, ed., *Oliver Mowat's Ontario* (Toronto: Macmillan 1972); Christopher Armstrong and H.V. Nelles, *The Revenge of the Methodist Bicycle Company, Sunday Streetcars and Municipal Reform in Toronto, 1888–1897* (Toronto: Peter Martin Associates 1977); and Susan E. Houston, 'The "Waifs and Strays" of a Late Victorian City: Juvenile Delinquents in Toronto,' in Joy Parr, ed., *Childhood and Family in Canadian History* (Toronto: McClelland and Stewart 1982).

143 *Daily British Whig*, 7 May 1883; *London Advertiser*, 3 March 1883; *Whitby Chronicle*, 4 April 1884; and *Manitoba Free Press*, 29 March 1887

144 *London Advertiser*, 17 July 1883; *Belleville Daily Intelligencer*, 4, Dec. 1883; and *Hamilton Spectator*, 25 Jan. 1884

145 *London Advertiser*, 17 July 1883; *Petrolia Advertiser*, 28 June 1884; and *World*, 17 Dec. 1883

146 *London Advertiser*, 30 Nov. 1882; *Northern Advance*, 25 Oct. 1883; and *Hamilton Spectator*, 5 May 1884

147 For a discussion of maternal feminism see Kealey, *A Not Unreasonable Claim*, and Carol Bacchi, *Liberation Deferred? The Ideas of the English-Canadian Suffragists, 1877–1918* (Toronto: University of Toronto Press 1983).

148 In the midst of her difficulties with hostile male medical students, Smith notes in her diary that 'the Salvation Army has marched on Kingston.' Veronica Strong-Boag, ed., *'A Woman with a Purpose': The Diaries of Elizabeth Smith, 1872–1884* (Toronto: University of Toronto Press 1980), 291

4 The Alchemy of Politicization:

Socialist Women and the Early Canadian Left

Janice Newton

A few months ago I looked upon socialism with horror. Today I honour it above all other movements working for the betterment of mankind ... A friend of mine who lives a domestic, secluded life on a farm, held up her hands in surprise, when she learned that I actually attended socialist meetings. She asked me in real earnest if I was not afraid that 'some of those foreigners would stick a knife in me.' She seemed to think that socialists were a set of men who went around with bombs in their pockets and knives in their belts, anxious and ready to commit murder. Alas, how we are maligned.[1]

These words of Mary Cotton Wisdom, editor of the Woman's Column of Canada's largest selling socialist newspaper in 1909, hint at some of the challenges she faced in becoming politically active in the early Canadian left. As a white English-speaking woman, she clearly felt a need to reassure herself and her readers that socialists were not 'foreign murder[er]s.' To overcome this fear of socialism, she identified the Christian ideals that she thought represented socialism: 'Socialists are bound together in a great cause. They are trying to help the weak, to raise the fallen, to lift the burden of oppression, to overthrow crime and bind up the broken hearts, trying to fulfil the teachings of Christ in truth.'[2] In these beliefs, she was not alone. Other women who shared Wisdom's commitment to Christian ideals were drawn into the socialist movement before the First World War in Canada.

But Wisdom's words also hint at other challenges, especially the challenges that foreign or non-Christian women would confront in becoming politically active in a socialist movement when faced with comrades such as Mary Cotton Wisdom.

This paper will explore the political convictions that drew women into the early Canadian left, concentrating mainly on prominent women socialists who left their mark in the historical record. We will focus primarily on three questions: What political and social concerns led these women into the socialist movement? How did these concerns shape their involvement in the left? And did a concern for 'women's issues' provide a bond that strengthened socialist women's commitment to the left? In exploring these questions, three themes will emerge as important in women's lives: religion, prohibition, and women's suffrage. Some women socialists demonstrated commitment to these causes, but their socialist convictions at times alienated them from conservative allies in other movements. Socialist women carried political and social concerns with them into the socialist movement, but their concerns did not always fit comfortably with the politics of the male-dominated parties. Furthermore, differences in ethnicity, religion, and class sometimes aided, but sometimes fragmented, the coherence of women's interests within the left. Vastly outnumbered by male comrades, and in a movement that did not value women's interests, socialist women faced considerable odds in developing a common voice to articulate women's concerns within the left.

Male English-speaking socialists dominated the leadership of key left organizations like the Canadian Socialist Leagues (CSL), the Socialist Party of Canada (SPC), and the Social Democratic Party of Canada (SDPC). English-language party papers, like the *Western Clarion* and *Cotton's Weekly*, were distributed by party members across Canada. The majority of women socialists identified in this press were married.[3] Some identified themselves as housewives and mothers by lamenting the domestic duties and family responsibilities that prevented then from doing more for the socialist movement.[4] Few of these socialist women worked for wages. Of the wage-earning women mentioned, Jewish garment workers were prominent, especially in the larger cities like Montreal, Toronto, Winnipeg, and Edmonton.[5] Many Finnish women were socialists and also participated in the labourforce, but they were seldom acknowledged in the English left press.[6] The dual demands of employment and domestic responsibilities, compounded with barriers of language and ethnicity, helped to silence these socialist women; their voices or presence were seldom acknowledged in the English left press. Most of the women known to be active in the English-speaking left were primarily engaged in unpaid domestic labour. Overall, women probably never exceeded 10 per cent of the English-speaking left.[7] Their small numbers doubtless inhibited women's ability to influence a male-dominated movement.

Women were involved in the Canadian socialist movement from its inception. Prior to 1904, the largest socialist organization in Canada was the Canadian Socialist League (CSL). This was a loose organization, with membership from all but two provinces. At its organizational peak in 1902, the CSL had sixty-five locals.[8] Some of the members of the CSL were involved in other social causes, notably trade unionism, suffrage, prohibition, and the social gospel.[9] For example, George Wrigley edited a temperance paper before he became editor of *Citizen and Country*, a paper that supported the CSL. His wife, Sarah Wrigley, was the Ontario superintendent for temperance in Sunday schools in the Woman's Christian Temperance Union (WCTU), and she also edited the woman's column in *Citizen and Country*. Her column, 'The Kingdom of the Home,' appeared only briefly, but she raised issues that echoed those raised by women's organizations of the time, including suffrage, charity, prohibition, intemperance, war, the servant problem, prostitution, and immorality. She specifically urged WCTU women to subscribe to the paper, and she headlined a theme that was characteristic of maternal feminism: the values of the home sphere, love and purity, should become the guiding principles in the political realm.[10]

Margaret Haille, a prominent activist in the CSL, also had prior experience in the WCTU, and claimed that her commitment to socialism stemmed from her experience in the temperance union.

Before coming to Toronto, Margaret edited the first woman's column in an English-language socialist publication in the United States. She was described as one of those socialist women who 'still clung to the notion of the home as a traditional source of woman's power, [and to] domesticity as a special feminine preserve.'[11] In 1902 Haille became the CSL's candidate in North Toronto for the provincial election, and she promoted many of these views in her election speeches.[12]

The presence of these women in the early Canadian socialist movement confirms that Canada experienced a trend similar to one in the United States: important women activists in the American left had their early political training in the women's movement, especially the temperance movement.[13] A number of women in Canada who were active in these organizations later became active in socialist or trade-union organizations.[14] Women's organizations of the time, like the WCTU, articulated a form of feminism that legitimized woman's place in the public sphere by stressing the important contribution woman's maternal qualities would make to politics. While these organizations propounded maternal feminism, we must not assume that a concern for the domestic and maternal roles of women necessarily reflected a middle-class bias. At this time, domestic concerns largely shaped women's lives, even the lives of working-class women and women who worked for pay. The development of a more radical feminist voice at this time would require some ability to transcend middle-class biases, but it would not necessarily entail a rejection of women's concerns about their domestic and maternal roles. These were concerns that working-class women might also share.

Although these women were able to rise to prominence within the CSL, their commitment to suffrage, prohibition, and Christianity did not fit comfortably with the socialist party that followed the CSL. By 1904 the Socialist Party of Canada (SPC) had eclipsed the CSL. The SPC had locals across Canada, but much of its political leadership came from British Columbia, where the party had elected a socialist member to the provincial legislature. Known as the 'impossibilist party,' the SPC consistently disparaged political parties that supported reform measures. While the party emphasized the need to educate the working class to vote for socialism, its conception of the working class focused narrowly on male workers. The party platform eschewed any reference to reforms and limited itself to the call for workers to vote for socialism. This change in the character of the socialist movement had dramatic implications for issues like woman's suffrage, Christian socialism, and prohibition. Members who were committed to these issues, including women members, were sometimes compelled to make tactical choices when reconciling their interest in these issues and their integration within the party.

The most prominent woman's issue of this time period was woman's suffrage. The international socialist movement was hesitant to support woman's suffrage, viewing women as politically conservative and bound by religious views. The SPC reflected this attitude by refusing to include woman's suffrage in its party platform, calling it a reformist measure. On several occasions, suffrage groups approached the SPC for its support and the party refused, claiming it was for socialism, not reform. When the Political Equality League of British Columbia asked the SPC to endorse woman's suffrage and to provide financial assistance for the cause, the party refused. The editor of the party paper explained his position: 'Not that we are violently opposed to your having the vote, even though we know you would use it against us. We know of no good reason why you should not have a vote and it would matter nothing if we did. We simply don't care a cuss ... We know only two kinds of people. Not men and women, but masters and slaves. Our "financial assistance," if any, is devoted to making slaves aware of the fact.'[15] The party insisted that the class struggle – between workers and bosses – took priority over the sex struggle.

Despite this official stance on suffrage, several prominent party members did support suffrage. Most notably, J.H. Hawthornthwaite, the SPC member of the provincial legislature in British Columbia, introduced private members' bills to extend the franchise to women. In 1908, after a heated debate, the Ontario SPC convention voted to endorse woman's suffrage and to encourage locals to bring in women lecturers. They also urged the dominion executive to follow suit and provide literature on working women.[16] Despite such examples of support for woman's suffrage among some party members, the dominion executive refused to change party policy.

The SPC never officially endorsed suffrage; in fact its hostility to suffrage in the party press became more pronounced over time. Prominent suffragists were criticized for their upper-class backgrounds or for their political persuasions. Nellie McClung, for example, was criticized for lending her support to the Liberals.[17] After 1912, the party press did not cover or endorse suffrage politics, nor did it acknowledge the attainment of woman's suffrage at the federal or provincial levels. It did note that in the 1917 federal election, working women had been influential in the outcome, but not to the party's advantage. Ironically, the party paper concluded that the SPC had been 'right all along. Women need to be educated to use the vote.'[18]

The SPC also claimed Christianity was incompatible with socialism, but this argument took different forms in the party press. The most extreme form argued that a Christian who believed in individual salvation could never be a socialist, and a socialist who believed in the collective power of the working class could never be a Christian.[19] Such an attitude shows clearly the effort of the SPC to distinguish itself as much as possible from the intellectual heritage of late Victorian reformism in Canada and to reject any specifically Christian justification for social change. The SPC also ridiculed the reform efforts of specific religious groups and argued that only socialism, not religion, would solve the world's problems.[20] Others simply argued that religious convictions were of no consequence to socialism, and that the party should refrain from attacking Christian socialists.[21] Such attacks on Christianity clearly offended Christian socialists, who sometimes protested the attacks through letters to the party paper. While rejection of Christian socialism might have alienated many Christians, this position might equally have made the party more attractive to non-Christians, especially Jewish and Finnish socialists. Women formed a significant portion of the latter group.

The SPC's hostility to Christian socialism should be understood in a larger sense than simple rejection of Christian socialism. The party identified religious devotion with political conservatism. In rejecting Christian socialism, the party was also rejecting the radical potential of the social gospel. Furthermore, women were deemed more religious than men. The SPC's paper described women as particularly subject to religious dogma and less able to think 'clearly' for themselves.[22] Despite this claim, the background of many socialist women in churches and Christian-based organizations like the WCTU helped to shape their political radicalism. The SPC's attack on Christian socialism denigrated the radicalism of Christian socialism and these socialist women in particular.

The SPC's hostility to Christianity was complemented by its opposition to prohibition. It expressed a profound mistrust of the middle-class bias of the WCTU, suspiciously viewing the goals of the WCTU as satisfying the bosses' need for 'sober slaves.'[23] The party press opposed the WCTU's local option and prohibition campaigns because it claimed they were reformist and failed to attack the cause of the liquor problem. The SPC focused predominantly on a class perspective, while ignoring or ridiculing the women's perspective on drinking offered by the WCTU. Sometimes, the party simply defended the individual right of workers to indulge in alcohol without interference from the state, contending that it was a necessity of life for the working man, but ignoring the consequences that excessive drinking might have on the wife of the working man.[24]

While such opposition to prohibition might be expected from the SPC, given its opposition to reforms in general, the party went beyond mere verbal attacks on prohibitionists. Socialist MPP Hawthornthwaite opposed the restriction of the sale of alcohol to miners, alcohol was served at party events, the party paper carried advertisements for alcohol, and some party members were expelled for joining a local option league. In one instance there were complaints that a party organizer appeared drunk on stage.[25] Such activities would have outraged and alienated those socialists with strong prohibitionist convictions who had earlier been drawn to the socialist movement, including those women with ties to the WCTU.

The party's opposition to prohibition must be understood on a deeper level than its opposition to the reformist or middle-class elements in the prohibition cause. Consumption of alcohol was predominantly a male activity, not only in the sense that women, for the most part, did not drink, but also because men who did drink tended to do so in exclusively male environments.[26] Since consumption of alcohol was associated with masculinity, prohibition was one means for women to exert influence over masculine behaviour. This connection, well understood by the WCTU, helps account for the tremendous appeal of this organization among women, and the corresponding hostility it engendered in some men. Furthermore, the SPC actively relied on the association of masculinity with socialism to 'strengthen' the image of socialism. For the most part, this reliance was not self-conscious, but it was nonetheless crucial to the development of socialism's appeal to male trade unionists. An issue such as prohibition cut directly into this masculine image of socialism. Since opposition to drink jeopardized their efforts to connect socialism with masculinity, it is not surprising that some male socialists opposed prohibition in the same spirit that they opposed women's suffrage or Christianity.[27] This stance on prohibition also had significance for different ethnic groups involved in the socialist movement. For example, many early Finnish socialist organizations began as temperance societies.[28] With a high proportion of women in their ranks, Finnish socialists might have found tolerance of alcohol consumption was a significant barrier to cooperation with the SPC. As the CSL dissolved and the SPC rose to prominence, socialist women faced many challenges in adapting to these changes in the political character of the Canadian socialist movement.

Ruth Lestor provides us with an example of a woman socialist who endured some cost while embracing the SPC's platform fully.[29] Coming to Canada from Britain, Lestor and her husband gained prominence from 1909 to 1911 during a speaking tour for the SPC.[30] Touted as the first lady socialist lecturer in Canada, Lestor claimed to speak 'naturally from the standpoint of the woman's interest in social conditions.'[31] Despite this claim, an analysis of her speeches and writings shows that, like the SPC, she saw women's issues as relevant only when construed from a class perspective that put the male worker at the centre of the class struggle. Her commitment to the SPC platform created difficulties in promoting solidarity among women socialists.

Drawing on here experience of women workers in Manchester, England, Lestor often focused on women workers in capitalist society. She assumed that only women who worked like men – in the paid labour force – would have the most interest in socialism, but this assumption ignored, among other things, the reality that the lives of most women in Canada, even working-class women, revolved around domestic labour. Her emphasis on paid labour reflected the tendency of the SPC to focus on those areas in which women's interests corresponded to men's, without allowing women's concerns and experience legitimacy in their own right. Characteristically, she concluded one article by stating that women were going to 'march alongside the men ... Companions and Comrades, marching for the conquest of the world, for the workers.'[32] Typically, 'workers' did not include the women who worked without pay within the home.

Her arguments about women's suffrage provide one illustration of her tendency to use male experience as a model for analysis of women's issues. Lestor used women in the paid labourforce as the basis for her analysis of suffrage. Women's demand for suffrage was the direct result of the development of capitalism. 'The working woman, like the working man, is denied the right to develop herself because she is poor,' but 'the vote given to the working women would be the means of making them class conscious.' She saw revolutionary potential as resting naturally with the women in the paid labourforce. In contrast, Lestor expressed barely concealed contempt for the women working without pay within the home. These women 'have a narrower outlook than those who work outside. Their work is monotonous in the extreme, they are victims of custom. They spend their lives in a round of uncomplaining unpaid drudgery. Superstition has them in its paralysing grip.'[33] Capitalism had reduced these women to 'simply breeding slaves for the capitalist market.'[34] Women not in the labourforce were reactionary and disruptive. Their demand for woman's suffrage sprang mainly from 'a desire to perpetuate permanently woman's follies and slavery to capital.'[35]

Alongside here emphasis on women in the paid labourforce, Lestor sometimes used the rhetoric of maternal feminism to support suffrage. Even without a political voice, she argued that 'the mother's instinct for the protection of her young ought to send them forth on a holy crusade against the evils [of capitalism].' In the meantime, women 'can nevertheless hurl countless votes through their influence on their friends and relatives of the opposite sex. The man who will not listen to the pleas of woman for the child is not entitled to receive woman's co-operation in producing children.'[36] Overall, her use of the rhetoric of maternal feminism was overshadowed by her commitment to the SPC's party line: 'the true revolutionist loses all sight of sex ... A woman is a man – that's all.'[37]

Lestor also shared the SPC's contempt for the views of moral reformers who blamed social problems on alcoholism or sin. Drawing on her years of experience as a nurse in mental institutions in England, she argued that madness was not caused by sin or alcohol, but by the monotony of the factory girl's life: 'The monotony of their former employment had worked on their nerves to such an extent that they always believed themselves to be at work. Some of these ... were always begging pitifully for the engine to stop.' In contradiction to her other claims, about the advantages of women working, she blamed working mothers for the problem of lunacy, because they could not care properly for their infants. She concluded that capitalism breeds lunacy and that ridding the world of capitalism would make it sane.[38]

Another article provided a cogent glimpse of her attitudes towards women and religion. Lestor stated that initially she thought the SPC tried to keep women out of its ranks and she made every effort to encourage women to join. On reflection she decided this had been the wrong course of action – the party needed not just women, but women who were 'mentally equipped with knowledge sufficient to understand what they are doing.' On the whole, she observed, 'woman ... is so ignorant that she does not yet possess that knowledge that entitled her to membership in our ranks.' Echoing assumptions commonly held in the international socialist community, Lestor described women as conventional, ignorant, cruel, and bound by religion and fashion. 'Religions seems to cling to a woman longer than it does to a man; perhaps it is that woman goes to church, more especially when she has anything new to go in.'[39] Her views of women and religion would have been alien, if not antithetical, to women like Mary Cotton Wisdom, who were drawn into the socialist movement from a tradition of maternal feminism or out of the conviction that socialism would make a Christian life possible.

At the same time, Lestor acknowledged the price she paid for her strict adherence to the SPC line. She lamented going for years without female companionship in the socialist movement, because she 'rarely found one of my own sex worth talking to.' She claimed that truly revolutionary women, such as herself, had a difficult time because they were ostracized by other women in the movement, although she found the comradeship of men was adequate compensation.[40] Lestor was isolated from those Canadian women socialists whose political roots overlapped with the women's movement. Despite her prominence as a woman socialist, it is abundantly clear that Lestor did not identify with other women socialists or with women's issues. Many of her remarks about women were more misogynist than the views of male socialists. Her experience demonstrates the difficulty a woman socialist would face in supporting the SPC line while at the same time trying to advance women's interests within the left.

The stridency of the SPC's line was shared by other prominent women socialists. Though from a very different background than Ruth Lestor, Sophie Mushkat also supported the SPC's line on suffrage and religion, but she broke with the party in her support of prohibition.[41] A Russian emigrant of Polish descent, Mushkat and her father, William, came to Canada in 1905 and settled in the Maritimes. Mushkat had not been a member of a socialist organization in Russia, but had been a sympathizer for many years. She joined the Canadian Socialist party around 1908, and both she and her father became active party supporters.[42]

Mushkat was first noted for her activities in organizing and speaking in the Maritimes. Most of the information about her early work comes from the regular reports of Roscoe Fillmore, the Socialist party organizer in the Maritimes in 1909 and 1910. According to Fillmore, she spoke on several occasions, sometimes drawing crowds of 1200.[43] She even faced violence, as hostile crowds or police tried to disrupt socialist meetings. Fillmore commended Mushkat for her courage: 'She persisted in attending the meeting and speaking even when we were all sure we would be "pulled in." '[44] The topics of her speeches ranged from poverty, 'The Class Struggle,' 'Socialism and Trade Unionism,' to 'The Materialist Conception of History,' but she also spoke on women's issues, such as 'On Woman's Place in the Socialist Movement.'[45] We were assured by Fillmore that her speeches were not frivolous; he commended her for talking 'plain straight socialism without ever once mentioning ice-cream, bon-bons, directoire gowns or peach basket hats.'[46]

Since her soap-boxing would have been an unusual activity for a woman, reports of her speaking style are of interest. Reputed to be the only lady socialist speaker in Canada, she was labelled the 'Mother Jones of Canada.' In some sense this was apt, for she was not described as a genteel speaker: 'Miss Mushkat, her sleeves rolled up to the elbows, vigorously pummelled the various bogeys created ... by the capitalist papers to frighten people from taking part [in socialism].'[47]

One soap-box speech in Moncton led to a disturbance that involved the police, and Mushkat subsequently appeared in court as a witness. The account of her testimony at the trial revealed the basis for her commitment to socialism. In taking the witness stand, Mushkat refused to swear on the Bible. Without revealing that she was Jewish, she explained that she did not believe in the afterlife, but she believed she would be punished by her conscience for misdeeds.[48] When asked by the lawyer the aim of the SPC, she replied that she was proud to be a member of the SPC whose aim was 'To give the workers the full value of their labour.'

Her answers drew applause from the audience and a reprimand from the judge, who dismissed her testimony because she did not swear on the Bible.[49]

In late 1910 Mushkat travelled west to Calgary. She continued her speaking tours under the auspices of the SPC and hustled subscriptions for the party paper.[50] While on tour, she made good use of her facility in English, Russian, and Polish,[51] even providing a translation for the party press of the experiences of a Russian serf who moved from Russia to Canada and tried to establish himself as a farmer.[52] She was also active in organizing the campaign to elect socialist T. Edwin Smith from Taber, Alberta.[53] Her speaking ability and her facility in languages made her an asset for the SPC. However, the SPC did not organize fund-raising drives for its women organizers as it did for the men, so, despite Mushkat's popularity, the expenses of her tours often exceeded the money she raised. On one tour, for example, she reported expenses of $200, which exceeded the $108 she raised during the tour.[54] When she reported making money another one tour, she was criticized for mishandling of funds. The matter was apparently resolved by the local involved.[55]

The last official report of her activities is a brief mention in the minutes of the SPC's Dominion Executive Dommittee in 1915. She became involved in the prohibition campaign in Alberta, despite the SPC's rule that prohibited members from participating in reform causes or sharing the platform with other parties.[56] The dominion executive reviewed her activities and endorsed the action of the Alberta executive to expel her from the party. No further mention is made of her actions during this campaign or of the party's reasons for expelling her.[57]

Mashkat's life is fascinating for several reasons. Judging from the evidence, she was clearly an exceptional woman. Her speaking style was doubtless influenced both by her class and ethnic background. That such an indefatigable party worker should have been expelled is a reflection of the sectarian spirit that dominated the SPC during these years. While popular among working-class and mining communities, her agnostic and anti-religious sentiments would not have been popular among socialists with strong

Christian socialist convictions, nor would her speaking style have appealed to all socialist women. The sectarian climate of the SPC, differences in class, ethnic, and religious backgrounds, as well as different commitments to social issues provided a difficult context for prominent socialist women to cohere a voice for women within the SPC.

Some socialists disagreed with the SPC platform and tried to work within the party to make it more receptive and supportive of issues like suffrage and prohibition. The best example of such a woman is Bertha Merrill.[58] Unlike Ruth Lestor, Merrill was committed to socialism, feminism, and prohibition, and she struggled to integrate these concerns in her political activities whenever possible.

In 1900 Merrill moved to British Columbia and became active in the socialist movement in Nelson. She was the first woman executive member of the Socialist party in the province, and participated in such local activities as writing and giving speeches. In July 1903 she moved to Vancouver and took up a position on the editorial board of the *Western Clarion*, as editor of the woman's column. She was a signatory to the establishment of the Western Socialist Publishing Company, active at the founding convention of the Socialist Party of Canada, and was an executive member of the party. These activities made her one of the leading figures in the development of the early socialist movement in British Columbia. In addition, she had the distinction of being the most widely published female writer in the Canadian socialist press.

In December 1903 she and Ernest Burns, treasurer of the Socialist party, travelled to Seattle and were married. Thereafter, like many feminists of her day, she referred to herself as Bertha Merrill Burns, retaining her maiden name as a middle name. The party press published a brief biography of Ernest Burns, which provided an account of his political background.[59] Born in Birmingham, England, he studied the works of Edward Bellamy, Henry George, William Morris, Edward Carpenter, and H.M. Hyndman. In 1885 he became a socialist and a charter member of the Birmingham Social Democratic Federation. In 1889 he left England for Washington and became active in the Knights of

Labor and the Populist party, endorsing socialism from their platforms. He returned to British Columbia in 1899, worked in logging and fishing, and, as president of the Fisherman's Union, he was prominent in the Fisherman's strike of 1900–1. From 1900 on, he was active in socialist politics in British Columbia.

Burns's socialist politics were marked by a considerable amount of tolerance and an abhorrence of sectarianism. Unlike the leadership of the Socialist party, he endorsed reforms and criticized party members for treating Marxism like a creed that could not be questioned. He endorsed women's suffrage, and was one of the few male socialists to give speeches on women's issues such as 'Women and the Labour Problem.'[60] In March 1907 J.T. Mortimer moved to strike Ernest Burns from membership of the Socialist party because of his views. Bertha was not included in the motion. The initial vote rejected suspension, but a subsequent motion did suspend him until 'he could conscientiously support the platform and programme of the SPC.'[61] In later years, Burns claimed that the party's stance on women's suffrage was one of his grounds for discontent with the party. As the only member expelled for his convictions, Bertha claimed to be proud that he held that distinction.[62]

By all accounts, it appears that Bertha Merrill Burns shared many of her husband's political convictions. Like many other socialist women, she credited her awakening to socialism to her concern for young working women: '[M]y indignation over the treatment of certain young girls employed in the mechanical department of the paper where I worked first caused me to investigate the general conditions of women's work in that city and from that investigation sprung my first interest in socialism.'[63] From her articles and correspondence, it is clear Burns was well read in the socialist classics, as well as the works of other thinkers such as Charles Darwin and Edward Carpenter. She demonstrated a sound grasp of socialist principles, and did not shy away from talking about revolution. However, this did not inhibit her from exploring the social position of women. Unlike Ruth Lestor and Sophie Mushkat, Bertha Burns did not focus exclusively on wage-earning women, and she clearly acknowledged that women from different walks of life were important and welcome in the socialist movement. While she analysed the position of working women, she recognized the housewife as the woman to whom socialists had to appeal. Consequently, her woman's column often discussed the socialist transformation of domestic labour.

Her religious convictions were never made paramount in her columns or articles, but she did acknowledge in private correspondence that she considered herself unaffiliated with any church, preferring the labels socialist, agnostic, or freethinker. She complained that the census takers would not accommodate her desires in this respect.[64] Despite this attitude towards religion, she did not draw the ire of Christian socialists by publicly attacking their views.

Burns publicly disputed the party line on several issues: she favoured reforms such as prohibition and woman's suffrage, she challenged the Socialist party's lack of internal democracy, and she endorsed local plebiscites on prohibition and 'the social evil.' While sharing these political views that clashed with the SPC's, Bertha and Ernest initially worked within the SPC trying to persuade party members to change the party. At the same time, however, they actively supported these other causes. Burns, for example, chaired the meeting when Charlotte Perkins Gilman visited Vancouver, but she disclaimed any connection between the meeting and the SPC. She also organized a 'Pink Tea' at which Mrs Ramsay MacDonald, wife of the British labour leader, among others, discussed the idea of establishing an alternate party.

In private correspondence with Mrs MacDonald, Burns acknowledged as early as the summer of 1906 that she was involved in a party called the Social Democratic party in Vancouver that she distinguished from the SPC, which she claimed was in the full control of the 'Impossibilists.'[65] She reported that half of the members for the new party were people drawn from the disenchanted ranks of the SPC, including many Finns. Burns indicated that the party as yet was small, but looked forward to developing into a provincial party. She also reported that they had a 'good percentage of women in our new party and we mean to so conduct ourselves that we shall keep them here.'[66] Bertha and Ernest were active in promoting their new party in British Columbia, and Bertha publicized its presence through correspondence with radicals across Canada.[67]

Both Burns and her husband managed to integrate their concerns for socialism and women's issues, but it was not without cost. Though they were active charter members of the SPC, they were unable to persuade the party to support issues like woman's suffrage or prohibition. While there is no record that Burns was expelled from the SPC, it is clear her convictions on suffrage and prohibition were disapproved of by the SPC. She and her husband abandoned the party they had been active in forming, and worked to build an alternative socialist party that would be more amenable to such concerns.[68] Other socialists across Canada who shared their disenchantment with the SPC joined the Social Democratic Party of Canada (SDPC), which finally established a national structure in 1911. The SDPC avoided the 'impossibilist' stance of the SPC, and was more willing to include some reforms in its political platform. It was also more receptive to permitting ethnic locals to form within its ranks than was the SPC. Some members who shifted their allegiance to the new party had been outspoken critics of the SPC for its crude attacked on Christian socialists.[69] The SDPC paper, *Cotton's Weekly*, debated the merit of Christianity, but the overall tenor of the debate accepted the compatibility of socialism and Christianity. Unlike the SPC, the SDPC provided intellectual continuity for socialists rooted in the heritage of Christian reformism. As the party paper stated, only socialism would permit people to live Christian lives.[70] This attitude was also reflected in actions, as the SDPC cooperated with the Christian Socialist Fellowship, organized in Toronto.[71]

The SDPC was also more flexible on prohibition, and did not go as far out of its way to offend prohibitionists, as did the SPC. *Cotton's Weekly* had a temperance column for the first year, reflecting the strong prohibitionist convictions of its editor, William Cotton. He became a less strident supporter of temperance over the years, but continued to refuse liquor advertisements and even made appeals to members of the WCTU to vote for socialism.[72] Cotton also rebutted some of the more strident claims of the SPC on prohibition. For example, to those who argued that prohibition would cause unemployment, one article retorted that the abolition of prostitution would do the same, yet this was not an adequate reason to refrain from endorsing the end to prostitution.[73] The paper also carried an article on prohibition by Mary E. Garbutt, vice-president of the U.S. National Socialist Union and an active member of the WCTU for over twenty-five years. Rather than ridicule the prohibitionists, she argued that only socialism would accomplish the ends they desired.[74] The socialist men and women who were alienated from the SPC, given its stance on temperance, were more likely to have been drawn to the SDPC once it was formed.

Mary Cotton Wisdom provides us with an example of a prominent woman socialist who also had strong ties to the woman's movement and strong Christian beliefs. She was born in 1878, the oldest child of Charles Cotton, member of a prominent family in the Eastern Townships of Quebec.[75] His wife Alice MacKay was a direct descendant of the United Empire Loyalists. When Mary was fourteen, her mother died and she took charge of the household and her three younger siblings: Alice, Charles, and William. Her brothers were well educated, each having spent a year in France on scholarships and earning law degrees in Canada; she received singing lessons in New York. By all accounts, the entire family was keenly interested in politics and economics, often debating issues of the day.

Her husband, an engineer, travelled a great deal and she accompanied him on his trips to remote mining camps where, at times, she was the only white woman in the area. Between trips they lived in a house in Sweetsburg, called the 'Anchorage,' which her father had bought for her. While completing his education to become an engineer and metallurgist, her husband had worked as a labourer in mines and smelting plants in Sydney, Nova Scotia, the eastern seaboard, and Northern Ontario. He worked twelve-hour shifts, and every two weeks when the shift changed he worked twenty-four hours straight. These working conditions profoundly affected their thinking in favour of labour unions, despite their middle-class status.

In 1908 Wisdom's youngest brother, William, bought a newspaper called the *Observer* and turned it into *Cotton's Weekly*, a socialist newspaper. She wrote for the paper and edited the woman's column in 1908 and 1909. Fortunately, she provided her readers with an account of her first experience of a political meeting with three other 'plain women' from the Eastern Townships of Quebec (two writers, one society woman, and one home body), who met to discuss politics. Her account is interesting for what is revealed in its disclaimers. The women were not meeting to discuss styles, gossip, men, or each other's clothes, though as a measure of their serious-mindedness Wisdom reported that the ladies wore simple shirt waists, short skirts because it was a rainy day, and plain hats. They earnestly discussed matters in which all women should be interested: 'signs of the times, the economic questions of the day, the old age pensions, poverty and crime around us.' They left with plans to establish a study group: 'To study the ways and means, to help remedy if we can be our united or single efforts, the appalling conditions with which we are surrounded.'[76] This account of middle-class women organizing a political study group reminds us of the timidity some women of the time must have felt, even when organizing among themselves, and to what extent political actions constituted a challenge to their sense of femininity. It further underscores the deterrent effect that the sexist language and behaviour in mixed groups would have had on such women and allows us to appreciate the value of separate organizations for women.

Wisdom's writings focused less on issues of economic exploitation than on the problems of male domination and woman's role in society:

> I will confess just among ourselves that though I believe earnestly in socialism I have not the energy to keep keyed up to the high pitch of pulling my hair in desperation over the evils of capitalism ... This is a free country in which every man has the vote (I just wish every woman had) and if the men want socialism they can have it simply by casting their vote at the next general election that way ... In the meantime we women must do our housekeep-

ing and the dishes have to be washed and the floor swept and the children put to bed, despite all the political agitators around us. We must continue to do our duty, each in her own small way, thus we will continue to be for a while longer the salt with which this old world is savoured.[77]

Her columns never exhibited an extensive understanding of socialism, although she did have a wide-ranging interest in current social issues, empathizing with the poor and deprived. Her commitment to socialism, such as it was, was not paramount. One article, entitled 'My View of Socialism,' clarified her views. She took exception to a prominent socialist's argument that socialism would result in the perfect world. She stated that she believed in socialism and looked forward to the coming of the cooperative commonwealth, explaining that 'No one will doubt ... that they will be better off when we cease to eat each other financially.' Nonetheless, she insisted that no form of government by men would ever be perfect. Only when the 'Messiah himself shall come and take the reins of government into his own hands, will the perfect government be ushered in.'[78]

Wisdom's involvement with socialism did not last. With the onset of the First World War, many social democrats who were also pacifists found themselves deeply torn between their socialist convictions, which applauded the struggle of workers against their oppressors, and their pacifist convictions, which disdained war in any form. This general conflict took on a particular significance for those women socialists whose pacifist and socialist views had been strongly linked with maternal feminism. In addition, the Russian Revolution, which marked the transition to revolutionary socialism for many in the Canadian left, put to the test the political commitment of those Anglo-Canadian women, like Mary Cotton Wisdom, whose political heritage rested in church organizations, the women's movement, and the socialist movement. Women who were unable to withstand the concerted pressures of pro-war propaganda, virulent propaganda directed against 'foreign' radicals, and church-based support for the war effort found themselves further alienated from socialism during the war years. Not surprisingly, some chose to abandon socialism altogether. One such person was Mary Cotton Wisdom.

As noted in the opening quotation of this article, before the war years Mary Cotton Wisdom urged women to overcome their fear of 'foreign' socialists. Little is known of her activities during the war, but through her responses to her brother's activities after the war she reveals a xenophobia that contradicts her pre-war comments. Her brother, William, maintained his commitment to socialism until 1930. After the war he edited the *Maritime Labour Herald*, an official newspaper for the miners in Glace Bay, Nova Scotia, during which time he was arrested for political activities.[79] Wisdom's letters to him provide us with interesting insights into her political views. She claimed: 'I don't object to your radical ideas or your defending the weak,' but she objected to the strong language he used in his papers, reminding him that he was a gentleman and 'a gentleman doesn't call names' to people who disagree with you.[80]

Like some reformers of her time, Wisdom believed in spiritualism and claimed to have psychic powers with which she could relay messages from their dead father to William.[81] Using 'automatic writing,' she sent William letters which included passages supposedly written by their deceased father. In this spirit she wrote: 'The idea has been impressed upon me to tell you that you had better impress upon your readers that you are *not* any immigrant, – for by the taunting you have been doing they may think you are – say you are a staunch Britisher and you had better wave the dear old flag (figuratively) pretty lively – you honour the King and love your Country but dislike the way the laws are administered.' She then recapped the long list of distinguished ancestors from their family tree to provide him with evidence that he was no 'foreigner,' but descended from '*British* loyal, educated gentlemen.' As 'father,' she further cautioned William to be more careful: 'when your head is in the lion's mouth be careful, be polite until you crack his jaw.'[82] She insisted that if he remained a loyal Britisher he could not be called a 'seditionist,' 'disloyal,' a 'Red or some other dreadful character.'[83]

In many respects, Wisdom characterized the women of her

generation and class who were involved in the early Canadian women's movement and also drawn to the left. Her early affiliation with socialism reflected her understanding that socialism would complement Christianity and foster improved, equitable social conditions. She also believed that socialism should address the problems that concerned many women of this era, such as woman's suffrage and prohibition. Her views on Christianity and women's issues conflicted with the SPC's platform, and doubtless also contributed to her disenchantment with socialism. Her sense of superiority over 'foreigners' was also an important part of her rejection of socialism. Although she remained sympathetic to her brother's efforts as a 'mighty man of valour for men of law degree,' her later politics were decidedly Liberal as were her father's. She continued to be active in women's organizations, such as the local Women's Institute, the Women's Guild, and the Woman's Christian Temperance Union, and she continued her religious commitment as a devout Anglican, philanthropist and supporter of the Salvation Army until her death.[84]

So far, we have discussed the views of women who attained some prominence in the Canadian left, but this tells us little about the ordinary women who joined the socialist movement. Fortunately, we have information about one working-class woman who could be described as an ordinary socialist. Mary Norton joined the Social Democratic party in 1912 and became secretary for her local. Like many socialist women of her era, she cited Edward Bellamy's work as an early influence on her thinking. During the same decade she maintained involvement in the women's movement; she joined the Pioneer Political Equality League, campaigned for the suffrage referendum in British Columbia, and joined the Women's International League, the organization that sent a peace mission to Europe during the First World War. She also became involved in the struggle for workmen's compensation after her husband died as a result of an industrial accident. Throughout her life and until her death in the 1970s, she maintained her interest in these three issues: socialism, women's issues, and trade unionism.[85]

Unlike the other women socialists discussed in this paper, Norton's family did not share her support of socialism. When she joined the Social Democratic party she was already married and had children, but neither her husband nor her children were interested in socialism. Later in life she reflected that her activities probably meant that her husband suffered at home, but he did not interfere with her political activities. However, to maintain her political life, even after she was widowed, Norton's family must have provided 'passive' support for her political activities, at minimum by not opposing her work, or by taking over some responsibilities while she attended meetings or campaigned. Without family support, it would be difficult for a married woman to be politically active.

Norton did not think there was sex discrimination in the SDPC. She insisted that the party did not ban their separate meetings at all. The women members developed 'aggressive spirits' and learned a lot from the various out-of-town and university speakers who addressed them. She did observe that men had advantages in not being house bound; women socialists had to make special accommodations for these constraints. In forming a socialist women's committee of suffragists, Norton stressed the convenience of the afternoon meeting times because women usually wanted to stay home in the evenings. While the party scheduled regular party meeting times for the convenience of its male members, Norton took it for granted that the party would not make similar accommodations for women. The women found regular meeting times inconvenient, but they considered the party nondiscriminatory because it allowed them to make other arrangements. This reflects the extent to which some assumptions about gender distinct roles remained fundamentally unchallenged within the party, even by a woman who fought for women's rights.

Norton confirmed that the SDPC was much more supportive of women's suffrage than was the SPC. After she joined the SDPC, Norton campaigned for the suffrage referendum by stopping the farmers on the way to market. Although she did not have to hide her suffrage sympathies from her socialist comrades in the SDPC, she tried to keep her socialist activities from the suffrage women, for fear they would discriminate against her. Norton admired

Helena Gutteridge, a local activist for women's rights and trade unionism, but she judged Gutteridge too conservative and never joined Gutteridge's suffrage organization. When Norton held a tea for her suffrage colleagues, she refused to invite Gutteridge for fear that the suffragists would show 'disfavour for anybody that was holding night meetings or speaking on the street.' She recounted that 'Mrs. [Helen Gregory] MacGill once saw in the newspaper the election of the officers of the socialists and I happened to be on the list for some office. To her eternal credit she said to me 'If I couldn't have a good standard of life under this government I'd be a socialist too.' But all the others [suffragists] that I met thought that [socialism] was the last association they wanted to [be associated with].'[86] Norton's life testifies to the support socialist women in the SDPC gave to suffrage, but it also reveals the difficulty of forming alliances between suffragists and socialists.

The socialist women discussed in this article struggled on two fronts: to change the world and to change their socialist comrades. Each was drawn to the socialist movement, believing it could change the world, but the socialist movement did not always welcome women's perspectives on issues. Many socialist women had to make tactical choices between their interest in socialism and their interest in issues like prohibition, suffrage, and Christian socialism. Commitment to women's issues meant alienation from the left, or alienation from allies in other organizations. Furthermore, socialist women did not always speak with one voice. As demonstrated elsewhere in this book, racism and ethnocentrism were crucial components of turn-of-the-century feminism; similar views also fuelled the radicalism of the left, and of some socialist women within the left. This leads us to conclude that radical class politics did not solve the problems of racism or sexism at this time. Socialist women were as enmeshed in these contradictions as were their male comrades and their middle-class feminist sisters.

Political activism for socialist women was initiated and sustained in complex ways. Many have approached the study of women's political activism from the perspective of the social and economic constraints that shape women's lives. At the turn of the century, and even today, women face important constraints in becoming politically active, ranging from the double burden of domestic and paid labour to the constraints imposed by male-dominated political institutions. In this article, we have shifted the focus away from such constraints, to the political ideas that drew women into the early Canadian left and the ways in which those ideas both mobilized and dampened their political participation. This is not to suggest that ideas alone account for the politicization of women. Rather, by looking at the political ideas of women, we can see how women struggled to come to terms with a range of social issues that profoundly affected the lives of women of their day. Whether their concern was the presence of women in the labour force, the decline in importance of the domestic sphere, the lack of a political voice for women, the problems of alcohol, or the perceived threat of waves of immigration, these socialist women struggled to understand and to change the world they found themselves in.

NOTES

1 'Socialism and Ignorance,' *Cotton's Weekly*, 20 May 1909
2 Ibid.
3 Of the 376 women mentioned in the English left press whose marital status could be identified, 76 per cent were married. This is consistent with the general population of the time, for in 1911 women were roughly 13 per cent of the paid labour force. Noah M. Meltz, *Manpower in Canada, 1931–1961* (Ottawa: Department of Manpower and Immigration 1969), table A-4, 61
4 Letter from M.D. Armstrong, *Western Clarion*, Oct. 1915; letter from Mrs Owen, *Cotton's Weekly*, 27 Nov. 1913; Mrs E. Sharpe, 'Montreal Active,' 4 Dec. 1913. For an excellent discussion of a woman who combined here domestic duties with her socialist activities see Anne B. Woytika, 'A Pioneer Woman in the Labour Movement,' *Alberta History* 26 (winter 1978): 10–16.
5 *Cotton's Weekly*, 16 Oct. 1913, 20 July 1911; *Canadian Forward*, 13 Jan. and 24 March 1917. See also *Der Yiddisher Zhurnal*, 25 and 31 Aug.

1919, courtesy of Ruth Frager; and Frager, 'Uncloaking Vested Interests: Class, Ethnicity and Gender in the Jewish Labour Movement of Toronto, 1900–1939' (PhD thesis, York University 1986).

6 Varpu Lindström-Best, 'Defiant Sisters: A Social History of the Finnish Immigrant Woman in Canada, 1890–1930' (PhD thesis, York University 1986)

7 For a more complete breakdown of women's marital status, ethnicity, and political activities within the parties see Janice Newton, 'Enough of Exclusive Masculine Thinking: The Feminist Challenge to the Early Canadian Left' (PhD thesis, York University 1987).

8 *Canadian Socialist*, 19 July and 16 Aug. 1902; *Western Clarion*, 2 Dec. 1905

9 Phillips Thompson and George Wrigley are two such people discussed by Ramsay Cook in *The Regenerators* (Toronto: University of Toronto Press 1985). For a discussion of the concerns of early women's groups in Canada see Linda Kealey, ed., *A Not Unreasonable Claim: Women and Reform in Canada 1880s–1920s* (Toronto: Women's Press 1979); Susan Mann Trofimenkoff and Alison Prentice, eds., *The Neglected Majority* (Toronto: McClelland and Stewart 1977); Ramsay Cook and Wendy Mitchinson, eds., 'Organizations,' in *The Proper Sphere* (Toronto: Oxford University Press 1976), 198–223; Michael Bliss, 'Neglected Radicals,' *Canadian Forum* (April–May 1970): 16–17; Jennifer Stoddard and Veronica Strong-Boag, '... And Things Were Going Wrong at Home,' *Atlantis* 1, 1 (1975): 38–44; Carol Bacchi, *Liberation Deferred? The Ideas of the English Canadian Suffragists, 1877–1918* (Toronto: University of Toronto Press 1983); Veronica Strong-Boag, *The Parliament of Women: The National Council of Women of Canada, 1893–1929*, Mercury Series, History Division Paper No. 18 (Ottawa: National Museum of Man 1976).

10 *Citizen and Country*, 13 May 1899, 13 and 27 April 1900; *Western Clarion*, 9 Feb. 1907

11 Mari Jo Buhle, *Women and American Socialism* (Chicago: University of Illinois Press 1981), 94–117 passim

12 National Archives of Canada, Ontario Socialist Platform, adopted by the Ontario Socialist League by Referendum Vote, Jan. 1902; *Citizen and Country*, 16, 30, and 9 May 1902

13 Buhle, *Women and American Socialism*

14 Alice Chown's biography provides us with one example of a woman

making the transition from conventional women's organizations to activism within trade unions: *The Stairway* (Boston: Cornhill Company 1921).

15 *Western Clarion*, 22 April 1911 and 17 October 1908

16 Ibid., 26 Sept. 1908

17 Ibid., 21 Sept. 1912, 27 Sept. 1913, 4 July and 1 Aug. 1914, Aug. and Dec. 1915, May 1916, and June 1917

18 Ibid., Jan. 1918

19 This was argued by Moses Baritz, a Jewish member of the small, sectarian Socialist Party of North America: *Cotton's Weekly*, 6 Oct. 1910. Another socialist, Fred Faulkner, recalled that 'many socialists in those days, spent too much time (killing God) as it was called.' University of British Columbia Library, Angus MacInnis Collection, Fred Faulkner, Letters, 5 and 10 March 1910

20 The party paper attacked the Salvation Army, the Catholic church, and the Methodists. Some of this hostility may be attributed to the direct competition that organizations like the Salvation Army posed to the socialists in their propaganda efforts directed towards the working class. For example, see *Western Clarion*, 6 June 1908, 15 May 1909, 19 Dec. 1914.

21 The articles by William Shier, before he left the Socialist party, are a good example. See *Western Clarion*, 31 Aug. 1907, 29 May 1909, and 1 Aug. 1908.

22 Ibid., 22 Dec. 1906

23 'Red Herring Season,' ibid., 26 June 1909

24 Bars or saloons did serve important functions for working men. In logging camps, they could be the only place where men could socialize; in towns where working men were not permitted in the social clubs reserved or the middle and upper clases, bars were important social meeting places for itinerant worker; and sometimes the saloon would be the only place a worker could cash his pay cheque. For examples of the attitudes of the SPC on prohibition see 'The Drink Evil from a Proletarian View Point,' *Western Clarion*, 7 Dec. 1907, 9 Dec. 1905, 2 May 1908, 26 Feb. 1910 and Aug. 1915.

25 Ibid., 13 Feb., 13 March, and 16 Oct. 1908, 24 May 1913, 14 March 1914, Oct. 1915; *Cotton's Weekly*, 4 May 1911

26 For example, at one socialist picnic where alcohol was served, the barrel

was placed at the opposite end of the field from the women and children. *Western Clarion* 24 May 1913

27 See, for example, 'The Woman's Place,' ibid., 10 Dec. 1910.

28 Lindström-Best, 'Defiant Sisters,' 362

29 The discussion of Ruth Lestor is based on *Western Clarion*, 13 March 1909, and the following articles in this newspaper: 'Calgary,' 19 June 1909; 'The Woman's Place,' 10 July 1909; 'How Capitalism Breeds Lunacy,' 11 Dec. 1909 and 23 July 1910; 'With the Reds of the Prairies,' 4 March 1911 and 1 April 1911; 'Woman and the S.P. of C.,' July 1911 and Sept. 1917; *Cotton's Weekly* 6 and 13 May 1909, and the following articles in this newspaper: 'Comrade Lestor Coming East,' 6 Jan. 1911, and 'Lestor at Dundurn,' 19 Jan. 1911.

30 We know more about Lestor's husband, Charles Lestor, than we know of her. He was born in England in 1876 and had turned his hand to many occupations: blacksmith, solicitor, labourer, showman, actor, and water-works manager. He touted himself as a socialist, writer, and student of history and social problems. He joined the Canadian Socialist party in 1908. 'Comrade Lestor Coming East'

31 'Calgary'

32 'The Woman's Place'

33 Ibid.

34 'Calgary'

35 'Woman and the S.P. of C.'

36 'Calgary'

37 'Woman and the S.P. and C.'

38 'How Capitalism Breeds Lunacy'

39 'Woman and the S.P. of C.'

40 Ibid.

41 The discussion of Sophie Mushkat is drawn from the following sources: Roscoe Fillmore, 'Strike Situation in Eastern Canada,' *International Socialist Review*, 10 May 1910; 'Moncton,' *Western Clarion*, 7 Aug. 1909, and other ariticles in that newspaper: 'O Righteous Judge! O Learned Judge!' 9 Oct. 1909; 'Springhill, N.S.' 12 March 1910; 'Random Remarks,' 16 Aug. 1913; 'Comrade Mushkat Reports,' 23 May 1914; 'In Vindication,' 4 July 1914; 'The Argument of a Russian Serf,' 18 July 1914; 'Erskine, Alta,' 30 Jan. 1915; 'Dominion Executive Committee,'

Aug. 1915; 'Later News,' *Cotton's Weekly*, 30 Sept. 1909; and the following articles in that newspaper: 'N.B. Socialists Prosecute Disturber,'
30 Sept. 1909; 'Good for Comrade Mushkat,' 24 March 1910; 'Socialists Invading White Hills, N.B.,' 11 Sept. 1913; and 'Socialism in St
John, N.B.,' 25 Sept. 1913. See also Linda Kealey, 'Sophie,' *New Maritimes*, Nov. 1987, and Newton, 'Enough of Exclusive Masculine
Thinking,' 426–35.
42 'O Righteous Judge!' and 'N.B. Socialists'
43 'Moncton,' 'Springhill,' 'Strike Situation in Eastern Canada,' and *Eastern
Labour News*, 4 Dec. 1909
44 'Later News'
45 'Socialists Invading,' 'Socialism in St John,' and *Western Clarion*, 4 Sept.
1909
46 'Moncton'
47 *Cotton's Weekly*, 24 March 1910
48 In other public speeches, she pragmatically employed the argument that
only socialism would abolish all evils and make it possible for 'men to
live a Christian life.' See 'Good for Comrade Mushkat,'
49 'Oh Righteous Judge!' and 'N.B. Socialists Prosecute'
50 *Western Clarion*, 5 Nov. 1910, 20 April 1912, 29 June and 19 July 1913
51 Ibid., 14 March 1914
52 'The Argument of a Russian Serf'
53 *Cotton's Weekly*, 15 May 1913
54 'Random Remarks,' and 'In Vindication'
55 *Western Clarion*, 16 Jan. 1915
56 If the spc was consistent, she was probably expelled fo supporting prohibition or local option. Several party members in British Columbia had
been expelled for the same reason.
57 'Dominion Executive Committee'
58 The discussion of Bertha Merrill Burns is drawn from the following
sources: articles by B.M. Burns and Ernest Burns published in *Western
Clarion*, *Cotton's Weekly*, *Citizen and Country*, *Candian Socialist*, *Western Socialist*, *Vancouver World*, *B.C. Federationist*, *Independent*, and papers in the
MacInnis Collection, University of British Columbia Library, and the
Ramsay MacDonald Collection, National Archives of Canada.
59 *Western Socialist*, 14 Feb. 1903. The left press published brief biographies

of a number of the leading male socialists, but did not publish similar articles for leading women socialists.

60 *Canadian Socialist*, 19 July 1902

61 *Western Clarion*, 2 and 9 March 1907

62 *B.C. Federationist*, 20 May 1912; Ramsay MacDonald Collection, Bertha Merrill Burns to Mrs Ramsay MacDonald, 29 April 1907

63 Ramsay MacDonald Collection, Bertha Merrill Burns to Mrs Ramsay MacDonald, 29 April 1907

64 Ibid.

65 Ibid., 26 July 1906

66 Ibid., 29 April 1907

67 Phillips Thompson mistook her for a man. See *Western Clarion* 18 May 1907.

68 Bertha Burns became a public speaker for the Social Democratic party and she was elected as provincial secretary to the party's women's committee in British Columbia. Her activities, however, were cut short in 1914 because of illness.

69 William Shier criticized the party for its crudeness and its attacks on Christian socialists, then shifted his allegiance to the Social Democrats. See *Cotton's Weekly*, 28 Nov. 1912.

70 Ibid., 12 Jan. 1911

71 Ibid., 20 Aug. 1911

72 For example, ibid., 2 July 1914

73 Ibid., 7 May 1914

74 'Poverty the Cause of Intemperance,' ibid., 2 July 1914

75 This account of the life of Mary Cotton Wisdom is based on her articles published in *Cotton's Weekly* and papers held in the author's private collection, including Mary Cotton Wisdom's letters to her brother, William Cotton, circa 1922; 'Biographical Memo,' by William Cotton, 1943; letter to author, 30 Aug. 1983, from Harriet Beech, granddaughter of Mary Cotton Wisdom (all courtesy of Harriet Beech); interview with Mary Ford, niece of Mary Cotton Wisdom, 1983; and 'Family History' compiled by Mary Ford, 1983.

76 'Four Plain Women,' *Cotton's Weekly*, 4 Feb. 1909

77 Ibid., 28 Oct. 1909

78 'My View of Socialism,' ibid., 30 Sept. 1909

79 William Cotton, 'Biographical Memo,' 26 June 1942
80 Letter by Mary Cotton Wisdom to William Cotton, 27 Feb. 1922
81 Ramsay Cook discusses the significance of spiritualism among late Victorian reformers: *The Regenerators*, 56–85.
82 Letter by Mary Cotton Wisdom to William Cotton, 27 Feb. 1922
83 Letter from Mary Cotton Wisdom to William Cotton, nd
84 In later years, Wisdom developed an interest in her family history and wrote a biography of the Rev. Charles Cotton. Surviving her husband and two children, she died at the age of eighty-four.
85 Material for this discussion of Mary Norton is drawn exclusively from a taped interview with Mary Norton, 1973, Women's Labour History Project, British Columbia Archives and Record Service.
86 Ibid.

5 Wounded Womanhood and Dead Men:
Chivalry and the Trials of Clara Ford and Carrie Davies

Carolyn Strange

Residents of Toronto in the late nineteenth and early twentieth centuries might quite legitimately have assumed that women could get away with murder. In two highly publicized trials in that period, female defendants were acquitted on charges of murder in spite of the fact that both had confessed to the deed. The first of these women, Clara Ford, was a mulatto seamstress who, by her own admission, had shot and killed a wealthy white youth in 1894. After the verdict of 'not guilty' was announced to a crowded Toronto courtroom at the spring 1895 Criminal Assizes, the acquitted murderer led a throng of well-wishers to a downtown restaurant. 'I thank you for the way you stood by me,' she announced to the largely male gathering: 'This does the boys of Toronto credit.'[1] Twenty years later, Carrie Davies, a teenaged British immigrant, left the prisoner's dock under similar circumstances. The young servant had confessed to the murder of her master, yet, like Ford, she left the courtroom a free woman to cheering and tumultuous applause. Judge William Mulock was teary-eyed when he discharged the prisoner, adding, 'you are now a free woman.' 'Thank you, Judge,' Carrie Davies replied, 'and thank you gentlemen of the jury.'[2] Both defendants recognized that they had been treated mercifully, and made a point of thanking the men without whose help they would not have been acquitted.

At the time of these trials, commentators generally assumed that chivalry accounted for the acquittals. In a post-trial interview with the jury in the Ford case, for instance, the men revealed that they shrank from the thought of convicting the defendant because she was 'a defenceless woman who was bluffed and coddled by turns.'[3] Similarly, Davies' sex softened the hearts of her male peers who, according to the *Evening Telegram*, cried along with the chief justice at the announcement of the verdict.[4] In subsequent accounts of these cases the theory of chivalric justice has continued to provide journalists and popular historians with a convincing explanation for the acquittal of two women who admitted to having killed men.[5]

This assessment of the Ford and Davies trials seems to confirm what one criminologist has called 'the most widely held assumption' about women in the criminal justice system – that men treat them leniently.[6] From the late nineteenth to the mid twentieth century, the 'fathers' of criminology translated this popular belief into criminological theory in their studies of female offenders. Cesare Lombroso, W.I. Thomas, and Otto Pollak refined the theory that women escaped their rightful share of punishment because their sex buffered them from the full brunt of the law. Thomas, for example, wrote in 1907 that '[man] exempts [woman] from anything in the way of contractual morality, or views her defections in this regard with allowance and even with amusement.'[7] Pollak, one of the most influential 'fathers,' articulated the theory of 'masked' female crime in the context of a male-dominated legal system. He asserted that female conviction rates were artificially low because men were more forgiving of women than of offenders of their own sex. Women could freely commit crime because they set off a kind of domino effect on chivalric law enforcers: 'Men hate to accuse women and thus indirectly to send them to their punishment, police officers dislike to arrest them, district attorneys to prosecute them, judges and jurors to find them guilty and so on.'[8] Pollak identified men as the orchestrators of chivalric justice, but condemned their gentlemanly behaviour because it befuddled their sense of right and wrong and quite literally allowed women to get away with murder.

Feminist legal historians have been relatively quiet on the question of chivalry. They have been more eager to show women, including those who clearly broke the law, as victims in the patriarchal system of injustice. Those feminists who have addressed the issue of chivalry offer a variety of theories to account for apparent male lenience. There are some who attest, on the basis of quantitative research, that conclusive evidence for leniency towards all female offenders does not exist.[9] More common are arguments that chivalry is a privilege conferred upon white, middle-class women offenders who conform to acceptable feminine roles.[10] Some feminists argue further that the stereotypically feminine behaviour of the privileged sets impossible standards that most women offenders cannot or will not follow to extract favours from men in the criminal justice system.[11] Finally, there are a few theorists who have asserted that the ideological underpinning of chivalry – the notion that men must protect women because they are weak, defenceless, and therefore less responsible than men – damages all women, even if a handful receive the benefits of lenience.[12]

Straightforward and, in some cases, simplistic models of patriarchal oppression cannot explain why two poor, self-confessed murderers, one a mulatto woman, were exonerated. Their acquittals suggest that feminists must rethink their analysis of chivalry. In particular, they must account for the motivations of men and sharpen their sensitivity to the importance of race and class in judicial decisions that may appear to be exclusively gender related.[13] Chivalric justice perpetuates female and male stereotypes since it upholds equally the ideals of feminine frailty and masculine heroism; at the same time, it reaffirms the class and race privilege of the men who wield the power to protect and the option to pardon. The class, race, and gender of a defendant may influence men towards rendering a chivalrous verdict. Acquittals contribute not to the correction of sexism, racism, and classism in the justice system but rather to their obfuscation.[14]

In the nineteenth and early twentieth centuries, the revived medieval code of chivalry, expressed in heroic literature, art, and even the castle-building craze, was evident in the criminal justice system as well.[15] As a guide for gentlemanly conduct, the modernized chivalric code provided a discourse of selective mercy.

Just as knights had been charged with the duty to protect their inferiors and to uphold honour, so nineteenth-century gentlemen affirmed their status by protecting the defenceless. The difference between the strong and the weak was class-based, but gender also organized the distinction: men alone could become knights. The gender-encoded script of chivalry dictated contrasting roles for men and women. While men were to be brave and decisive, women were expected to be pure and submissive. Thus, for the nineteenth-century gentleman to realize his subjectivity, the 'true woman' had also to play her part. So dominant were these ideals in turn-of-the-century Toronto, a city which prided itself on its 'goodness,' that the newspapers, the men of the court, and the defendants, guided by their counsel, used the language of 'honour besieged' to confer meaning to the cases of Clara Ford and Carrie Davies.[16]

As a matter of working-class, masculine pride, wage-earning men borrowed the language of chivalry and applied it to their struggles against capitalist exploitation. Gentlemanly rhetoric can be heard in nineteenth-century, male trade unionists' demands for the right to support their dependants on a family wage and in their objections to night work for women and children. Trade unionists measured male bosses' sexual exploitation of women workers and the miserly wages of capitalists against the chivalric ideal to substitute working-class men as the true gentlemen.[17] In their modified version of chivalry, they defined masculine honour as the male breadwinner's ability to support and protect his dependants – women and children. For their part, women were to preserve their purity and to resist by any means the lecherous advances of upper-class rakes.[18] The plight of penniless, self-supporting women in the prisoner's dock, on trial for their lives, thereby excited considerable emotion among the city's working class. Moreover, the allegedly dishonourable conduct of wealthy men in both cases confirmed their suspicion that men of gentle birth did not uphold the gentlemanly ideal. Although working-class Torontonians lacked money and access to formal avenues of power, they also contributed to the acquittal of the two women.

Finally, by adhering to the conventions of femininity, Clara

Ford and Carrie Davies helped to save themselves. On being apprehended by the police, both initially confessed they had shot a man as a matter of feminine honour. Yet only Davies, an English maid with a saintly reputation, and not Ford, an eccentric woman of mixed race, was permitted to tell this tale of chastity under attack at her trial. While both were eventually acquitted, the importance of race and respectability in the course of their trials shows that chivalric justice cannot be reduced to a formula of gendered mercy. In the end, although each woman testified at her trial, neither woman could present her own story once she stepped into the masculine domain of the courtroom and surrendered her fate to the men of the bar, the bench, the jury, and the gallery.

The Drama Cast

The main stage of justice is the trial. Lawyers don dramatic costumes and joust with oratorical skills while an elevated judge, also robed, looks on and arbitrates. The highly mannered proceedings are grave in every case, but especially so when a life hangs in the balance. The drama heightened whenever lawyers fought to determine the fate of a woman, as they did in the Ford and Davies trials. At the turn of the century, when women could not yet sit on juries and female lawyers rarely appeared in court, the masculine domination of the judicial process was overwhelming. The battling lawyers were men, the judges were men, the jury members were men, the victims were men, but the lives to be saved or claimed in the name of chivalric justice were women's. The female defendants, although apparently at centre stage, were little more than foils for the male characters in these ritual courtroom battles.

Ford's and Davies's lawyers were not only aware of the dramatic elements in the trials: they wrote the scripts. E.F.B. (Blackie) Johnston was a highly skilled trial lawyer who earned a reputation in the 1890s for crafting persuasive defences that sometimes outweighed the effects of evidence on the minds of the jury. He saw the Ford case as an opportunity to put his talents to an exacting test. His first move was to represent the impoverished woman without fees. At once he demonstrated his selfless offering of services to a poverty-stricken defendant. His adversary, B.B. Osler, had not the same opportunities to present himself as a chivalrous gentleman, since he faced the unpleasant task of asking twelve men to see that a poor woman be hanged. Yet Osler, after he successfully prosecuted Louis Riel, had a reputation (at least among Anglo-Protestant Canadians) for loyal and faithful service to his country. He balanced his stalwart reputation as an uncompromising fighter in the courtroom with a remarkably tender domestic life that revolved around his invalid wife, whom he had rescued from a burning building. 'This chivalry,' commented a journalist, 'was a notable factor in his family life,' but it was equally evident in Osler the legal man.[19] Johnston's goal in the Ford trial was as much to trump this paragon of chivalry as it was to have his client acquitted.

Clara Ford was in her early thirties when she was arrested for the murder of Frank Westwood in November 1894. It was rumoured that she had been married for a short while, but she had lived as a single woman for at least a decade prior to the murder. She lived above a 'negro restaurant' on York Street, one of the main thoroughfares of 'The Ward' and the centre of Toronto's small, black community. On 20 November 1894 two detectives visited her tiny apartment looking for evidence in connection with the shooting death of Westwood six weeks earlier. They found a suit of men's clothes, a fedora, and a hand gun of the same calibre as the bullets that killed the young man. Detective Reburn and Inspector Stark of the Toronto police force questioned her for several hours until she broke down and gave a detailed confession of her activities on the night of Westwood's shooting.

Ford stated to her accusers that she had visited a friend in the garment district near Spadina and Adelaide streets. She had announced to her hosts that she was going to the Toronto Opera House to see 'The Black Crook' with a girl who was reputed to be her illegitimate daughter. In fact, she broke her engagement. Ford told the detective she had donned men's clothing and proceeded south to the lakeshore, where she continued for two miles until she reached Jamieson Avenue in Parkdale. Under cover of darkness she stood by the bushes in front of 'Lakeside Hall,' the Westwoods's palatial home, and rang the bell. When eighteen-year-old Frank came to the door she shot him twice, then fled the scene of her crime. She told the police she wished him dead because he had taken 'improper liberties' with her the previous August and had 'insulted' her.[20] She had not gone to the police to report the incident because she knew it was 'no use for a woman of [her] colour going to the police for justice.'[21]

The events leading up to the trial of Carrie Davies were no less sensational. Davies was an eighteen-year-old maid from Bedfordshire, England. She had obtained a good position as a servant in the home of Charles (Bert) Massey, his wife and son. Despite the Massey family's reputation as righteous pillars of Toronto's elite, Bert fell short of the gentlemanly ideal. He was, in fact, a sport who preferred fast cars and pretty women to the slow pace of his Methodist upbringing. He had behaved with propriety towards his maid until the first weekend in February 1915, when Mrs Massey was away visiting friends. Davies later testified that he became drunk at a Friday night dinner party and made lewd remarks to her. More alarming in her estimation, though, were his attempts the following day to kiss her and his insistence that she accept a ring from him. When he tried to wrestle her onto a bed she was making she felt sure she was in danger. On Sunday, 7 February, she visited her sister and brother-in-law in Cabbagetown to tell them of her troubles. They advised her to return, since it was her duty, but to be careful. Overcome by fear that Massey would succeed in disgracing her, she took a revolver from the house and shot her master as he came up the walk to his home on Monday evening. She made no attempt to escape or to deny her crime. Her confession to the detectives was straightforward and concise: Massey had behaved so disrespectfully towards her that she felt he would 'disgrace' her unless she stopped him.[22]

A groundswell of public support rose for Davies immediately after her police court appearance on 9 February. Leading counsel competed for the case, but Davies's brother-in-law had already secured the services of Maw and Company. Ironically, Maw's senior partner, Hartley Dewart, took the case. Twenty years earlier he had been B.B. Osler's junior partner in the Ford case and had taken over entirely when Osler's wife died during the trial. The notoriety of the Ford case had elevated him from the rank of promising young crown attorney to that of prominent lawyer in his own right. His adversary in the Davies case was E.E.A. Du Vernet, a distinguished senior member of the Toronto bar who had made many appearances both for the prosecution and the defence in capital cases. The presence of Chief Justice William Mulock on the bench lent additional gravity to the proceedings.

Character on Trial

The Toronto daily newspapers were instrumental in spinning chivalric yarns out of the circumstances surrounding these two murders of men. Because Clara Ford initially claimed to have been 'insulted,' her trial was, in part, a posthumous test of Westwood's character. Two days after the shooting, when the young man struggled vainly to live, the *World* commented that Westwood was 'generally spoken of as an inoffensive and agreeable young man, and [was] not known to have had a quarrel with anyone.'[23] Women were particularly touched by his death. At his funeral, 'half the feminine population of Parkdale was present.' Young girls, children, and mothers pushing baby carriages waited in the melancholy drizzle to see the funeral procession.[24] At that point, no one yet knew the identity of the assailant because Westwood had been unable (or unwilling, as many speculated) to identify his killer in an antemortem statement. The absence of this crucial fact in Westwood's murder provided an opening for journalists eager to narrate a melodramatic tale of gender conflict that led to death.

Westwood had described his attacker as a slender, moustached man, dressed in dark clothes and wearing a fedora. He concluded his description enigmatically with, 'mum's the word.' The *Empire* offered several tales to compensate for Westwood's reticence. Perhaps the murderer was a jealous lover, a rival for a woman's affections. Or perhaps he was a longshoreman whom Westwood had previously caught trying to break into his family's boathouse. Or the murder, as Westwood's parents maintained, was a case of mistaken identity.[25] The police, however, were inclined to favour the theory that, as with most contests between men, a woman was somehow involved. The *World* cautioned its readers that the police '[gave] out no reason for their belief,' and that they could extract nothing from his friends or family to support their explanation of the crime: 'The theory which the police are now inclined to credit is that the shooting is the outcome of the entanglement of the victim with a woman, that it was for her sake that the crime was committed, and they claim that in a few hours the father of the girl will be arraigned at the bar of justice to face whatever penalty the law might inflict upon him.'[26] Torontonians, deprived of a suspect, were free to let their imaginations roam over the motives that drove characters to murder in both the highbrow retellings of Arthurian legend and in the popular melodramas of the day. Love, jealousy, and revenge must surely have played a role in this tragedy, too, but how?

Westwood's statement that he had been shot by a man diverted most of the city's amateur and professional detectives from a plot line that Torontonians would have found plausible. As Ruth Harris has shown, romantic melodrama drew theatre-goers from all classes in the nineteenth century. Characters were larger-than-life embodiments of good and evil, while plots generally turned around virtue as a perpetually embattled ideal. The plight of the heroine, 'made desperate by the insensitivity, deceitfulness or even villainy of men,' lent dramatic tension to the simple tales.[27] The absence of the hero or his inability to rescue the heroine could add a further twist to the plot. When the poor girl, wronged by a rich villain, found herself without a champion, she turned to self-defence.

Theatre critic and journalist Hector Charlesworth observed in his 1925 retelling of Westwood's murder that 'at the cheap melodramas then popular ... the heroine often dressed in boy's clothes and shot the villain.'[28] Thus, the revelation in police court that a women disguised in men's clothes had shot a scion of a rich family was sensational but far from implausible to contemporary observers. It confirmed the police theory that a woman whose honour was at stake was involved in the crime, and it followed the familiar plot line of 'cheap' melodramas where working-class heroes and heroines seized the opportunity to right the wrongs inflicted by their rich exploiters. The *Globe*, initially an upholder of Westwood's good name, reluctantly turned, after Ford's confession, to a different assessment of the man. Her tale of revenge, the paper admitted, '[did] not reflect credit on the reputation of the youth whose life was so ruthlessly cut short, [yet] it offer[ed] at least a more reasonable explanation of the crime.'[29]

If it was possible for Torontonians to imagine a wronged heroine shooting a villain to avenge her shame, most of those who commented on the case argued that the players had been miscast. 'I thought Westwood did not treat me respectfully,' Ford had stated as the motive for her crime, but would this odd, mixed-race woman be able to convince a group of white men that she was worthy of respect and that Westwood was actually a villain?

Pre-trial speculation focused on the question of Clara Ford's character, for her respectability was crucial to her credibility as a wronged heroine. Ford hardly gave the impression of an innocent maiden driven reluctantly to violence. 'She is a woman who at times has exhibited terrible ebullitions of temper, and it transpires that she has threatened the lives of at least two persons,' claimed the *Empire*. The newspaper found it unlikely that 'the supposed insult offered by Frank Westwood' was anything more than a 'passing remark.' Ford was not a demure maiden but a tough Ward dweller who 'took pride in exhibiting her fearlessness of everything earthly.'[30] Several of the dailies unearthed or invented damning stories about Ford's eccentricities that confirmed her as a violent-tempered 'man-woman' of a lesser race.

The *World* and the *Empire* attempted to outdo each other with fantastic tales of the wild creature who asked that she be given the role of the wounded woman. The newspapers credited Ford with, among other unfeminine quirks, a taste for raw meat, an ability to mount streetcars at a fast clip, and a brief stint as an Anglican choir 'boy' during a sojourn in Chicago. The *Empire* printed stories about Ford's penchant for men's clothes, which she first wore to work in livery stables, then came to prefer over womanly garb. She carried a revolver and did not hesitate to exercise her 'pugilistic skill' when roused by 'teasing and ridicule on account of her colour.'[31] The *World* went much further, labelling Ford as a 'sexual psychopath.' She was 'addict[ed] to parading in male attire,' it began. Had Westwood interfered with a masquerade that was 'one of her dearest pleasures' he could have incited feelings of 'jealousy and rage sufficient to instigate the murder of the young man of itself and requiring no other incentive whatever.'[32]

In spite of Ford's checkered past, she would not be judged on the same standards as a white person. In the late nineteenth century, white Canadians considered themselves more enlightened than their racist American cousins; nonetheless, most harboured a strong sense that blacks were linked more closely to animals than to humans.[33] While scientific theories engendered notions of race hierarchies, popular entertainments contributed to the perpetuation of racist stereotypes. Minstrel shows that packed Toronto's theatres in the 1880s and 1890s typically featured romantic depictions of slave life where the childish, outlandish 'jigaboos' had nothing to worry about but their own pleasures. It is likely that Torontonians would have encountered more blacks on stage than in the streets, since in 1891 they accounted for less than 1 per cent of the city's population. Outright hostility was not as common an attitude among whites in this period as were amusement and pity. Portrayals of 'the Negro' as childish and outlandish framed whites' perceptions of blacks' behaviour. That neither the defence, the crown, nor the newspapers suggested that Clara Ford required psychiatric assessment to determine her fitness to stand trial is noteworthy.[34] Apparently, few Torontonians considered her bizarre conduct to be abnormal for a person with 'African blood.' Spectators were inclined to see the mulatto defendant as ludicrous before she ever took the stand.

The defendant had clearly not lived up to the standards expected of a chaste, white woman, yet stories of her irrational outbursts and violence did uphold her contemporaries' racist assumptions about blacks' inferiority. The *Globe* contributed to the rumours about her unmaidenly past, but it remained sympathetic to Ford on account of her race and class. Ford's mother, it told its readers, had been a black servant and her white father was the son of an 'old and highly respected Toronto family.' As an infant, she had been left on another family's doorstep, and it was a black washerwoman who eventually took her in. The suspected mother of an illegitimate child herself, Ford had understandably developed a 'strong aversion to men, she having keenly felt the disgrace of her shame.'[35]

The *World*, in contrast, doubted that any woman who 'had conducted herself exactly as one of the superior sex' could possibly feel shame. It did, however, share with the other dailies a degree of sympathy for her as a mulatto, much in the way that it might have pitied a dumb animal: 'She had come to regard herself as a sort of social Pariah ... [U]shered into a world by whom she knew not, she had been buffeted about with no more comprehension of cause or reason than has a dog; nay, not so much, for she knew not friends from foes. As she grew older she realized that it was to the presence of African blood in her veins that many of the rebuffs she received were due.'[36] These tales of a woman burdened by poverty and racial inferiority undoubtedly elicited sympathy among those who felt that life had dealt her a cruel blow. That sympathy did not translate automatically, however, into an acquittal for this woman, who was almost comically miscast as an innocent maiden. It was up to Ford's defence counsel, Johnston, to appropriate her melodramatic tale of wounded womanhood as his masculine quest for chivalric justice.

There were no such ambiguities about heroes and villains in the Davies case, for Charles Massey and Carrie Davies were more suited to their roles in the courtroom drama that unfolded in February 1915. Davies was the picture of working-class respectability and Massey the prototype of the wealthy cad. Since Davies had shot Massey in front of witnesses and made her confession hours after the murder, the press had not the same narrative vacuum to fill with colourful speculation. Pre-trial publicity nonetheless confirmed that, once again, character more than fact would become the crucial issue in the trial of a woman accused of murder.

Bert Massey resembled Frank Westwood in that he came from a respectable, wealthy Methodist family. Beyond these similarities, they differed significantly. There was no one in Toronto at the time of the murder to whom the Massey name would have been unfamiliar. His grandfather, Hart Massey, had founded a massive farm implements firm and his father, in whose memory Massey Hall had been built in 1894, had helped to turn it into a worldwide enterprise. The family set such a strict tone of upper-class respectability that they were never entirely integrated into Toronto 'society' in spite of their considerable wealth. Bert, unlike his elders, did not fit the Massey mould. The *Globe* noted on the morning after his death that he was not 'intimately known by his neighbours,' although he was 'well known about town.' The *World* called him 'quite a popular figure among the younger society set.' As a sales agent for York Motors, he had abandoned his grandfather's sluggish tractors for speedy automobiles. 'He was fond of motoring, and took much enjoyment out of life,' commented the *Globe*.[37] On the night he died he was wearing a diamond stick pin, a symbol not only of his wealth but his vanity.

The background of Massey's assailant starkly contrasted with his class and his character. Carrie Davies's impoverished family lived in Bedfordshire, England. When her invalid father, a disabled veteran of the Boer War, died in 1913, she had been sent to service in Canada at sixteen so she could help support her purblind mother and three younger sisters. She had worked since her arrival in Toronto as a general servant at the Massey household. By scrimping and rarely going out, she had managed to pay back the $45 she had borrowed for her passage and to send home $5 to $10 per month out of her monthly wage of $16. On the night of the murder she was carrying a letter addressed to her mother in which she had enclosed $30 for the support of the fatherless family. The immigrant maid had briefly seen a young man who had signed on with the Canadian Expeditionary Force shortly after they had met in the summer of 1914. A writer of melodramas could hardly have created a more virtuous heroine.

Davies stood out from the crowd of vagrants, drunks, thieves, and prostitutes who appeared with her at the women's court. The *Telegram* judged that Davies was virtuous because she had a shy manner and wore dowdy, sensible clothing: 'The slight, girlish figure in its long brown coat and black velvet hat ... was in the midst of a number of well dressed, care-free women ... More like a mild and gentle Sunday School pupil did she look, and very subdued and sorrowful.'[38] Her costume confirmed her plausibility in the role of the dutiful young servant, just as Ford's habit of cross-dressing raised doubts as to her credibility as a wounded woman.

Although Bert Massey was something of a black sheep, he was still a Massey. In the trial of a servant, the honour of a respectable family would be tested as well. The *Star* was the most vocal supporter of the victim's gentlemanly reputation when it argued that 'there is absolutely no truth in any report that credits him with any indiscretions.'[39] A more likely explanation for Davies's violent outburst, it offered, was her unbalanced mental state. Under the headline 'No Motive Known for Awful Deed,' the *Star* introduced the theory that Davies had shot Massey because she was insane. The upright servant may have had an unblemished past, but she did have a history of epileptic 'fits,' the last bout having occurred the previous summer when she had 'carried on like an insane person,' according to the victim's brother: 'we feel sure that the crime was committed in a fit of temporary insanity, and many things that puzzled us in the past seem very clear now,' added A.L. Massey on behalf of the family. The *Star* speculated that the 'strain of carrying the family in the Old Country [had] worked on her nerves' and left her unable to cope with separation from her soldier sweetheart. The thought that he might have been killed on the front 'played upon her mind until she worked herself into a frenzied condition where she did not know or realize what she was doing.'[40]

The *Star* supported the Massey family's hopes that all might be forgiven without exposing the dead man's reputation to the scrutiny of the trial. If Dr Beemer of the Mimico Asylum, whom they had hired to examine Davies, were to determine that she was insane, she would have been incarcerated indefinitely and not accorded the benefit of a trial. The allegations that a master had attempted to disgrace a defenceless maid could accordingly be dismissed as the ravings of a madwoman, and not the testimony of an embattled heroine.

Davies's many supporters, particularly working-class, British immigrants, rejected the insanity theory as a dishonourable ploy of a rich and influential family eager to escape justice. The Masseys had thrown down a gauntlet and Davies's champions rose to the challenge. Her principal defender, in the absence of her soldier hero, was the Bedfordshire Fraternal Association (BFA), a group of working-class Englishmen who had emigrated from the same area of England as Davies. The group initiated a defence fund for the accused, who they realized could not afford to hire a lawyer on her own. The *Telegram* coordinated the collection of donations that came from hundreds of supporters, who frequently sent along a letter with their money. 'A Loyal Canadian,' 'East End,' 'One Who Knows,' and 'Another English Working Girl' were among the pen names of the men and women who felt drawn to Davies's defence. The 'ones who knew' and the 'English working girls' were likely women who had experienced the harassment Davies had described. Working-class men found different reasons not only for defending her against her enemies, but also for adopting her cause as their own. One male contributor to the BFA defence fund described how the trial of a woman could be interpreted as an unchivalrous attack against the honour of men loyal to the empire: 'I appeal to every Englishman, Welshman, and soldier, to every British subject who is worthy [of] the name to give the price of a cigar or a glass of beer and not let this scandal be upon them of a poor, friendless girl condemned because she was too poor to bring out evidence in her own favour.'[41] It was up to her beer-drinking compatriots, in other words, to fight a David and Goliath battle against the mighty Masseys on her behalf. Even before the trial that would be argued by men and decided by men, the Carrie Davies case, like the Ford case twenty years earlier, took on the shape of a chivalrous drama where the issue of male honour superseded a woman's claim of sexual assault.

The Trials

Pre-trial publicity generated immense public interest in the trials of Clara Ford and Carrie Davies. The *Globe* noted at the beginning of Ford's trial that officials had to hold back 'the immense number of the public for whom standing room only could not be provided.'[42] She was 'the all-absorbing topic of public attention,' and 'dramatic interest' in her case steadily increased through the five-day trial.[43] When the verdict was announced, the *World* observed that 'young girls, middle-aged women and men of all classes crowded around to get a look at the heroine of the drama of the day.' Davies did not possess Ford's flair for the dramatic, yet her trial was equally noteworthy. A headline in the *Daily News* described a 'Disgusting Scene when Women Mobbed Corridors and Courtroom to Satisfy Curiosity.' These were not the usual habitués of the courts, as the front-page story continued: 'Many of the women were well-dressed and evidently of the "upper" stratum, but they pushed and jostled with the rest, intent on satisfying a more or less morbid curiosity.'[44] The *Telegram* added that three additional police officers were required to hold back the crowds.[45] The *Star* declared that the 'mob' at Davies's police court appearance included 'hatless girls, furred and expensively gowned matrons, street urchins and young men idlers of the lower type.'[46] For those who could not squeeze into the courtrooms, all of the dailies provided front-page coverage, and whether comfortable in the role, like Ford, or reluctant to take centre stage, like Davies, both of the confessed murderers became 'heroines of the hour' through their dramatic trials.

On 30 April 1895 two worthy opponents, 'the famous Osler' and Blackie Johnston, met in court to determine the fate of a woman who had confessed to murder but changed her plea after her lawyer's 'friendly remonstrances.'[47] Osler based his case on three elements: Ford's police court plea of guilty and her confession to detectives; striations on the fatal bullets matching etchings on cartridges fired from Ford's gun; and, finally, a witness who claimed she had heard Ford threaten to shoot Westwood if she found him with another woman. Johnston countered with a defence that denied the validity of Ford's initial confession, including her testimony that she had been 'insulted.' He claimed that villainous men had tricked his client into inventing a story and that the detectives had been led to the defendant by the malicious gossip of liars, pickpockets, and drunkards.[48]

Despite the crown's apparently strong case, Osler was hampered from the start, for he had little but evidence on his side in this contest of character. Johnston, however, seized his opportunity to wax heroic in his defence of a poor, mulatto seamstress, one who was, according to the artificial hierarchy of class, race, and gender, his inferior. It would be an unpleasant task indeed for a gentleman to hang such a defenceless creature.

Ford had confessed that she had shot Westwood because he had knocked her down and 'insulted' her. For a young gentleman to behave in such a manner was not only unchivalrous but possibly criminal as well, since 'insult' was a euphemism for sexual assault in the nineteenth and early twentieth century.[49] Both the prosecution and the defence dismissed Ford's melodramatic motive for revenge. To argue that the defendant had been raped would have required Osler to smear the reputation of the slain man and Johnston to present Ford as a woman against whom sexual assault might be considered an 'insult.'[50] In spite of her confession's resonance with the plot lines of romantic melodrama, neither legal adversary asked the all-white male jury to believe that an apparently respectable white man had raped a mulatto woman.

Osler opened with his 'usual terse, clear and simple outline of the evidence to be presented.'[51] His most powerful ammunition in his fight to bring a killer to justice was Ford's confession, but how to use it without confirming the humble woman's motive and thereby staining the good name of the dead youth? The prosecution, he informed the jury, was under no obligation to prove a motive for a criminal act to secure a conviction, yet he realized that he was more likely to win his case if he could show the jury that the accused had a reason to shoot Westwood. '[His] story is the old one of love and passion, condemned by the law of God and man,' he offered: 'It is the story of a mulatto girl who had been the play thing of an apparently respectable young man. Discarded by him for another, she deliberately shot him to death.' He promised the jury that the crown would call a witness who would corroborate his theory and help to establish that there was 'evidence of a certain relationship of an improper kind' between Westwood and Ford.[52] Osler allowed for a certain degree of indiscretion on Westwood's part, yet he carefully expunged her claim that the youth had sexually assaulted her. Although he was compelled, as a gentleman, to upbraid Westwood for dallying with a woman so evidently beneath him, he commended him for having done the right thing by spurning her. Tragically, Ford was not a woman to be spurned and, for her response to Westwood's rejection, she would have to face the law.

The crown presented an unprecedented number of witnesses to establish that Ford had shot Westwood in cold blood. Included among the thirty-three crown witnesses were the family and friends of the victim, whom they described as 'an exemplary son.'[53] The remaining witnesses were associates of Ford's, who confirmed that she had both the inclination and the opportunity to kill the young man. Finally, the detectives who had arrested and interrogated Ford testified that she had freely confessed to committing the crime after being cautioned that any of her statements might be used in evidence against her. Inspector Stark related Ford's claim that Westwood had been in the habit of saying offensive things to her and that he had 'attempted liberties' with her several months earlier. Detective Reburn testified that he had asked her if she wanted a lawyer, but she thought it would do her no good since she was guilty. It was not new for one of her colour to be teased and ridiculed, she had informed her interrogators, but the 'insult' had been too much to bear. 'If you had a sister and she was treated as I was, would not she have done the same thing?'[54] After three-and-a-half days of seemingly conclusive evidence, the prosecution rested.

Osler had ably represented the Queen in his case against Ford;

Johnston, however, emerged as the superior champion of a much humbler woman. He decided, once Justice Boyd allowed the confession into evidence, that he would tread on shaky ground if he tried to convince the jury that his client had shot a respectable white man because he had tried to rape her. Ford, the woman who paraded in men's clothes, brandished a revolver, and jumped onto streetcars 'like a man,' was simply incredible as a wounded woman. As the *World* had earlier explained, Ford's alleged motive was unbelievable unless one granted: 'that Clara Ford was a virtuous woman, so virtuous, in fact, that she was shocked at the approaches of a boy fourteen years younger than herself; that she led a moral life and was extremely sensitive of her reputation for morality. The evidence so far does not establish this fact. On the contrary, it looks as if the prisoner had passed through a very checkered career.'[55] Johnston could ill afford to take chances with his eccentric client; instead, he tried to establish that, as a woman and a person with 'African blood,' she had made an easy target for unchivalrous detectives who had badgered her and duped her into making a false confession.[56]

Clara Ford's flair for the dramatic was put to the test when, in a surprising move, Johnston called her as the first witness for the defence. All, including her detractors, agreed that her performance rivalled those of the finest tragedians of the day:[57] 'she enjoyed the fact that she was at length the central figure in a drama, even though it were being played on life's stage and the finale was fraught with momentous results,' the *World* dramatically commented.[58] Johnston's junior, Mr Murdock, led her through her revised story of having been deceived by the detectives into admitting lies: she had neither shot nor even known the dead man, she now claimed. Ford alleged that the detectives had not told her she was under arrest when they searched her room and that, despite her denials of responsibility for the crime, they had subjected her to seven hours of brutal interrogation at the police station. She told the hushed courtroom how she had been tricked:

Sergeant Reburn continued to press me to confess, and said that if I said Frank Westwood insulted me, nothing would be done to me. No one, he said, will know to the contrary; he is dead, and won't come back again ... He kept repeating I was in a net and could not get out. The more I denied, the more he pressed me to confess. At last, I said I did it.[59]

Ford's sensational testimony helped establish the defence's case: she was not a murderer but an unschooled mulatto woman who had been outwitted by big city detectives eager to advance their careers. Dewart tried in vain to shake her from her new story with a cross examination that lasted over three hours. Johnston ended the day with anticlimactic testimony from witnesses who supported Ford's alibi; what remained in the jury's and the spectators' minds, however, was the dramatic performance of a woman on trial for her life.

Ford temporarily upstaged Johnston's role as the orchestrator of her defence, but in his closing remarks, Johnston managed to re-establish her trial as a battle between men over male honour. He began his speech with a thunderous reminder that the jury must return a verdict of 'Murder or nothing.'[60] Were they to convict his client, they had to accept the awful responsibility of sending her to the gallows.[61] He cautioned the jury that convicting Ford required that they rely on the word of self-interested detectives who had swooped down on his client on the advice of drunkards and thieves. These detectives had pursued a dishonourable course in their desire for fame at the cost of a lesser being. 'Was it any wonder that she, womanlike, would say anything to get out of the clutches of those vultures?' Johnston asked the jury, whom he hoped would interpret 'womanlike' to mean easily cowed. In a forthright appeal for the men of the jury to share his sense of gentlemanly outrage, he concluded that the detectives' unchivalrous behaviour had made him 'ashamed to be a man.'[62]

Johnston bridged class boundaries when he addressed this jury of wainwrights, cobblers, and farmers as fellow gentlemen.[63] He urged them to act in a way that would do them credit as men of honour: they alone had the power to right a wrong by upholding the code of chivalric justice and allowing his client to go free. Here was a rare opportunity for humble artisans to become heroes by saving a poor, badgered woman. They could side with the crown and its villainous henchmen, or they could support Johnston and his falsely accused, much maligned client. The defence, unlike the crown, had declared that Westwood and his client had never met. To acquit his client would accordingly exonerate Westwood from the unseemly charges of indiscretion reluctantly brought before the court by the crown. Johnston reiterated that he had taken the case without fees because he believed that Ford was innocent and because, as he underlined in his closing address, she had had 'not a dollar.'[64] The jury's decision, then, would determine Ford's fate as well as reflect upon Johnston's reputation, the jury's, and that of Westwood who was not alive to defend himself. By the time he finished his appeal to masculine honour, several members of the jury were said to have been in tears.[65]

Dewart, having taken over the case for Osler, faced the unenviable task of following Johnston's performance with the crown's summation. Johnston had boxed him into a corner and forced him to develop the prosecution's theory that there had been a dishonourable connection between a bizarre 'man-woman' and an 'apparently respectable' man. Dewart concentrated on the weighty, circumstantial evidence against Ford and questioned the defence's claim that she had been coerced into a false confession. In light of her calm and glib manner after six hours on the witness stand, including more than three hours of close cross examination, could the jury believe that two detectives had been able to break her indomitable will? He reminded the all-white jury that her word was not to be trusted and suggested that her 'African blood' gave her almost supernatural powers of trickery. Dewart compared her self-possession on the witness stand to the 'devilment and recklessness' shared by her race equivalents such as 'Mexican bandits and stoic Indians.' Her testimony was not the protestation of an innocent heroine but the bravado of a half-savage.[66] Justice Boyd bolstered the crown's case with a charge in which he declared his belief in Ford's initial confession. It did little good. In less than one half hour, the jury sided with Johnston and the code of chivalry rather than with the crown and the letter of the law.

Carrie Davies's trial was much less a struggle to determine the guilt or innocence of a defendant than a gentleman's agreement to recognize a heroine. The case had made front-page news for two weeks before the trial and, unlike Ford, Davies had been the target of little unfavourable publicity, save the Massey's suggestions that she was mentally unstable. Dr Beemer laid those rumours to rest, though, when he established her fitness to stand trial. Davies's pristine character, her race and ethnicity led the lawyers involved in her trial to construct a case that starkly contrasted the arguments presented in the Ford case. Although both defendants were poor women who had confessed to having killed rich white men who had sexually assaulted them, their defenders pursued different courses in their attempts to win their case. It was possible for Dewart, now a lawyer for the defence, to present his client's confession as the truth because, unlike Ford, she possessed all the qualities of an innocent maiden. Yet even Davies's story in court did not assert women's right to be free from sexual harassment, nor did it indict the criminal justice system for its routine dismissal of women's allegations of sexual assault. By the time that Davies's case went to trial her story was no longer her own. Dewart masterfully crafted the servant's tale into a defence of the empire, British values, and the honour of the men who were oversees fighting the forces of barbarism.

In the early months of the war, Torontonians indulged in an orgy of patriotism. Voluntary enlistments were among the highest in the nation, and it still seemed possible to secure a swift, honourable victory over the evil 'Hun.' Pulpits, classrooms, and the press helped generate almost unanimous support for the British cause. Women's groups, such as the Young Women's Christian Association, the Local Council of Women, and the Imperial Order Daughters of the Empire constructed a highly publicized, feminine support role as their contribution to the war effort. Women were to keep the home fires burning and to preserve the civilized, British values that their men were fighting to protect. Newspapers reminded readers that Davies's own sweetheart was one of the brave lads who had volunteered to risk his life in defence of Britain. Davies seemed to have performed her part by waiting patiently for her soldier boyfriend and faithfully supporting her impoverished mother and sisters who lived in England. To ignore the plight of a beleaguered British 'girl' in Toronto in 1915 would have bordered on treason.

Working-class Britishers turned the Davies case into a patriotic exercise. The BFA spoke on their behalf with the assistance of the Toronto *Telegram*, which gave the BFA a great deal of favourable publicity. The men of Davies's homeland were not, however, the only group to support her. The Toronto Local Council of Women (TLCW) had, since 1913, supplied women to act as advocates for women who appeared in court. Their objection to the lenient treatment of men who were guilty of morals offences prompted them to form a standing committee on the Equal Moral Standard. The TLCW leapt to Davies's defence once Dr Margaret Patterson, the chair of the Equal Moral Standard Committee, told the executive about Massey's alleged sexual assault.[67] The women managed to secure the services of 'a prominent KC,' but they were rebuffed by Davies's brother-in-law, who had already hired a lawyer on his own.[68] He preferred the help of his working-class neighbours, including William Goldsmith, the secretary of the BFA. He and the rest of the BFA executive considered it a matter of pride to shoulder the burden of Davies's defence without the help of the 'ladies of the upper stratum.'[69] The triumph of the British working-class defenders over the bourgeois female philanthropists helped to translate Davies's trial into a wartime test of her class and compatriots. The BFA's muzzling of the TLCW left the presentation of the defendant's story in the hands of men.

Just as hundreds of the city's sons had rushed to answer the call to defend the empire against the kaiser, so Toronto's lawyers scrambled for the privilege to defend this wronged English servant. 'The competition among the legal fraternity to represent Carrie Davies is said to have been amazing,' the *Telegram* informed its readers.[70] There could perhaps have been no better time for a Canadian lawyer to have come to Davies's defence,

[handwritten margin note: defendants used as political bargaining support.]

nor a less propitious moment for the crown to have sought a conviction.

The prosecution's heart did not seem to have been in the case. Crown counsel Du Vernet's opening remarks, in fact, sounded remarkably like a plea for the defence. 'I have never had a more unpleasant duty than to prosecute such a young girl on such a serious charge,' he began. He noted the defendant's spotless reputation and commended her for obeying her mistress's order to remain at the house. His only hope in winning the case was to convince the jury that Massey had merely made advances that were not in themselves sufficient justification for murder: 'It is for you to determine if there was sudden provocation. You must judge whether this girl was insulted.'[71] Davies herself had admitted that Massey 'did not really assault her.' Du Vernet suggested to the jury that Davies had over-reacted, and that they must, at the very least, find her guilty of manslaughter. He tried, weakly, to appear merciful in carrying out his unpleasant duty to prosecute her. 'Give the benefit of the doubt to this girl as far as you can under your oaths,' he graciously implored Davies's peers.[72]

Twenty years after losing the Ford case to E.F.B. Johnston, Hartley Dewart had a chance to play the coveted role as defender of wounded womanhood. 'Never before had there been such a charge against an innocent and honourable girl fighting against unequal odds and a treacherous assailant,' he opened. His exaggerated claim not only heightened the drama of the trial; in addition, it erased the similarities between Ford's and Davies's claims of sexual assault as the provocation for their crimes. The defence would not dispute that Davies had killed Massey, but it would strive to convince the jury that her upright background and unsullied character justified her extreme response to Massey's advances. Dewart spoke to the jury members, most of whom were over fifty, as fathers while he repeatedly referred to the defendant as 'the little girl.' He told them that Davies's father had been a 'man of fighting blood in whose home there was wholesome discipline, where daughters were brought up as daughters should be.' As a teenager, Davies had come to Canada to help her widowed mother, only to find herself the victim of a dishonourable man. The gentlemen of the jury must, as he did, surely feel an obligation to protect her now. Dewart suggested to the jury that they were obligated to right the unchivalrous Massey's wrong: 'We have placed upon ourselves as Canadians the duties of trustees and guardians for girls who come from homes such as this to Canada.' Massey, a man who should have been a member of this fraternity of trustees, had, instead, tried 'to accomplish the ruin of this girl.' Dewart shared with the jury his realization that men can hardly imagine what it must be like to be disgraced: 'It is hard,' he admitted, 'to bring a man to put himself in the position of an innocent and honourable girl of eighteen.'[73] How much easier, though, for these middle-aged men to imagine themselves in the place of Davies's recently deceased father.

Du Vernet tried to build his case on facts, whereas Dewart made a sentimental appeal for fatherly forgiveness. The prosecution brought forward several witnesses who testified that Massey had been walking towards his front door when his maid emerged and fired two shots at him, one of which struck him in the heart and killed him instantly. Like Dewart in the Ford trial, Du Vernet relied principally on the defendant's confession, which he interpreted as an admission to having over-reacted to Massey's indiscrete attentions. Dewart countered with only three witnesses: the first, Dr Arthur Harrington, testified that he had examined Davies at the request of the defence, and that he could certify she was a virgin; her brother-in-law, the second witness, corroborated her statement that she had complained to her relatives about Massey's advances; and the final witness was Davies herself. All three, in effect, acted as character witnesses. They constructed for the jury the picture of a modest girl, torn between duty and fear, but driven in the end to protect her chastity at any cost. Her virginity was proof that she had succeeded where Massey had lost. Dewart's decision to put 'the slight pathetic figure' on the witness stand to relate her fears of disgrace only heightened the already dramatic proceedings.

The closing remarks of the defence were a masterpiece of chivalric oration. Dewart's summation was, at once, a request to spare a defenceless woman, an argument for chastity as a woman's dearest possession, and a call to defend embattled British values in time of war. He recounted in dramatic detail the advances of the man whom Davies had every reason to fear. She had not erred in her assumption that he 'meant to accomplish his purpose no matter what obstacles he met with' and that he might 'follow up his attack with violence if necessary.' She was forced to use a gun because he was a strong man 'against whom her puny strength could not resist.' Dewart conceded that Massey had not threatened her life, yet he had put her in peril of losing something as precious – her chastity: 'The attack gave the girl only one alternative ... If she did not defend herself against this man she would have been a fallen woman, an outcast, one more sacrifice. Let that sink into your mind. *It was not manslaughter. It was bruteslaughter.*'[74]

Dewart implied that had Massey 'accomplished his purpose,' his client would not have been a credible witness. He had opened his defence, after all, with medical proof of her virginity. Since the loss of her chastity would apparently have rendered Davies an 'outcast,' Dewart would have had to resort to a different defence. Ironically, he used the fact that Davies had *not* been raped to prove that she had just cause to kill.

Honourable men had a duty to punish brutes, as loyal Canadians knew well, and soldiers who joined the army to kill Germans were decorated, not indicted for murder. The duty of men to fight, however, also meant that Davies's protectors were either dead or fighting on European battlefields. In time of war, she had been forced to come to her own defence. Dewart implied that the acquittal of his client would amount to a patriotic act. Davies may not have been fighting on the front for her country, but she had tried desperately on the home front to uphold the values that Canadian soldiers, including her sweetheart, were willing to die for: 'While this girl's lover is at the front fighting for the honour of Britain, this girl was fighting just as strongly for the principle which *is* the British Empire – honour.'[75]

Torontonians read every day of men's bravery in the trenches, but a case such as Davies's showed that women were also doing their part to preserve the moral standards that elevated the British Empire above its enemies. Of all the soldiers fighting for the King, Dewart estimated, 'none of them more faithfully defended the honour of the Empire than this girl defended her own honour.'[76] In effect, Dewart told the members of the jury that unless they considered themselves treasonous scoundrels, they had no choice but to acquit Carrie Davies.

Neither the lawyer for the defence nor the imposing Justice Mulock overlooked the importance of class in the determination of the case. Dewart commended her not only for her patriotic defence of her chastity but also for her unswerving sense of duty. She had left the Massey household after her master took liberties with her, but she had returned because she had promised Mrs Massey that she would look after her husband and son in her absence. She was not a murderer, therefore, but 'a girl possessed of a sense of duty, a faithful servant, and imbued with principles that make our national greatness.'[77] In Mulock's charge to the jury he reiterated Dewart's admiration of her loyalty to her mistress. Perhaps conscious of the perennial lack of 'good help' for bourgeois homes, he added: 'It is, I think encouraging and pleasing to find some person so devoted to respect one's promise as the prisoner seems to have been.'[78] Nor was she a 'care-free' working girl but an old-fashioned, trustworthy servant whose primary concerns were to preserve her chastity and obey her mistress.[79] She had, in other words, acted in a manner appropriate to her gender and class and might, accordingly, appeal to the mercy of the court.

Du Vernet played the same unpopular role that Dewart had adopted in the Ford trial, and he too tried in his closing remarks to reassure the jury that a conviction would be an unpleasant yet just verdict. He courageously tried to counter Dewart's emotional appeal with his own interpretation of the role that chivalry might play in the decision of the jury. The chivalric code demanded that the defenceless should not be attacked, as Dewart had ably argued in reference to 'the little girl' defendant. Yet Davies had shot to death an unarmed man without any immediate provocation. Although Du Vernet did not explicitly discredit Davies's story, he reminded the jury that Massey had died before he could give his side of the story. The murdered man had been deprived of his right to give his word as a gentleman. Why should the jury excuse Davies after she had summarily imposed the death penalty on a man who, had he been convicted of indecent assault, 'would possibly have got six months'?[80] If the jury ignored the law, he warned, then Canada would sink into barbarism: 'We must not let down the bars of law and order and we must do our duty even if it is hard ... the law in its efforts to be fair and reasonable has a merciful side, but it must protect the public.'[81]

Du Vernet's attempt to call an assailant to justice was valiant. His skill was wasted, though, for the jury needed only a few minutes to render their verdict of 'not guilty.' Their decision, Justice Mulock commented to the jubilant crowd, was 'not absolutely in conformity with strict rules, but they have rendered substantial justice.'[82]

Getting Away with Murder?

No legal system maintains its legitimacy unless mercy tempers severity. Periodic compassionate judgments dramatize the power of the law to rectify inequalities outside the courtroom. They maintain the illusion that even the lowest citizens – women, the poor, and people of colour – are equal before the law. Merciful decisions do not, however, correct systemic inequality. In fact, as the trials of Carrie Davies and Clara Ford show, a generous verdict can mystify rich white men's generally unchallenged abuse of their powers.

The defendants, though, were well aware that gentlemen did not always behave as such. Both women had acted on the premise that obeying the law by asking the police to lay charges against their harassers would have been fruitless. When Ford confessed to detectives that she had not told the authorities about Westwood's alleged 'insult' because she felt it was futile for a 'woman of [her] colour' to go to the police, she exposed the authorities to charges of racism. She might have added classism as well.

Davies, for instance, did not even consider launching a formal complaint against her wealthy employer. She did not have to study the annual reports of the city police to guess that her chances of success would have been very low indeed.

Sexual aggressors, as Westwood and Massey were alleged to have been, were generally protected by the criminal justice system, particularly if they were well-to-do. For instance, from 1880 to 1930, not a single Toronto domestic who laid a complaint of indecent assault or rape against her master saw him punished.[83] At the root of the justice system's dismissal of female claims lay the belief that only an unchaste woman could induce a man to make a sexual advance. As Dewart emphasized in his closing remarks in the Davies trial, the word of a raped woman was worthless because her loss of chastity amounted to the irrevocable loss of feminine honour. Black women, whom whites considered to harbour insatiable carnal desires, could not even hope to attain the honour that men bestowed upon 'passionless' white women. Had either Ford or Davies complained to the police that they had been sexually assaulted by wealthy white men, it is extremely unlikely that the crown attorney would have pressed charges.[84] The historically low conviction rates for rape suggest that the criminal justice system is actually more inclined to be merciful towards men who dishonour than towards dishonoured women.[85] Ironically, the verdicts in these two trials lent tacit approval for women to kill villains whom men routinely exculpated. Vigilantism, as these women discovered, was more effective than litigation as a remedy for sexual violence.

It is equally doubtful that either of these women would have been acquitted had they not attracted the services of highly skilled, prominent lawyers. At the turn of the century, most humble people in conflict with the law were without legal representation of any kind and, consequently, pled guilty in the hope of swifter justice. Those who did find advocates whom they could afford had to settle for inferior service, even in capital cases. Both the men and the women who were convicted of murder and executed in nineteenth- and twentieth-century Canada were poorly represented in court, as Neil Boyd has revealed.[86]

[handwritten margin note: again, defendants used as proxies in political matter.]

It is difficult to explain why self-confessed murderers of low social station attracted men of Johnston's and Dewart's calibre unless one asks what the lawyers hoped to gain by taking on their cases. Johnston made an open secret of the fact that he had defended Ford without payment. Victory would enhance his reputation as a lawyer and a gentleman, and not his pocketbook. Dewart was, perhaps, eager to vindicate his loss in the Ford case when he jumped at the chance to defend Carrie Davies. By stirring up working-class, British pride in his overblown speeches and appealing to the judge's well-known patriotism, he bridged the gulf between the elite and 'the people.' Professional pride also factored into Johnston's and Dewart's decision to take these cases. A lawyer who successfully defends his client against a seemingly unbeatable charge of murder is the envy of his peers and the talk of the town. Neither man defended a murderer because he was 'mesmerized' by her charms. Both took on their case with their eyes wide open to the opportunity to enhance their reputation within the legal fraternity.

The defence lawyers did not ask for a straightforward, merciful verdict but, instead, couched their pleas in the language of chivalry. This strategy was likely to be effective in a period when chivalry was a cultural ideal; in addition, it inspired the men of the jury, the defence lawyers, and the judges to live up to that ideal in performing their duties. Johnston's references to his client's vulnerabilities and his shame over the behaviour of the detectives would have meant little to a jury unschooled in the proprieties of gentlemanly conduct. Similarly, Dewart made an explicit appeal for paternal protection of a 'little girl' who had narrowly escaped the clutches of a 'brute.' In the Davies trial, men too old for war found their chance to be heroic in defending the British servant – all without the unpleasant task of killing a man themselves. The trials showed that women needed men to save them because of their 'puny strength' and 'womanlike' frailties. Hence, their acquittals did not send a signal that women had the right to be free from the threat of sexual assault; on the contrary, the verdicts confirmed men's prerogative to defend weaker beings.

Because the courtroom proceedings were essentially masculine dramas, the women's stories were muted. In the Davies case, Dewart downplayed the young woman's obvious ability to subdue her male attacker. The defence in the Ford case strayed even further from the defendant's confession when it erased both the 'insult' and her deadly response altogether. Their trials transformed what might have been a chilling warning to male harassers into a confirmation of women's need for heroic men. Again, the message was more comforting to men than women. If apparently respectable men such as Westwood and Massey were potential rapists, how might a woman tell the heroes from the villains against whom she required protection? The answer came too late, as rape victims realized. Lawyers, judges, and juries may mete out mercy to isolated individuals such as Davies and Ford, but such a pattern of mercy is not justice. In the end, judicial chivalry merely obscures and perpetuates injustice beyond the stage of chivalric courtroom dramas.

NOTES

I am grateful to the Osgoode Society and the Department of the Solicitor General of Canda for their generous financial assistance. Among those who have helped to make this a better paper are John Beattie, Clifford Shearing, and the members of the Centre of Criminology at the University of Toronto; the faculty and students at the School of Criminology at Simon Fraser University; John McLaren; and the other contributors to this volume, who will no doubt be happy not to hear any more homicide stories – for a while.

1 Toronto *World*, 6 May 1895. The newspapers of the period, along with trial transcripts and secondary accounts in periodicals and journalistic studies of murderers, were the principal primary sources for this study.

2 Ibid., 28 Feb. 1915

3 Ibid., 6 May 1895

4 The story headline on the day after Davies's acquittal was, 'Both Judge and Jury in Tears.' Toronto *Evening Telegram*, 27 Feb. 1915

5 More has been written about Ford than perhaps any other woman tried for murder in Canada. Included in the secondary material on her case

are Hector Charlesworth, *Candid Chronicles: Leaves from the Book of a Canadian Journalist* (Toronto: Macmillan 1925); George Taylor Denison, *Recollections of a Police Magistrate* (Toronto: Musson 1920); W. Stewart Wallace, *Murders and Mysteries: A Canadian Series* (Toronto: Macmillan 1931); and Albert R. Hassard, *Not Guilty and Other Trials* (Toronto: Lee-Collins 1926). The latest recountings of her trial were a Canadian Broadcasting Corporation radio play entitled 'Dressed to Kill,' broadcast in March 1990, and the lead article in the Toronto *Star*'s series on 'Deadly Women,' 19 Feb. 1989. Both were written by Frank Jones. Aside from extensive coverage of the Davies trial in newspapers of the period, I have been able to find only one study of her case in the form of a semi-fictionalized monograph about the trial. See Frank Jones, *Master and Maid: The Charles Massey Murder* (Toronto: Irwin 1985). Her case is also featured in Genevieve Leslie, 'Domestic Service in Canada, 1880–1920,' in Janice Acton et al., eds., *Women at Work: Ontario, 1850–1930* (Toronto: Canadian Women's Educational Press 1974), 71–126.

6 Susan S.M. Edwards, *Women on Trial: A Study of the Woman Suspect, Defendant and Offender in the Criminal Law and Criminal Justice System* (Manchester: Manchester University Press 1984), 183

7 W.I. Thomas, *Sex and Society* (Boston: R.G. Badger 1907), 234

8 Otto Pollak, *The Criminality of Women* (Philadelphia: University of Philadelphia Press (1950), 151. For a comprehensive appraisal of classical criminology see Carol Smart, *Women, Crime and Criminology: A Feminist Critique* (London: Routledge and Kegan Paul 1976).

9 See Smart, *Women, Crime and Criminology*, and Ilene Nagel et al., 'Sex Differences in the Processing of Criminal Defendants,' in D. Kelly Weisberg, ed., *Women and the Law: A Social Historical Perspective*, vol. 1: *Women and the Criminal Law* (Cambridge, Mass.: Schenkman 1982), 259–83. For studies that show the historical and jurisdictional variation in conviction and punishment patterns see N.E.H. Hull, 'The Certain Wages of Sin: Sentence and Punishment of Female Felons in Colonial Massachusetts, 1673–1774,' in Weisberg, ed., *Women and the Law*, 7–26, and Barbara Hanawalt, 'Women before the Law: Females as Felons and Prey in Fourteenth-Century England,' in Weisberg, ed., *Women and the Law*, 165–96. Neither of these last two studies found any special preference shown towards women charged with capital crimes, including murder. John Beattie found that in early modern Surrey, women were slightly

more likely to be found guilty of murder than men, although they were less likely to be convicted of property offences. John M. Beattie, *Crime and the Courts in England, 1600–1800* (Princeton: Princeton University Press 1986), 437

10 The best-known historical studies that interpret chivalry in this light are Mary Hartman, *Victorian Murderesses: The True History of Thirteen Respectable French and English Women* (New York: Schocken Books 1977), and Ann Jones, *Women Who Kill* (New York: Holt, Rinehart and Winston 1980). For feminist criminological theory on the subject see Carol Smart, 'Criminological Theory: Its Ideology and Implications Concerning Women,' *British Journal of Criminology* 19, 1 (Jan. 1979): 50–9; Etta Anderson, 'The "Chivalrous" Treatment of the Female Offender in the Arms of the Criminal Justice System: A Review of the Literature,' *Social Problems* 23, 3 (1976): 350-7; Barney Bardsley, *Flowers in Hell: An Investigation into Women and Crime* (London 1987); and Frances Heidensohn, *Women and Crime* (London: Pandora 1985).

11 Barney Bardsley has argued this point in terms of the class and race privilege that protects white, 'respectable' women, and stigmatizes women of colour and working-class women who 'refuse to humble themselves, or acknowledge their place.' Bardsley, *Flowers*, 143

12 See Susan S. Edwards, *Gender, Sex and the Law* (London 1985), and Hilary Allen, 'Rendering Them Harmless: The Professional Portrayal of Women Charged with Serious Violent Crimes,' in Pat Carlen and Anne Worrall, eds., *Gender, Crime and Justice* (Philadelphia: Open University Press 1987), 81-94. Ruth Harris's excellent work will set the standard for historical studies of chivalric justice. See her 'Melodrama, Hysteria and Feminine Crimes of Passion in the Fin-de-siècle' *History Workshop Journal* 25 (spring 1988): 31–63.

13 Mary Hartman claims that women who were acquitted 'mesmerized' judges and jurors by manipulating popular stereotypes of female frailty. See Frances Heidensohn's critique of this argument in *Women and Crime* (London: Macmillan Education 1985), 108. For an anecdotal account of underclass British women who could not 'mesmerize' male law enforcers see Patrick Wilson, *Murderess: A Study of the Women Executed in Britain since 1843* (London: Joseph 1971). Sixty-eight women were hanged for murder in the period of Wilson's study.

14 The work of Douglas Hay on the image of justice has laid the ground-

work for this analysis. See especially his seminal article, 'Property, Authority and Criminal Law,' in Hay et al., eds., *Albion's Fatal Tree: Crime and Society in Eighteenth Century England* (London: Allan Lane 1975), 17–63.

15 The most comprehensive work has been written by Marc Girouard, *The Return to Camelot: Chivalry and the English Gentleman* (New Haven: Yale University Press 1981).

16 Recent work on masculinity in nineteenth- and early twentieth-century Europe and North America has begun to right the imbalance in the historiography of gender identities where only women were presented as gendered subjects. A Canadian example is Joy Parr, *The Gender of Breadwinners: Women, Men, and Change in Two Industrial Towns, 1880–1950* (Toronto: University of Toronto Press 1990).

17 For an exploration of working-class chivalry see Karen Dubinsky, ' "The Modern Chivalry": Women and the Knights of Labour in Ontario, 1880–91' (MA thesis, Carleton University, 1985). The labour organizers expressed their adherence to the chivalric ideal by choosing the honorary title of 'knights' to describe themselves.

18 The male, working-class defence of wage-earning women's honour was central to the assessment of the impact of industrialism in the *Report of the Royal Commission on the Relations of Labour and Capital* (Ottawa 1889). The pro-labour faction of the commission, for instance, contrasted female factory workers' heroic ability to resist the temptation of an 'easy life' to the number of adultery-related divorces among the upper classes.

19 Charlesworth, *Candid Chronicles*, 239

20 Testimony of Detective Reburn in Justice Boyd's bench book, 2 May 1895. Supreme Court of Ontario, Judges' Bench Books, Spring Assizes, 1895 (Criminal), 22 April–26 June 1895, Osgoode Hall

21 'The Case of Clara Ford,' in Wallace, *Murders and Mysteries*, 78

22 Archives of Ontario (AO), RG 22, series 392, box 270, Toronto (York) Supreme Court of Ontario, Criminal Assize Indictments, 1915

23 *World*, 8 Oct. 1894

24 Ibid., 13 Oct. 1894

25 Toronto *Empire*, 9 Oct. 1894

26 *World*, 9 Oct. 1894

27 Harris, 'Melodrama, Hysteria,' 44. For a comprehensive analysis of mel-

odrama and the Victorian mind see Peter Brooks, *The Melodramatic Imagination: Balzac, Henry James, Melodrama and the Mode of Excess* (New Haven: Yale University Press 1976).

28 Charlesworth, *Candid Chronicles*, 242

29 Toronto *Globe*, 24 Nov. 1894

30 *Empire*, 23 Nov. 1894

31 Ibid., 24 and 29 Nov. 1894

32 *World*, 22 Nov. 1894

33 Robin Winks, *The Blacks in Canada: A History* (Montreal: McGill-Queen's University Press 1971), 288–92. There is little secondary material on the history of blacks in Canada. Most of it is written in a liberal framework that highlights the advances of individual blacks and minimizes racism as a persistent problem. Winks is one of the few historians who has argued that racism was central to the emergence of (white, Anglo) Canadian nationalism, 292.

34 It was uncommon, but not unknown, for Canadian lawyers in the 1880s and 1890s to argue that their clients were not guilty of crimes because of 'moral insanity.' The defence in the Valentine Shortis case, tried only a few months before Ford's case went to trial, for example, demanded a psychiatric assessment of the accused murderer, who had had a history of irrational outbursts. Although the defence failed, Shortis was not executed, but was incarcerated for decades in psychiatric wings of penitentiaries and in asylums. See Martin Friedland, *The Case of Valentine Shortis: A True Story of Crime and Politics in Canada* (Toronto: University of Toronto Press 1986).

35 *Globe*, 22 Nov. 1894

36 *World*, 29 Nov. 1894

37 *Globe*, 9 Feb. 1915, and *World*, 9 Feb. 1915

38 Toronto *Telegram*, 9 Feb. 1915

39 Toronto *Star*, 11 Feb. 1915

40 Ibid., 9 and 11 Feb. 1915

41 *Telegram*, 22 Feb. 1915

42 *Globe*, 2 May 1895

43 Ibid., 1 and 4 May 1895

44 Toronto *Daily News*, 16 Feb. 1915

45 *Telgram*, 16 Feb. 1915

46 *Star*, 16 Feb. 1915

47 'Not Guilty,' in Hassard, *Not Guilty*, 7

48 The police had been tipped off about the possibility of Ford being Westwood's murderer by Gus Clarke, a pickpocket and thief. The woman who told the detectives about Ford's threats was Libby Black, a frequent prisoner in the Toronto jail, who had been arrested several times for drunk and disorderly behaviour.

49 This expression was apparently not restricted to genteel literature, as it was used by working-class women in a number of rape cases from Toronto in the period. An example is the rape trial of John Barnes in 1899. His twenty-year-old maid, Minnie Robson, claimed that four days after she started to work for him, he attacked her. The verbatim transcript reads as follows:

Q. [from crown attorney Mr Curry] What happened?
A. I was insulted.
Q. What did he say to you?
A. He didn't say anything to me. He dragged me up the stairs.

She proceeded to describe his having 'had connection' with her against her will. The defendant's lawyer, later the prosecuting attorney in the Davies case, successfully discredited the maid by asking why she did not leave if he had posed a threat. Barnes was acquitted. County Court Judge's Criminal Court, Indictments, AO, RG 22, 1899

50 Jacquelyn Dowd Hall has shown that black men accused of raping white women were lynched in the American South without the benefit of trials or, in many cases, evidence to link them to the crime. Black women raped by black or white men, in contrast, found it next to impossible to bring their attackers to trial. In both cases, racist assumptions of blacks as sexually savage supported notions of black men as beasts and black women as indiscriminately lustful. To be 'insulted,' then, was the privilege of respectable, white women, since only the 'honourable' could be 'insulted.' The fate of women who refused chivalric protection exposed 'the importance of the sexualy constrained [white] woman to the preservation of the mores of white supremacy.' Hall, *Revolt against Chivalry: Jessie Daniel Ames and the Women's Campaign against Lynching* (New York: Columbia University Press 1979), 153

51 *Globe*, 1 May 1895

52 *World*, 1 May 1895

53 *Globe*, 1 May 1895

54 Justice Boyd's bench book, 2 May 1895

55 *World*, 26 Nov. 1894

56 The venerable police magistrate, who heard both Ford's and Davies's confessions in police court, wrote extensively about the 'interesting and amusing' blacks who appeared before him in his forty-two years on the bench. In a chapter on 'The Negro Element' in *Recollections of a Police Magistrate*, he shared his opinion that blacks were 'a source of amusement in the court because of their many peculiarities' (39). Although he was, as a former cavalry officer who had fought for the South in the Civil War, possibly more open about his racist attitudes than other Torontonians, it is likely that most of his contemporaries identified blacks or people of mixed race with the ridiculous caricatures that minstrel artists of the period popularized.

57 Hassard gave Ford's court appearance rave reviews that sounded more like the overwrought praise of a threatre critic: 'Enthroned on her high stage, she commenced a battle for her life, the like of which has few parallels in history.' *Not Guilty*, 18

58 *World*, 4 May 1895

59 Court testimony of Clara Ford, quoted in Wallace, *Murders*, 86

60 Hassard, *Not Guilty*, 25. There was no reason for the public or the jurors to assume that these defendants would be spared the gallows simply on account of their sex. A woman was hanged for murder in 1873 and two more were executed in 1899. The last hanging of a woman in Canada did not take place until 1953. See Alan Hustak, *They Were Hanged* (Toronto: James Lorimer 1987), 49.

61 In fact, the jury had a number of alternatives in their decision and, at any rate, the judge and not the jury set the punishment. Most juries who convicted with reluctance usually rendered a guilty verdict with a 'strong recommendation for mercy.'

62 *Globe*, 6 May 1895

63 The *Globe*, 1 May 1895, reported that the jury consisted of two wagon makers, two farmers, two cobblers, one painter, one carpenter, one blacksmith, one weaver, one 'hardware,' and one tailor.

64 Ibid., 6 May 1985

65 Ibid.

66 Ibid.

67 AO, series A, box 1, MU6362, Toronto Local Council of Women, 'Minutes,' 17 Feb. 1915
68 *Daily News*, 16 Feb. 1915
69 *Telegram*, 20 Feb. 1915
70 Ibid.
71 *News*, 26 Feb. 1915
72 Ibid.
73 Ibid., 27 Feb. 1915
74 *Telegram*, 27 Feb. 1915
75 *Globe*, 1 March 1915
76 *Telegram*, 27 Feb. 1915. While it was more common during the First World War for patriotic propaganda to show women as caretakers or workers, a gun-wielding woman occasionally appeared in defence of the nation. An illustration in the Montreal *Daily Star* showed a sturdy, bourgeois matron holding a gun on whose barrel was the word 'Vote.' It suggested that the female franchise would be an effective weapon to win the war, since she pointed her gun at evil Turks and 'Huns' who lurked on the other side of her parlour window. William Werthman, ed., *Canada in Cartoon: A Pictorial History of the Confederation Years, 1867–1967* (Fredericton: Brunswick Press 1967), 72
77 Ibid.
78 AO, RG 4-32, Ontario, Attorney-General Central Registry Files, no. 327 (1915). Mulock was also likely to be vulnerable to Dewart's portrayal of the case as a wartime melodrama. A few days after the war broke out, Mulock was elected president of the York County Patriotic Fund, the city's primary fund-raising and morale-boosting organization. An auxiliary group, the Toronto Women's Patriotic League, contributed to the war by, among other charitable activities, recruiting unemployed women to be domestic servants. For a survey of the city's patriotic response to the war see Hubert Groves, *Toronto Does Her 'Bit'* (Toronto: Municipal Intelligence Bureau 1918), 39, 49.
79 Mulock's sentimental excesses in the Davies trial did not, apparently, characterize his usual attitude towards cases that involved charges of sexual assault. A prominent lawyer, John J. Robinette, recalled in 1975 an earlier encounter where he had appeared before Mulock to appeal a client's penitentiary sentence for an indecent assault: 'Sir William was most sympathetic to my client, treating such matters as sexual offenses

as the effervescence of youth, and the Court reduced the sentence sub-
stantially.' Robinette continued, presumably in a humorous vein, with a
contrasting story of Mulock's 'very hostile' attitude towards another of
his clients who was a chicken thief. Quoted in John D. Arnup, *Middle-
ton: The Beloved Judge* (Toronto: McClelland and Stewart 1988), 168
80 *Telegram*, 27 Feb. 1915
81 Ibid.
82 *Globe*, 1 March 1915
83 Detailed statisics are contained in Carolyn Strange, 'The Perils and
Pleasures of the City: Single Wage-Earning Women in Toronto,
1880–1930' (PhD thesis, Rutgers University 1991).
84 Feminists have argued that rape is the most under-reported crime
against the person because women feel that the attack will reflect badly
on their own reputation, expecially if the case comes to trial, or because
they doubt that their story will be believed. On rape in contemporary
Canada see Lorenne M.G. Clark and Debra J. Lewis, *Rape: The Price of
Coercive Sexuality* (Toronto: Women's Educational Press 1977).
85 Acquittal rates have varied in different jurisdictions, but it appears that
in countries with common-law legal foundations, as many as 80 per cent
of accused men have gone free. This was the case in mid eighteenth- to
mid nineteenth-century England, for instance. Douglas Hay, 'Prosecution and Power: Malicious Prosecution in the English Courts,
1750–1850,' in Hay and Francis Snyder, eds., *Policing and Prosecution in
Britain, 1750–1850* (Oxford: Clarendon Press 1989), 343–97, 377. In Ontario, the rate appears to have been about the same, ranging from 10 to
32 per cent between 1840 and 1892. Constance Backhouse, 'Nineteenth-
Century Canadian Rape Law, 1800–92,' in David Flaherty, ed., *Essays in
the History of Canadian Law*, vol. 2 (Toronto: Published for the Osgoode
Society by the University of Toronto Press 1983), 200–47, 222
86 A typical example of a woman who could not afford chivalric justice
was Elizabeth Workman, who was convicted in 1872 for the murder of
her drunken husband who had abused her for years. She was a washerwoman who could not afford to hire a lawyer. In the end she was represented by an inexperienced man who had only a few hours to prepare
her case. She was hanged on 19 June 1873. National Archives of Canada, Capital Case Files, RG 13, vol. 1410, no. 64A. The vast majority of
the 701 Canadians who have been executed since Confederation could

not afford adequate legal counsel. The poor are overrepresented among the hanged, but so are aboriginal Canadians, French Canadians, blacks, recent immigrants, and homosexuals. Hustack, *They Were Hanged*, xv. For an historical overview of murder and its sanctions in Canada see Neil Boyd, *The Last Dance: Murder in Canada* (Scarborough, Ontario: Prentice-Hall Canada 1988).

6 Class, Ethnicity, and Gender in the Eaton Strikes of 1912 and 1934

Ruth A. Frager

At a giant New Year's Eve party for the T. Eaton Company's Toronto employees in 1898, Timothy Eaton announced his hope that the word 'employees' would be 'done away with' by the end of the century. As Mr Eaton wished his 'fellow-associates' a happy New Year, 2475 of them were sitting down together for the celebratory dinner. The dinner tables occupied the Yonge, Queen, and James streets areas of the second floor of the famous Eaton store, and almost fifty thousand pieces of china and silverware were used to serve the meal. The tenor of this gala event, explained the Eaton public relations experts, 'was just the prevailing spirit of good will existing between the head of the business and his helpers.'[1]

But as the next century unfolded, certain 'fellow-associates' gave a sharply contrasting account of labour-management relations at the Eaton Company. 'Discrimination, intimidation and subjection to the worst prison-like system has been and is the predominant rule of this firm,' declared defiant cloakmakers in 1912 as they struggled to mobilize support for their strike at the company's Toronto garment factory.[2] Twenty-two years later, protests again mounted against the Eaton Company's 'tyrannic barbarism,' as another group of the firm's Toronto clothing workers went out on strike.[3]

The unfolding of these two strikes reflects much more than conflicting perceptions of workplace relations at this firm. In the history of the labour movement in Toronto's needle trades, these two strikes stand out, in particular, because of the activists' unusually far-reaching efforts to forge cross-class, cross-ethnic, and cross-gender alliances in their struggle against one of the most powerful Canadian corporations. In the battle against the T. Eaton Company, strike leaders laboured not only to unite the garment workers themselves but also to forge broader coalitions to support the strike. At both levels, they faced formidable difficulties, and even when they did succeed in hammering out temporary alliances, the alliances were fraught with ambivalence.

Women workers were centrally involved in both attacks on 'Fort Eaton,' and strike activists struggled to forge alliances between female and male garment workers as well as between Jewish and non-Jewish workers in this sector. During both disputes, the strike leaders laboured to garner support not only from the broader labour movement but also from middle-class women's organizations. The strikers hoped to win further support from members of the general public who objected to the big-business practices of the 'Eaton Octopus.' However, the class, ethnic, and gender biases of these groups sharply limited the activists' abilities to forge strong coalitions.[4]

In the present day, the manifest failure of narrow, workplace-centred versions of class politics has produced calls for coalitions with 'the new social movements.' As the Eaton strikes demonstrate, such coalitions are not unknown in Canadian labour history. The experience of these two strikes indicates that these kinds of alliances have been sources of both hope and frustration. Without the unusual alliances that developed, these strikes would never have generated such momentum. Yet the contradictions and tensions in the alliances that emerged during these strikes sound a cautionary note for those today who promote progressive coalitions. As the strikes unfolded, these contradictions and tensions were never adequately resolved. Based on the crisis of the moment, these alliances were a temporary coming together for strike-support work rather than the kind of enduring coalitions that could support a broad-based progressive political formation. The two strikes at Eaton's point to some of the dangers and the possibilities the left faces today.

The 1912 Strike

In mid-February 1912 more than one thousand workers from the T. Eaton Company's garment factory walked off the job over a dispute in one of the women's clothing departments. The International Ladies' Garment Workers' Union (ILGWU), a union for both females and males who made women's clothing, directed the strike. About a third of the strikers were women, and the ILGWU's head office sent two women organizers to Toronto to help lead the female strikers. The strike spread beyond the ILGWU to include members of a second union, the United Garment Workers, who worked in the men's clothing departments of the same factory. And it spread beyond Toronto: some workers at the Eaton clothing factory in Montreal also struck in sympathy with the Toronto workers, and Hamilton's garment workers threatened to join the strike if any of Hamilton's clothing firms attempted to do any work for the Eaton Company. The strikers were now locked in combat with one of the most powerful employers in the country.[5]

The causes of the strike are not difficult to find. Extremely low wages and harsh working conditions characterized the notorious garment industry in these years. Long hours, speedups, periodic unemployment, unsanitary conditions, and wage cuts plagued workers struggling to eke out a living in this sector. Women workers in particular were systematically confined to the lower-paid, supposedly less-skilled jobs. Although working conditions in the Eaton Company's garment factory were better than most in this arduous sector, the 1912 strike dramatically dispelled the idyllic image that was so carefully crafted by the Eaton family and their public relations experts.[6]

The Eaton clothing factory had been established in Toronto in 1890 and had expanded rapidly to supply the company's retail stores and mail-order business. By the end of the 1910s, the company boasted that its Toronto factories, which produced mainly clothing, 'cover over 19 acres, operate over 5,000 electric power machines and employ 6,411 workers.'[7] At the start of this decade, however, discontent among the Eaton garment workers was already mounting. At that time, the Eaton garment factory was probably the largest clothing factory in the country, and most of the firm's clothing workers were Jews. Although management's policy was one of 'instant dismissal' in response to 'any attempt on the part of an employee to so much as dare to protest,' the firm's Jewish workers had been cautiously organizing themselves through the International Ladies' Garment Workers' Union.[8]

The 1912 strike at the Eaton clothing factory stemmed not only from deep-seated discontent with low wages and long hours; it stemmed as well from the exploitation of child labour. The union charged: 'in this very Kingdom of the Eaton Company, frail children of fourteen years, in busy seasons, work from 8 a.m. to 9 p.m. ... in slack season, skilled working women, connected with the firm for six, eight or more years, can earn only Five, Four or even less Dollars per week; [and] girls are forced at times to take "homework" to do at night, after the long day in the factory.' The strikers also objected to 'Graft for Foremen,' protesting that 'foremen and forewomen have power to discriminate most flagrantly in favour of their friends, or vice versa, and may cut wages, ruinously, by intention, or from careless distribution of piece work.' 'Insults to Girls' (sexual harassment) was another complaint against the Eaton Company. Hence the striking garment workers strove to teach 'Mr. John C. Eaton, "King of Canada" as he is generally called ... the A.B.C.'s of Industrial Democracy.'[9]

Management had triggered the strike when it ordered sixty-five male sewing-machine operators to sew in the linings of women's coats on their machines. The men refused. Although this was not a union shop, all of these men were members of the ILGWU. They had been making 65 cents per garment without sewing in the linings, and management was now insisting they do the extra work without any increase in pay. Previously, female workers known as finishers had sewn the linings in by hand. The employer's new directive amounted to more than a pay cut for the men: these women were going to lose their jobs. In protest, the sixty-five male operators sat down at their machines and refused to do any work. After several days, the Eaton administration fired them and physically threw them out onto the street. At that point, more than one thousand of their fellow workers walked out to support them.[10]

This strike provides a rare example of male support for goals that concentrated on women workers' interests. Although women and men often went out on strike together in Toronto's needle trades, particularly for across-the-board wage increases, it was unusual for strike demands to focus specifically on women's issues, partly because the men were regarded as the primary breadwinners for their families while the women were usually regarded as less important, temporary workers. The male-centred nature of the labour movement in the garment industry, as elsewhere, stemmed from deeply held patriarchal values.[11]

Yet, in this case, key supporters of the Eaton strike emphasized the men's solidarity with the women workers. The Toronto Trades and Labour Council, for example, stressed this aspect when it passed a resolution objecting to the firm's locking out workers for refusing 'in the interests of their sister workers, to do work which did not belong to them.'[12] This solidarity between women and men became one of the main themes of the strike. 'Remember,' Joe Salsberg (a Jewish immigrant who became a prominent left-wing labour activist), said in an interview in the 1980s, 'the Jewish tailors in Toronto went on their first big strike in defense of *undzere shvester* – our sisters.' He continued: 'The reasoning of the men who worked at Eaton's was a simple one: that these [women workers] will lost their jobs, and ... maybe they felt they didn't want to do these jobs that the women are now doing, maybe their wages will come down [if the men were to sew in the linings by machine] because the rates fixed for those operations were always traditionally lower because women did [those operations]. I never rule out the element of selfishness and self-interest – which is also human.' Salsberg stressed that one of the strike slogans 'became the folksy expression of simple, honest working men ... in Yiddish particularly: "*Mir vellen nisht aroycenemen dem bissle fun broyt fun di mayler fun undzere shvester*" [We will not take the morsel of bread from the mouths of our sisters].'[13]

Since the new production system clearly threatened to reduce men's earnings as well as deprive women of jobs, male self-interest and female self-interest coincided, fostering a notable alliance between the sexes. The ILGWU's newspaper stressed the men's solidarity with the women, portraying the men's action as more than a simple matter of self-interest. According to this newspaper, union officials believed in the early stages of the strike that 'management would have increased the price of operating [on] the garment, but the operators, with admirable solidarity, insist that the finishers shall not be deprived of their share of the work.'[14] Yet in the absence of a clear offer of extra pay for the men for doing the extra work, this was never put to the test. Indeed, given the company's obstinate refusal to negotiate as the strike dragged through the first two months, such an offer was highly unlikely.

Moreover, while the men's refusal to do 'women's work' supported their female co-workers, male reluctance may have stemmed partly from a sense that this work was beneath them. The men probably viewed the extra work not only as unremunerative but also as less skilled. The male strikers were, in effect, taking a stand to maintain the gender division of labour on the shop floor. This system of labour-market segmentation privileged the men themselves.

Female and male Jews from the Eaton garment factory remained united against the company, but their solidarity was not matched by the firm's non-Jewish clothing workers. The Jewish nature of the strike was, in fact, a central issue. As the ILGWU's newspaper explained: 'Those affected [by the dispute at the Eaton Company] are almost entirely Jewish: and the chief slogan by which it was hoped to cut off public sympathy was the report ... that this is "only a strike of Jews." The appeal to race and creed prejudice has succeeded, too, in so far as it has prevented the Gentile Cloak Makers from joining in the sympathetic strike.'[15] In order to weaken the strike further, management supplemented the local non-Jewish strikebreakers by bringing over 'a large shipment of English girls from England' to take the places of the defiant Jewish workers.[16]

The unwillingness of the Eaton Company's non-Jewish workers to join the strike was part of a wider pattern of tension between Jews and non-Jews in Toronto's garment industry. Although union activists in this sector were sometimes able to overcome the divisions between these two groups, there were other cases, as well, where non-Jewish clothing workers refused to join their Jewish co-workers' strikes. Particularly in strike situations, the garment manufacturers capitalized on anti-Semitism by pitting non-Jewish workers against Jewish workers.[17]

The labour movement in Toronto's needle trades was deeply rooted in the working-class immigrant Jewish community. Fleeing the virulent anti-Semitism and intense poverty of the Old World, East European Jews had begun to arrive in Toronto as the nineteenth century drew to a close. By 1911 there were almost 18,000 Jews in what was then a predominantly Anglo-Celtic city, and the number of Jews grew rapidly, amounting to over 45,000 by 1931. They congregated in the garment industry, partly because New World anti-Semitism sharply restricted the jobs that were open to them. While a significant number of these Jews had been radicalized by severe conditions in the Old World, others were radicalized on this side of the ocean by the hardships of immigrant life in Toronto, particularly as they toiled in the needle trades sweatshops on Spadina Avenue. They forged a dynamic Jewish labour movement that was dedicated not only to winning concrete improvements on the shop floor but also, in the words of the Yiddish version of 'The Internationale,' to fighting for a new 'Garden of Eden of freedom and equality.'[18]

The 1912 Eaton strikers received wide support within this immigrant Jewish community. The Associated Hebrew Charities provided food for the strikers, the Jewish mutual benefit societies donated funds, as did the Workmen's Circle (the socialist Jewish fraternal association), and the local Jewish women's organizations took up street collections for the strikers until city officials stopped them.[19] When the assault on Fort Eaton was reinforced by the call for a nation-wide boycott of the company's goods, many 'Jewish patrons of Eaton's ... transferred their custom to the Robert Simpson Co.' Reporting that 'the Jewish trade was no mean factor in the Eaton business,' strike supporters hoped that this switch would help wrest concessions from management.[20] The force of the boycott within Toronto's immigrant Jewish community depended on the support of Jewish women in particular, for they were the ones who were primarily responsible for the family shopping. Here, women's role as consumer was used strategically to support the struggles of producers of both sexes.[21]

Yet because of certain class divisions and ethnic subdivisions among Jews in this period, the city's entire Jewish community did not unite wholeheartedly behind the strikers. In addition to the East European Jewish immigrants, there was in Toronto an older community of more assimilated middle-class Jews who had come to Canada from England in the nineteenth century.[22] When the strike broke out, Rabbi Solomon Jacobs, who represented the interests of the more established Jewish community of English origin, tried to mediate. Together with Mayor George Geary and Magistrate Jacob Cohen, the rabbi sought to arrange a conference between both sides.[23] While the unionists apparently hoped that Jacobs would succeed in bringing management to the bargaining table, they must have remained suspicious of the rabbi himself. In fact, Rabbi Jacobs was already notorious for the 'ugly role' he had played during a strike of Toronto cloakmakers in 1910, 'with his sermons that Jews must not rebel and that this is a disgrace in the eyes of the Gentiles.'[24]

Despite the rabbi's efforts to play a more conciliatory role in the Eaton dispute to help work out a settlement, the Eaton Company refused to make concessions. When the rabbi's attempts to mediate the dispute failed, he and Cohen tried to persuade the strikers to repudiate certain negative statements about the company anyway, and the two of them issued a statement in which they 'assured [the strikers] that they could rely on the generosity and consideration of the firm and that they could expect nothing but fair and just treatment.'[25] The strikers had a different opinion of management's commitment to justice. Divisions within the Jewish community were heightened by the fact that Sigmund Lubelsky, an important member of Rabbi Jacobs's congregation, was a senior manager of the Eaton factory and a chief opponent of the strikers.[26] The strikers' source of strength was thus within the East European Jewish immigrant community itself, in contrast to the more established Jewish community Rabbi Jacobs represented.

Defiant Jewish strikers also sought support from the broader labour movement. They presented their case to the Toronto Trades and Labour Council, the city's central labour organization, which then raised money for the strike fund and promoted a national boycott of the Eaton Company. The Ontario labour press also took up the cause, warning its readers not to 'go after cheap Eaton bargains' because 'bargains at the expense of manhood, womanhood and childhood are expensive in the extreme.'[27] The *Industrial Banner*, a key labour newspaper, declared that the country's entire trade-union movement supported the strikers and that thousands of Eaton's mail-order catalogues had been sent back to the firm in protest. In the meantime, the 'stars' of the labour movement addressed a protest meeting of 4000 people at Toronto's Massey Hall, and the Toronto Trades and Labour Council led a massive strike parade through the streets of the city.[28]

Yet many of the strike supporters themselves were anti-Semitic: to the extent that they supported the Eaton strike, they did so despite the Jewishness of the strikers. Indeed, part of the appeal for public support raised a distinctly anti-immigrant note. This occurred in the context of reports that publicized the injustices perpetrated by the Eaton Company and stated that 'the boasted sanitary conditions leave much to be desired in the way of suitable wash-rooms, lockers for wraps, etc.' Allegedly, the lack of proper lockers was especially troublesome because 'wraps from all sorts and conditions of homes are to-day hanging packed together [in the Eaton factory] so that vermin and disease from the miserable homes of foreign immigrants are passed on to the clothing of the most delicate daughter of refined parents.' Appearing in such newspapers as *The Lance* (a Toronto labour paper) and *The Western Clarion* (the paper of the Socialist Party of Canada), this message thus used a nativist appeal to foster class opposition to Eaton's. Ironically, such nativism might instead have led people to question why they should support the unpalatable immigrants in the first place.[29]

While supporting the strikers, *The Lance* reported that recent pro-strike publicity 'did not keep the wives and daughters of Toronto labor men from going to the big [Eaton] store, and more's the pity.' 'Because a lot of foreigners, who may be good in their own way, call a strike,' explained this newspaper, 'it does not follow that Canadians are going to fall over themselves in getting into line.' The newspaper then veered in a more nativist direction, proclaiming that 'it is difficult ... to make the average Anglo-Saxon fall down and worship the far-eastern agitator.' 'The foreign agitator,' the paper warned, 'has few friends in Canadian labour circles.'[30] Thus, although this 'strike of Jews' did manage to obtain some significant support from the broader labour movement, the support was limited for nativist reasons. Such working-class nativism stemmed not only from prejudice but also from the ways in which the state and the employers used immigration to dampen wages by flooding the labour market with 'greenhorns' who were desperate for work.

Strike supporters also appealed for help from women's groups in particular. The Toronto Trades and Labour Council asked 'Women's Clubs [and] Suffrage Associations ... to defend the rights of the [Eaton] workers,' and the ILGWU's newspaper optimistically reported that 'Women's Lodges and Women's Auxiliaries of men's trade unions, and associations of leisure class women' promised to support the strike.[31]

The head office of the International Ladies' Garment Workers' Union sent Gertrude Barnum, an organizer, to Toronto to rally the female strikers and to recruit support from women's organizations. The daughter of a prominent American judge, Barnum was leading member of the National Women's Trade Union League, an American organization consisting of a cross-class alliance of women dedicated to improving the lot of female workers. As well as 'making a special effort to bring the Jew and Gentile workers closer together,' Barnum especially worked to promote the boycott of the T. Eaton Company.[32] At a mass meeting in support of the strikers, she urged the unionists 'to seek the cooperation of the women.' 'If employers would not treat their employees fairly,' she declared, 'women would retaliate by refusing to purchase goods from the unfair employer.' In Toronto, Barnum sought to persuade members of women's groups to do just that, explaining the Eaton strike to meetings of women.[33]

In particular, Barnum 'attended [a meeting of] the Equal Franchise League, which was subsequently turned into a gathering of interested consumers.' Here, she stressed 'the part women must play in the real life of the world by means of her industrial ballot, less talked of than the municipal franchise but more powerful to redress wrongs.' 'Every time you make a purchase,' she explained, 'you cast a vote for the conditions under which the article bought has been manufactured.' She then went on to describe the effectiveness of a boycott of certain Cleveland garment factories, which forced the firms to make important concessions to the ILGWU.[34]

Nevertheless, according to Alice Chown, a local women's rights activist, 'leisure class women' were not always persuaded. In a thinly disguised account of Barnum's meeting with the Equal Franchise League, Chown recalled that the audience was not sympathetic to the strikers: 'During the [Eaton] strike I had to preside at a meeting of the Woman's Political League. I asked [the woman], who had been sent from New York to conduct the strike, to speak to our association. She made a very wise and illuminating speech. I did not expect an audience who had never considered that justice to working people was a higher virtue than charity, to respond any more cordially than it did.' As Chown explained, many of the women suffragists were especially unwilling to support the female strikers because they feared that 'their pet cause would be hurt through being linked with an unpopular one.'[35]

Chown stressed the difficulties she experienced when she tried to persuade middle-class women's groups to support the Eaton strikers: 'I tried to interest the various women's clubs, but I was amazed because they had no sympathy with the strikers, unless I had some tale of hardship to tell. The common, everyday longings for better conditions, for a life that would provide more than food, clothes and shelter, were not recognized as justifying a strike. I had to tell over and over the old, old story of the bosses who favored the girls whom they could take out evenings, girls who had to sell themselves as well as their labor to get sufficient work to earn a living.'[36] In this period, women's organizations were often immersed in the Social Purity Movement and hence especially concerned about sexual exploitation and sexual improprieties. They sought not only to end the 'white slave trade' (the forcing of women into prostitution) but also to regulate sexual behaviour rigidly so as to eradicate all 'improper' activities (such as 'lewd' dances and premarital sex). Club women thus responded to the portrayal of female workers as sexual victims, but they were far less interested in other hazards faced by women workers. The image of the downtrodden female sexual victim appealed deeply to them; the image of the assertive female striker, fighting for higher wages and better working conditions, did not.[37]

Chown was, however, able to gather together a small group of women to try to raise money for the 'displaced working girls.' Together with another member of the Equal Franchise League, several women from the University of Toronto, and one woman from the local branch of the National Council of Women of Canada (an influential federation of women's groups), Chown formed a committee 'to solicit funds and to interest the public in the protection of the women and the families of the [Eaton] strikers.' In addition to exhorting the public to use its purchasing power 'to obtain just conditions,' Chown thus called upon those who 'are keen to help forward the cause of arbitration and justice for working girls' to send donations to the committee. 'These women [at the Eaton Company] struck for a principle,' explained Chown, '[and] they believe they are suffering for a great cause.' 'Are they to be the only heroines in this strike, or will every woman stand by them and refuse to see them starved into the street?' she inquired.[38]

Chown's appeal was not notably successful. The ILGWU's newspaper, which had earlier hoped that middle-class women's groups would contribute significantly to the cause, made no mention of women's groups when it reported on the various organizations that had donated money to the strike fund. Issued half a year after the strike began, this report indicated that most of the money had been raised within the ILGWU itself. Additional contributions had come from other immigrant Jewish organizations and from the Toronto labour movement.[39]

The unpopularity of the strikers' cause in Chown's circles no doubt stemmed, in part, from the fact that the vast majority of the Eaton strikers were Jews. Nativism precluded stronger support not only from within the labour movement (where certain activists strove to overcome prejudice in the interests of class solidarity) but also from middle-class women's organizations. English Canadians were often intensely ethnocentric and suspicious of foreigners in this period, and Jews often bore the brunt of this prejudice. Even Chown herself felt that Jews were 'egotistical' and 'aggressive' and exhibited 'extreme emotionalism.' She added, though, that the Jews' 'great *atoning* qualities are their wonderful vitality, their keen sense of life, and their excessive feeling.' Many other Anglo-Celtic Canadians were far less generous in their assessments.[40]

In these years, the Canadian women's movement, like many other facets of Canadian society, was steeped in nativism. Organizations such as the main women's suffrage societies, the Woman's Christian Temperance Union, and the Young Women's Christian Association sought to uphold values that were, as many of their names suggest, explicitly Christian. In this context, first-wave feminists sometimes viewed Jews as a threat. The newspaper of the Woman's Christian Temperance Union, for example, even went so far as to reprint anti-Jewish material from Henry Ford's viciously anti-Semitic *Dearborn Independent*. More common was the standard suffrage argument that it was unfair for the 'ignorant' male 'foreigner' to have the vote when 'decent' Anglo-Saxon women did not. In this context, the members of the main women's organizations were hardly predisposed to make common cause with Jewish strikers.[41]

To offset the grave problem of nativism, the strike activists also hoped to capitalize on deep-seated public opposition to department stores in order to recruit extensive support. As Cynthia Wright's article in this volume indicates, there was an intense current of hostility to the department store in these years, stemming from the sense that department stores used 'unfair competition' to threaten local retailers and shamelessly manipulated the buying public.[42] The strike leaders hoped to move beyond the usual appeal for working-class solidarity and even beyond the unusual appeal for cross-class women's solidarity to create an even broader alliance against the Eaton Company. The ILGWU's newspaper trumpeted a 'stupendous scheme for uniting all the powers of democracy in a mighty struggle against the policy of this potentate [John C. Eaton].' 'From here, there and everywhere,' proclaimed the paper, 'are springing up men who have suffered at one time or another from the domination of this One-man-trust. [There are] not only members of all trade unions which the T. Eaton Company has endeavored to crush, but besides there are the shopkeepers he has undersold, druggists he has undercut, whole towns and cities he has manipulated.' 'All welcome the present opportunity to recoup themselves' by supporting the strikers, declared the newspaper.[43]

Although overly optimistic, the strikers did attract significant support precisely because their target was the Eaton Company rather than an ordinary garment manufacturer. Vigorous hostility to the Eaton Octopus thus brought the strikers aid from those who would not otherwise have supported 'a strike of Jews.' For example, the nativist *Jack Canuck*, a populist Toronto newspaper, missed no opportunity to criticize Eaton's and praised the strikers for tackling this villainous enterprise. While declaring, in another context, that 'a dirty Jew is about the dirtiest specimen of humanity in the world,' the editors promoted the cause of the Jewish strikers in article after article. They even set up a special 'Jack Canuck Strike Fund' to help the striking Eaton workers.[44]

Jack Canuck portrayed the T. Eaton Company as the 'bitter enemy' not only of the underpaid cloakmakers but also of the 'organized working class' as a whole, stressing a wide range of John C. Eaton's anti-labour activities.[45] One article scathingly declared that the head of the firm 'gives immense amounts of money to hospitals and other institutions to take care of the sick and indigent, and apparently tries very hard to keep these institutions supplied with patients by overworking and underpaying his employees.'[46] In addition, the newspaper repeatedly stressed that the company's employment policies led to 'the social evil.' While 'Jack Eaton is living in luxury,' explained the editors, 'the starvation wages he pays his employees [are] forcing hundreds of young women into lives of prostitution in order to obtain a bare living for themselves.'[47] The newspaper's sharp condemnation of the company was augmented by a letter to the editor, which argued that Eaton's was 'one of the public's worst enemies' because this 'trust store' was 'in a position to dictate to the manufacturers the price they are to receive for their goods, and [to dictate to] the sales clerks how much they are to receive for selling them.'[48]

Despite the strikers' best efforts to popularize their cause, however, public support was limited. When Gertrude Barnum and leaders of the local labour movement led a largely female strike parade through the streets of the city, for example, some of the bystanders scoffed while others cheered at the 2000 marchers.[49] Many who did not share *Jack Canuck*'s ferocious antipathy to the T. Eaton Company may have felt hostile to strikes in general. Such was the case, for example, with T.L. Wilkinson, a citizen who wrote an open letter to the Toronto Trades and Labour Council in response to receiving an appeal to support the Eaton strikers. Wilkinson declared that despite his sympathy for working people, he had 'very little sympathy' for strikes because he did not feel that 'strikes are in accord with the divine method of settling disputes.' Strikes 'seem to be in direct contravention of the golden rule,' he maintained. Wilkinson also disapproved of the boycott of Eaton's, arguing that it amounted to asking the public to endorse the strikers' 'mistaken and unchristian course.'[50]

Largely because of the weaknesses in the alliances across class, ethnic, and gender lines, the opposition proved to be no match for the powerful, intransigent employer. The adamantly anti-union John C. Eaton had the resources to recruit strikebreakers all the way from Britain and to weather any temporary drop in sales brought about by the boycott.[51] Despite the formidable solidarity between female and male workers and despite the vigorous support of the immigrant Jewish community, the 'King of Canada' prevailed. Although the Toronto Trades and Labour Council provided considerable aid, the workers were forced to admit defeat after four months. The effect on the workers, especially the Jewish workers, was devastating. The ILGWU was seriously weakened, and 'for a long time' after this strike, a union official recalled, 'the T. Eaton Company would not hire any Jews.'[52] The company, in contrast, recovered so quickly from the strike that the administration made plans to erect a whole new factory building shortly after the dispute ended.[53]

Without the unusual solidarity between female and male Jewish workers and without the mobilization of consumers to boycott the Eaton Company, the strike would never have developed the powerful momentum it did. If the solidarity between the sexes had been matched by greater solidarity between producers and consumers and had been further supported by real solidarity between Jewish and non-Jewish workers, the 'King of Canada' would indeed have received 'the surprise of his life.' If, in addition, middle-class women's groups had vigorously supported the Jewish women strikers, 'Mr. Humpty Dumpty Eaton' might have had a great fall.[54] Instead, class, ethnic, and gender biases undermined the possibilities for forging strong coalitions. Even where activists succeeded in forming innovative alliances, the alliances were fraught with ambivalence, as was particularly apparent in the pages of the nativist *Jack Canuck*. The mobilization in support of the strike was not sufficient to turn around the legacy of these divisions.

The 1934 Strike

In mid July 1934, thirty-eight female dressmakers, members of the ILGWU, stopped work because the T. Eaton Company refused to grant an increase in the very low piece rates for certain dresses. Piece rates in this department were so low that no more than 64 per cent of the female employees were able to earn the legal minimum wage. The thirty-eight women dissidents left the factory to consult with their union officials, but when they attempted to return to work the next day, they found themselves locked out. They replied by declaring themselves officially on strike.[55]

The 1912 defeat shaped this unfolding of events. In the period following the 1912 strike, the garment unions had been unable to make much headway at this factory. The ILGWU had continued its efforts to organize Toronto's clothing workers, but found organizing Eaton's particularly difficult. In 1917, for example, Toronto's ILGWU had been carrying out an ambitious organizing campaign when some of the employers, including the Eaton Company, responded with concessions to keep the workers away from the union. Eaton's reduced the work week, increased wages, and instructed its supervisors to be more polite. According to the ILGWU's newspaper, 'these concessions, instead of keeping the Jewish workers away from joining the union, enthused them all the more, but [the concessions] influenced a certain number of the gentile women workers in the trade, mainly in the T. Eaton shops.'[56]

By the onset of the Great Depression, the ILGWU had still not succeeded in organizing the Eaton garment factory, and the Depression itself made difficult working conditions far worse, not only in this plant but throughout the needle trades. As the dramatic decrease in the purchasing power of the general public sharply reduced the demand for clothing, the garment workers suffered dramatic levels of unemployment and underemployment. At the same time, clothing manufacturers strove to slash their costs of production by instituting wage cut after wage cut and by speeding up workers on the job.[57]

Like many other employers in the needle trades in this period, the Eaton Company cut costs through numerous violations of the Minimum Wage Act. While the act stipulated that women workers in Toronto's needle trades should have been earning a minimum of $12.50 per week, the firm developed underhanded techniques for cheating its female workers out of this 'minimum.'[58] These management ploys were made easier by the fact that the Ontario Minimum Wage Board had too few inspectors to enforce the act, and the penalties for evasions of the act were so light they invited violations.[59] Moreover, Ontario's deputy minister of labour privately admitted reluctance, as well as inability, to enforce the legislation stringently, on the grounds that to do so would be too harsh towards the employers who were struggling in the midst of the Depression.[60]

Devastating and sometimes illegal wage cuts at Eaton's clothing factory went hand-in-hand with speedups so severe that one of the firm's female garment workers reported: 'I would go home nights and I would be so tired I could not eat my supper ... And I would be so tired and stiff going home on the street car, I would just dread getting a seat, because if I sat down, I could not get up again, my knees and my legs would be so stiff.'[61] One of her co-workers had had to be away from work for two months on account of 'nervous exhaustion.' Another co-worker, who had broken down several times and had had to go to hospital, explained: 'Well, you had to work so hard, you were driven so fast ... you were a nervous wreck.'[62] As 'a gray-haired veteran of 18 years in the Eaton factory' revealed, the speedup was so intense that 'you could not look up, take a glass of water or powder your nose.'[63] Another woman reported they were not even allowed to talk while sitting at their sewing machines.[64] In contrast, the youthful John David Eaton experienced the Depression decade as 'a good time for everybody,' for 'you could take your girl to a supper dance at the hotel for $10, and that included the bottle and a room for you and your friends to drink it in.'[65]

While the young Eaton heir was drinking and dancing, those in charge of the firm found themselves facing escalating public opposition to department stores. Although hostility to these stores had existed for years, the Depression itself sharply intensified this opposition. The cry of 'unfair competition' grew louder in the midst of the 'Dirty Thirties,' as so many small businesses went under and consumers found they could no longer afford many items. The T. Eaton Company was at the very centre of this controversy, for, by this time, the company was huge, encompassing not only the retail stores and garment factories in different cities but also such components as a stove factory, drug company, life-insurance company, and realty company. The antipathy towards the Eaton Octopus, which had been a significant feature of the 1912 strike, was to become an even more important feature of the 1934 strike.

H.H. Stevens, minister of trade and commerce until his resignation from R.B. Bennett's cabinet, played a key role in unmasking the practices of the department stores and rallying public opinion against them. As head of the Royal Commission on Price Spreads and Mass Buying, Stevens initiated intensive hearings in 1934 to investigate the divergence between production costs and selling prices. In this context, the commission scrutinized many aspects of the Eaton Company, vilifying the firm for such practices as using loss leaders to out-compete small retailers, using bulk orders to chisel down manufacturers' prices, and muzzling the press through heavy advertising. The investigation exposed the company's policies regarding a whole series of retail products, ranging from jams to tires and from canned milk to furniture. The commission particularly examined both the manufacturing and the retailing of clothing by the T. Eaton Company. Although the managers of Eaton's clothing factory tried to justify their policies by stressing that the factory had lost hundreds of thousands of dollars in the early 1930s, diligent questioning by the Stevens Commission elicited the information that the firm as a whole had averaged $3 million worth of profits annually for the past ten years.[66]

This ongoing exposé played a key role in arousing interest in the union. As Sam Kraisman, a Jewish ILGWU leader in Toronto, explained to the union's head office in New York in March 1934, the commission's investigation 'has brought out some startling evidence of the evils in the needle trades which has shocked the entire country and has been the means of creating great dissatisfaction amongst the workers. The investigation is primarily aimed against the mass buying powers of the larger department stores, particularly the T. Eaton [Company.] [This company] is attacked all along the line by those who appear before the [Commission] and the firm is on the defensive. The girls of [one of Eaton's dress-making] department[s] seem to know that, and they are ready to take advantage of the situation to make a grand onslaught on the firm for better wages.'[67] Some of the firm's female dressmakers joined the ILGWU at that time and actually won a wage hike and some other improvements. Their small victory was, no doubt, partly due to management's concern about all the negative publicity.[68]

Stevens himself increased the pressure on employers in the garment sector not only through the commission's hearings but also by speaking out against sweatshop conditions on other occasions. In June of the same year, for example, he addressed a large audience at Trinity Church in Toronto, stressing female clothing workers' low pay. The audience applauded enthusiastically when Stevens declared: 'I wonder what would happen in this City of Toronto if tomorrow morning all earnest and honest church women would cease buying the products of sweatshops!' He then condemned unscrupulous employers as un-Christian: 'Let me modernize the doctrine of the scriptures and say, if under our economic system powerful business concerns so operate their business that women and girls are forced to work under conditions that ought to shame any self-respecting people, then those operating such businesses come under the scathing condemnation of the Man of Nazareth.'[69] The garment workers themselves could read about this speech in at least four Toronto newspapers, and some were emboldened by it.

The strike broke out the next month, when the thirty-eight women walked off the job. This time, unlike in 1912, the strike did not spread to other clothing workers at the Eaton factory, despite the fact that a significant number of Eaton's cloakmakers had joined the ILGWU in early 1934. Whereas the 1912 strike had witnessed strong solidarity between female and male workers, in this case the thirty-eight women were out on their own. In contrast to the fact that the 1912 strikers were mainly Jews, the 1934 strikers were all non-Jews. One of the legacies of the 1912 defeat was that the Eaton factory still had not hired many Jews.[70]

These non-Jewish women had taken the bold step of joining the union despite the anti-Semitic appeals from the Eaton Company's management. As several of these women eventually informed the royal commission, their initial interest in the union had prompted management to 'bring in [the] racial question, about the Jewish people, telling us we should not belong to the union at all that was controlled by Jews.' According to this account, management told these female workers that the women were 'out of [their] class' because, in seeking the help of ILGWU officials, 'they were mixing with people on Spadina.'[71]

Over the years, deep strains between Jewish workers and non-Jewish workers in Toronto's needle trades had continued to plague those activists who promoted class solidarity in opposition to the bosses. Since the early days of the 1912 Eaton strike, clothing manufacturers had continued to manipulate these tensions to their own advantage. The heightened anti-Semitism of the depression decade, together with intense ethnocentrism, facilitated the bosses' machinations. The intensity of 'the Jew/Gentile problem' had become starkly evident during the large strike of Toronto fur workers in 1932, for example, when hundreds of Jewish fur workers went out on strike and their non-Jewish co-workers refused to join them.[72]

When the non-Jewish female dressmakers overcame Eaton's blatant attempt to 'divide and conquer' and signed up with the ILGWU, they received limited support from the union. Although the ILGWU eventually took the important step of hiring Jean Laing, a member of the Co-operative Commonwealth Federation (CCF), to organize the Eaton garment factory, the union's response was basically reluctant. This is apparent, for example, in Sam Kraisman's letters to the ILGWU's head office. When the women initially joined the ILGWU, Kraisman, the local union official, reported that 'we did not seek this trouble, but they came to us and we could not turn them away.' He feared that developments were proceeding 'to a point whereby these girls may any day walkout to enforce their demands.' 'How far shall we go into the matter?' he asked hesitantly.[73]

When the strike actually broke out several months later, Kraisman was not optimistic. In a letter to headquarters in which he described the lockout of the 'gentile girls,' he explained that 'what we feared finally happened.' 'We had all along gone very slowly and carefully to avoid getting into difficulties,' he indicated, 'but a dispute arose between the girls and the manager of the department over a price and they were thrown out.' Kraisman stressed his efforts to lobby the Ontario minister of labour to persuade the Eaton Company to reinstate the locked-out women, but the company would not budge. 'The girls,' Kraisman reported, were 'actively picketing the factory and the entire Eaton's district,' but 'it is quite apparent that the picketing will get them no where.' He clearly felt that the union had to do something to support the female strikers, even though he judged it a lost cause, and he inquired about the possibility of getting them jobs in union shops in other locales.[74]

Kraisman's assessment rested on the judgment that the union was too weak at the Eaton Company, and too weak among the Toronto dressmakers as well, to be able to help the strikers very much. Indeed, the thirty-eight strikers were in a vulnerable position, not least because more than one hundred and fifty of the other women who worked in the same dressmaking department had not joined the strike. More broadly, the earlier defeat at Eaton's garment factory probably made the union reluctant to risk committing scarce resources to fighting such a powerful company, especially in the midst of the Depression when there were so many unemployed clothing workers who were potential strikebreakers.[75]

Furthermore, the union's main resources were already committed elsewhere: the ILGWU was in the midst of a major organizing campaign in the city's cloak trade, and, one week after the Eaton strike had begun, hundreds of cloakmakers went out on a week-long strike. In addition, the Toronto cloakmakers found themselves embroiled in another major strike at this very time. This lengthy strike, which began a mere day after the Eaton strike, was of particular strategic importance to the union. Kraisman's attention was concentrated on these battles rather than on the thirty-eight Eaton strikers.[76]

The Jewish union leader's reluctance to provide more assistance to the Eaton strikers was perhaps also related to the fact that the strikers were non-Jews and women. The male Jews who led the ILGWU in these years commonly focused on organizing workers like themselves, not only because these were the people with whom they most identified but also because they viewed the others as less militant. By the mid 1930s, the fact that non-Jewish garment workers had sometimes refused to join Jewish strikers had led to the feeling that the former were generally not the best union material. Thus, in an ironic turnabout, the non-Jewish workers' lack of support for the Jewish strikers in 1912 led to the Jewish unionists' ambivalence towards the non-Jewish strikers in 1934. The ILGWU's history of difficulties in organizing non-Jewish women in particular probably contributed to Kraisman's unwillingness to back the thirty-eight strikers aggressively.[77]

In contrast to 1912, the Jewish labour movement was racked by factionalism in these years. Intense fights between Jewish Communists and anti-Communist Jewish socialists shook the very foundations of the garment unions, particularly in the period from 1928 to 1935 when the Communist Party of Canada officially maintained a dual-union policy. In 1928 the Sixth World Congress of the Communist International had instructed Communist parties worldwide to switch to organizing new radical unions, on the basis of the belief that humanity was entering a new revolutionary phase. This intensely sectarian policy meant that the Canadian Communists in the garment industry broke away to form their own union, the Industrial Union of Needle Trades Workers (IUNTW), which was designed to compete aggressively with the other clothing unions. Although the IUNTW was relatively ineffective in the Toronto cloak trade, it had captured most of the dressmakers in particular by 1934, making it difficult for the ILGWU to make any headway in the Toronto dress trade. The civil war within the Jewish labour movement seriously weakened the ILGWU and, more broadly, undermined the workers' ability to unite against the bosses. Although the ILGWU still engaged in certain battles against the cloak bosses, Kraisman's reluctance to mount an all-out offensive to defend the striking Eaton dressmakers was, no doubt, partly a product of this state of affairs.[78]

In fact, the Communist leaders of the IUNTW tried to persuade the Eaton strikers to join them and to repudiate the ILGWU. The Communist press announced it had warned the strikers of the devious nature of the ILGWU leaders. 'The members of [the IUNTW],' the Communist newspaper concluded, 'must bend might and main, through personal contact with the strikers ... to defeat the strike breaking, splitting tactics of Mrs. Laing.'[79] These pronouncements were part of a broader pattern whereby the Communist officials continually undermined ILGWU strikes by repeatedly denouncing the 'social fascists,' 'labor fakers,' 'betrayers,' and 'bosses' agents' of the ILGWU. This civil war within the Jewish labour movement thus made the Eaton strikers' situation all the more precarious.

The thirty-eight women strikers did, however, obtain some support from the broader labour movement, at least in Toronto. Although the official organ of the Trades and Labour Congress, Canada's national labour organization, carried a full-page advertisement for the T. Eaton Company in the midst of the strike, the Toronto Trades and Labour Council gave the strikers some assistance. The council apparently pressured the firm to make concessions and charged that the 'Hon. H.H. Stevens ... flatly refused to intercede on behalf of [the] girl strikers.' A number of the city's trade-union auxiliaries also helped the strikers, and, according to the *Toronto Telegram*, the marchers in the local Labour Day parade of this year 'dipped their flags in sorrow as they passed Eaton's.'[80]

The strikers also received help from the CCF, the forerunner of the New Democratic Party. Party officials apparently tried to negotiate with the firm on behalf of the strikers but were not successful. The party's provincial executive then met with the minister of labour specifically to put the strikers' case before him. The CCF delegation asked the minister to set up a board of conciliation to settle the strike and also called upon the minister to prosecute the Eaton Company for violations of the Minimum Wage Act. In addition, the Ontario CCF newspaper championed the strikers' cause, reporting extensively on the oppressive working conditions in Eaton's garment factory and stressing the firm's victimization of the pro-union workers. The newspaper especially helped publicize the boycott. Moreover, the paper proudly announced that the women strikers had been transformed through the process of organizing and fighting for their demands: 'To an outside observer, the most striking feature of the whole business is the change that has taken place in the girls themselves during a few short months. [Earlier] it would have been difficult to find a more frightened and forlorn bunch of girls anywhere, with thin, hollow cheeks, nervous as kittens, white faced and tired, and afraid to say a word for fear of losing their jobs. Today all this is changed. The girls are no longer afraid of their own shadows. They talk and act like free citizens, not serfs. They stand up straight where formerly they drooped.'[81]

In broad terms, the CCF's sympathy for the strikers stemmed, of course, from the social-democratic party's concern for the hardships faced by working people. But some of the CCF's interest in this particular strike may have stemmed from the hostility and competition between the social democrats and the Communists who, as mentioned above, were actively involved in organizing dressmakers through the IUNTW. Moreover, the CCF's focus on this specific strike was, of course, partly a product of the royal commission's exposé of the Eaton Company and was also partly a result of the role of key CCF women who mobilized to support the women strikers. Jean Laing, the CCFer who was hired as an ILGWU organizer, was probably the main link between these two female groups. Although Laing herself was one of the few female trade-union leaders in the CCF in the 1930s, certain other CCF women also took up the cause. This included Dr Rose Henderson, a former suffragist who, like Laing, was a socialist and a feminist.[82]

In order to generate active strike support, a committee of women, apparently from the CCF, organized mass meetings to publicize the injustices perpetrated by the Eaton Company. At a meeting in Queen's Park, for example, both Henderson and Laing played prominent roles. According to the CCF newspaper, the committee of women 'who stood by the strikers.... organized both park and street meetings, as well as three very successful dances in the Labor Temple to raise money to augment the strike pay.'

The CCF women may have decided to take such active roles particularly because the ILGWU itself was reluctant to support the Eaton strikers.[83]

Beyond this, the strikers received unusual support from the Local Council of Women. Since this Toronto branch of the National Council of Women of Canada hardly ever supported female garment workers' struggles in the first four decades of the twentieth century, this rare support emphasizes the crucial role of the royal commission in crystallizing public opinion against the T. Eaton Company. Indeed, when the council's president prepared her report for 1934, she stressed that the local council had tried to help the female garment workers and highlighted the role of the royal commission in exposing 'all the pitiable conditions' faced by women workers in certain sectors.[84]

The fact that the royal commission publicized the T. Eaton Company's unscrupulous practices was especially important in view of the strikers' frustrations with the daily press. During both the 1912 and 1934 strikes, strike activists repeatedly charged that the daily newspapers hesitated to publish labour's side because the press was so dependent on advertising revenue from the Eaton Company.[85] Although the labour newspapers strove to fill the gap, the role of the royal commission was central in 1934.

Earlier, the National Council of Women had been distinctly reluctant to address the plight of female needle-trades workers. In the late nineteenth century, for example, Lady Aberdeen (president of the council) had warned a member that it would not be wise to tackle this issue because, to do so, would 'arouse the wrath of some trades-people.'[86] In 1934, in contrast, the depth of popular opposition to Eaton's paved the way for the council's intervention on the side of the women strikers.

In addition to the role of the royal commission, the CCF women themselves played a key role in motivating the Toronto branch of the National Council of Women to support the 1934 Eaton strike. Laing brought the strike to the attention of the Local Council of Women. She was joined by Dr Henderson, who attended a special local council meeting to urge the council to undertake extensive strike-support work.[87] In contrast, the ab-

sence of an organized left-wing women's group in 1912 meant
that the 1912 Eaton strikers received less support from the wom-
en's movement.[88]

The Young Women's Christian Association (YWCA), one of the
local council's important affiliates, also helped to bring the 1934
strike to the council's attention. The YWCA's Winifred Hutchison
was in an especially good position to know about labour relations
in the needle trades, for she became an investigator for the royal
commission and eventually was to testify before the commission
concerning the appalling wages and working conditions of Toronto's female clothing workers. Hutchison urged the president
of the Local Council of Women to use the council's resources to
support the striking Eaton women.[89] Another link between the
local council and the women garment workers may have been
forged by Margaret Gould, a council member who came from a
poor immigrant Jewish family and who had worked as an organizer for one of the other garment unions in the early 1920s, before
anglicizing her name and moving into other circles.[90]

As a result of a special local council meeting that three of the
women strikers attended, the council decided to endorse the
strikers' demands prominently. The organization also offered to
arbitrate the dispute and attempted to influence government
officials. In a letter to the Ontario minister of labour, the president of the council stressed that the women workers in this
Eaton's department had been forced to accept a relentless series
of wage cuts and speedups. She indicated that council members
had investigated the situation, listening to both sides of the dispute, and were concerned that the constant speedups had led to
nervous breakdowns. 'At the end of the day's work,' this letter
declared, 'the girls were unfitted for any personal life, for recreation, or home duties, lacking even the energy to eat their
meal.' 'A good many of the women are married,' she continued,
'with children and homes to care for when they returned from
work. For these life was a constant torture.' The letter ended
with a strong statement of the council's position: 'We feel that
if the working conditions which the management wishes to impose are permitted, that these will lead to physical and nervous

breakdowns, and to greater social cost later. We feel that to impose such harsh conditions particularly on women, who are child-bearers, or potential child-bearers, is most deplorable.'[91] The council's concern thus focused particularly on the threat to the women's maternal capabilities and duties, stressing the women's role as mothers (or future mothers) rather than as workers. In addition, the council subscribed to the classic liberal position that present intervention was justified in the name of avoiding further social costs later on.

The strike built up considerable momentum, particularly because of the unusual support by women's groups, and, as in 1912, a special appeal was made to women shoppers. Union leaflets that were issued to publicize the dispute called on all women to support the female strikers and declared that before any woman buys a new dress, she should make sure it was made under fair working conditions. The leaflets indicated that, in addition to support from the Toronto Trades and Labour Council and a number of trade-union auxiliaries, the female workers were being supported by the Local Council of Women and two other women's organizations.[92]

However, the Eaton Company tried to pressure the local council to back down, implicitly threatening legal action against the council for publicly endorsing a strike placard that allegedly contained inaccurate statements about the company. The council stuck to its position, arguing that 'while mistakes in terminology had been made [on the placard], the fundamental facts as to lack of an adequate wage remained unchanged.' Hence the council allowed the picketers to continue carrying the disputed placard.[93]

The local council's willingness to support the women strikers in 1934 contrasts sharply with the suffragists' reluctance to support the women strikers in 1912. As Alice Chown explained during the earlier strike, the suffragists feared that strike-support work would tarnish the appeal of their main cause by alienating potential suffrage supporters. In these earlier years, the women's movement concentrated intensely on the goal of votes for women, whereas the women's groups of the interwar period lacked such a concentrated focus. In 1934 this worked to the advantage of the Eaton strikers, since it meant that the local council was freer to take up their cause.

However, despite the pressure from women's organizations, Eaton's management refused to meet with the union in 1934. As in 1912, the company would not budge. Thus, despite the unusual support the female strikers received this time, they were eventually forced to give up. The strike was fatally weakened by the failure of so many of the women workers in the same Eaton's department to join the strikers in the first place. In addition, since this department did not have a lot of orders to fill and since work could easily be contracted out, management was not forced to settle with the union. The strike failed.[94]

Some of the tensions among ambivalent allies became even more prominent in the aftermath of the defeat. More specifically, considerable tension arose between union officials and the committee of women that had been supporting the strikers and that was based apparently in the CCF. After the strike had been called off, the committee of women supporters raised money, independently of the union, to enable six or seven of the former strikers to set up a cooperative dress shop under the committee's leadership. Sam Kraisman, however, was disturbed by the situation and issued a statement denying that the official group of Eaton strikers was associated with any store. He insisted that no one was authorized to speak for these strikers except for legitimate union officials, and he complained that since the end of the strike, some people had been using the name of the Eaton women without any authority. In reply, members of the committee of women denied that they had acted in the name of the union or that they had stated the union was in any way associated with the store. The committee's members seemed quite troubled by Kraisman's lack of sympathy for their project.[95]

This friction between the two groups stemmed, in part, from competition for leadership and control of the non-Jewish, female garment workers. Friction also stemmed from the ideological differences between the CCF women's orientation towards producers' cooperatives and the Jewish union leaders' 'class-struggle' orientation.[96] No doubt Kraisman and the other union officials also felt that any post-strike fund-raising efforts should have gone to the coffers of the ILGWU instead of to the store.

Conclusion

Although the two strikes exhibit important parallels, they took place in very different political and economic climates. The relative buoyancy of the Canadian economy in 1912 contrasts sharply with the depression conditions of 1934. This basic difference was a source of both strengths and weaknesses. The intense hardships of the Great Depression were, of course, a major source of Eaton's power over workers: the threat of unemployment was terribly real. At the same time, however, these harsh economic conditions increased anti-monopoly sentiment and heightened public sympathy for impoverished workers. The populist crusade of the Stevens Commission particularly helped mobilize opposition to the T. Eaton Company. Beyond this, the context of broader political mobilization during the Depression lent additional significance to the strike of thirty-eight women, thereby helping the strikers elicit support that had been impossible to develop during the earlier strike. Garment workers were not the only ones who suffered from the Depression, and this contributed to the potential for a broader-based progressive alliance in the 1930s.

Whereas 'leisure class' women's groups offered little help in 1912, women's organizations provided considerable assistance in 1934. The willingness of middle-class women's groups to help the Eaton strikers in the second case was, no doubt, increased by the fact that these female workers were Anglo-Celtic rather than Jews. To the extent that middle-class members of women's organizations sympathized with the female strikers, either in 1934 or, to a much lesser extent, in 1912, their sympathies were based on a very particular reading of women's concerns. Hence they focused on the sexual harassment of female workers and on the health hazards that threatened the female workers' maternal capabilities and duties. Women's groups seldom aided Toronto's women garment workers in the first four decades of the twentieth century, and, when they did so in 1934, their help was clearly not enough to defeat such a powerful employer, partly because they were unable to convince enough female shoppers to join the boycott.

During the second strike, the CCF women, aided by other CCFers, played an important role, not only by helping to mobilize the Local Council of Women but also by organizing mass meetings and raising funds. However, the tensions that developed between the CCF women and the ILGWU leadership made these alliances tenuous.

One of the strengths of the first strike, by contrast, was the close alliance between the female and male workers. The male workers' formulation of their strike demands in terms of the issues affecting female workers was itself unusual in relation to the overall pattern of industrial disputes in Toronto's needle trades in the first four decades of this century. While women and men struck together on many occasions in the city's garment industry in these years, seldom did the strike demands centre on issues of special concern to the women in particular. In this case, the Eaton Company's failure to offer extra pay to the men for doing the women's work meant that female and male interests meshed together well. The female-male alliance in the Eaton strike of 1912 was the product of a special set of circumstances rather than the product of a major shift in female-male relations.

Although the firm thus missed an opportunity to divide female and male workers, the company was able to withstand such a large strike, chiefly because of the division between the Jewish and non-Jewish workers in 1912. The non-Jewish workers' refusal to join Jewish strikers in this instance was part of a broader pattern which, in turn, made Jewish union leaders reluctant to commit scarce resources to support the non-Jewish garment workers. The union's ambivalent support for the thirty-eight non-Jewish women strikers in 1934 was a product of this history.

It is the anti-Semitism of many of the 1912 strike supporters that perhaps best highlights the contradictions and tensions in the alliances that developed around these two strikes. The 1912 strike received significant support from the broader labour movement and from anti-monopoly populists such as the editors of

Jack Canuck. These groups aided the Jewish strikers in the fight against Eaton's, despite antipathy to 'dirty Jews.'

These two strikes of the Eaton family's 'fellow-associates' thus reveal unusual attempts to forge cross-class, cross-ethnic, and cross-gender alliances in the battle against one of Canada's most powerful employers. The difficulties of forging these alliances were compounded by the fact that employers deliberately manipulated divisions within the workforce, and within the broader public as well, in order to 'divide and conquer.' Class, ethnic, and gender biases filled the alliances that did emerge with tensions and contradictions. Yet these innovative attempts at coalition-building were critical to workers' power in both of these strikes: without such alliances, neither strike would have had any chance at all against Fort Eaton.

NOTES

I thank the other contributors to this volume, especially Cynthia Wright and Lynne Marks, for many helpful suggestions. I also thank Don Wells for all his help. In addition, I gratefully acknowledge financial assistance from the Social Sciences and Humanities Research Council of Canada. Part of this article constitutes an adaptation of a paper originally published in *Canadian Woman Studies/les cahiers de la femme* 7, 3 (fall 1986).

1 The T. Eaton Company Limited, *Golden Jubilee, 1869–1919: A Book to Commemorate the Fiftieth Anniversary of the T. Eaton Company Limited* (Toronto 1919), 222

2 *Western Clarion*, 20 April 1912

3 Toronto *Hush*, 18 Aug. 1934

4 On 'Fort Eaton' see International Ladies' Garment Workers' Union, New York *Ladies' Garment Worker*, June 1912. On the 'Eaton Octopus' see *Hush*, 18 Aug. 1934.

5 National Archives of Canada, Labour Council of Metropolitan Toronto Collection, vol. 3, Toronto District Labour Council Minutes, 7 March 1912; United Garment Workers, New York *Weekly Bulletin of the Clothing Trades*, 22 and 29 March and 12 April 1912; London *Industrial Banner*, March 1912; Canada, Department of Labour, *Labour Gazette*, March

1912, 856, 897–901; Toronto ILGWU's Cloakmakers' Union, *Souvenir Journal, 1911–1936*, A. Kirzner's speech (in Yiddish); *Ladies' Garment Worker*, March and April 1912; *Toronto Daily News*, 15 Feb. 1912; *Toronto Telegram*, 15 Feb. 1912

6 For additional background information on Toronto's garment industry see Ruth A. Frager, 'Uncloaking Vested Interests: Class, Ethnicity, and Gender in the Jewish Labour Movement of Toronto, 1900–1939' (PhD thesis, York University 1986), 14–23.

7 Eaton Company, *Golden Jubilee*, 54

8 The quotation is from *Western Clarion*, 20 April 1912. See also *Toronto Daily News*, 15 Feb. 1912 and Toronto ILGWU's Cloakmakers' Union, *Souvenir Journal, 1911–1961*, S. Kraisman's address.

9 *Ladies' Garment Worker*, April 1912; *Weekly Bulletin of the Clothing Trades*, 29 March 1912

10 *Labour Gazette*, March 1912, 856, 897–901; *Toronto Daily News*, 15 Feb. 1912; *Toronto Star*, 15 and 16 Feb. 1912; *Industrial Banner*, March 1912; *Souvenir Journal, 1911–1936*, A Kirzner's speech (in Yiddish) and Charles Shatz's speech (in Yiddish); *Souvenir Journal, 1911–1961*, S. Kraisman's address and Max Siegerman's address

11 For a fuller development of these themes see Frager, 'Uncloaking Vested Interests,' chaps. 5 and 6.

12 Toronto District Labour Council Minutes, 15 Feb. 1912. See also 7 March 1912.

13 Interview with Joe Salsberg, Toronto, 1984

14 *Ladies' Garment Worker*, March 1912

15 Ibid., April 1912. See also *Toronto Globe*, 16 Feb. 1912.

16 *Souvenir Journal, 1911–1936*, A Kirzner's speech (in Yiddish). (All translations from the Yiddish are my own.) See also Toronto *Jack Canuck*, 6 April 1912.

17 For a more detailed analysis of the relations between Jewish and non-Jewish workers in Toronto's needle trades see Frager, 'Uncloaking Vested Interests,' chap. 4.

18 For additional background information on Toronto's Jewish labour movement see Frager, 'Uncloaking Vested Interests,' chaps. 1 and 2. The statistics are drawm from Canada, Dominion Bureau of Statistics, *Census*, 1911, vol. 2, 248–9, and 1931, vol. 4, 268–71. The reference to

the new Garden of Eden is from an interview with Isaac Shoichet, Toronto, 1982.

19 Stephen A. Speisman, *The Jews of Toronto: A History to 1937* (Toronto: McClelland and Stewart 1979), 193–4; *Ladies' Garment Worker*, Aug. 1912

20 Toronto *Lance*, 2 March 1912. See also *Souvenir Journal, 1911–1936*, A. Kirzner's speech (in Yiddish).

21 For another example of the consumer activism of Toronto's immigrant Jewish women see Ruth A. Frager, 'Politicized Housewives in the Jewish Communist Movement of Toronto, 1923–1933,' in Linda Kealey and Joan Sangster, eds., *Beyond the Vote: Canadian Women and Politics* (Toronto: University of Toronto Press 1989), 264.

22 Speisman, *Jews of Toronto*, 15–16, 81

23 *Western Clarion*, 20 April 1912

24 *Souvenir Journal, 1911–1936*, A. Kirzner's speech (in Yiddish)

25 National Archives of Canada, Department of Labour, Strikes and Lockouts Files, vol. 299, file 3446, undated clipping from the *Toronto Empire*

26 Speisman, *Jews of Toronto*, 195

27 The quotation is from the *Hamilton Labor News* (reprinted in *Weekly Bulletin of the Clothing Trades*, 3 May 1912). See also, for example, Toronto District Labour Council Minutes, 15 Feb. and 4 April 1912; *Lance*, 20 April and 11 May 1912.

28 The quotation is from *Lance*, 30 March 1912. See also *Industrial Banner*, March and April 1912, and undated clipping from the *Toronto Empire* in Strikes and Lockouts Files, vol. 299, file 3446. For details on the role of the Toronto Trades and Labour Council during this strike see Susan Gelman, 'Anatomy of a Failed Strike: The T. Eaton Co. Lockout of Cloakmakers – 1912,' *Canadian Jewish Historical Society Journal* 9, 2 (fall 1985): 93–119.

29 *Western Clarion*, 20 April 1912; *Lance*, 30 March 1912

30 *Lance*, 9 March 1912

31 *Ladies' Garment Worker*, April 1912

32 The quotation is from *Lance*, 16 March 1912. See also *Weekly Bulletin of the Clothing Trades*, 22 March 1912; Nancy Schrom Dye, *As Equals and As Sisters: Feminism, the Labor Movement, and the Women's Trade Union League of New York* (Columbia, Missouri: University of Missouri Press 1980), 39 and 54.

33 The quotation is from an undated clipping from the *Toronto Empire* in the Strikes and Lockouts Files, vol. 299, file 3446. See also *Lance*, 16 March 1912.

34 *Lance*, 16 March 1912

35 Alice A. Chown, *The Stairway* (Boston: Cornhill 1921; Toronto: University of Toronto Press 1988), 153

36 Ibid., 151–2

37 On the Canadian Social Purity Movement see Mariana Valverde, *The Age of Light, Soap, and Water: Moral Reform in English Canada, 1885–1925* (Toronto: McClelland and Stewart 1991).

38 *Lance*, 30 March 1912

39 *Ladies' Garment Worker*, Aug. 1912

40 The quotations are from Chown, *The Stairway*, 225–6, 232 (emphasis added). On anti-Semitism in Toronto see, for example, Speisman, *Jews of Toronto*, 119–22, 318–23, and 332–5, and Cyril H. Levitt and William Shaffir, *The Riot at Christie Pits* (Toronto: Lester & Orpen Dennys 1987), 9–11 and 34–9.

41 See, for example, Carol Lee Bacchi, *Liberation Deferred? The Ideas of the English-Canadian Suffragists, 1877–1918* (Toronto: University of Toronto Press 1983), vii–ix and 52–5; Wendy Mitchinson, 'The WCTU: "For God, Home and Native Land": A Study in Nineteenth-Century Feminism,' in Linda Kealey, ed., *A Not Unreasonable Claim: Women and Reform in Canada, 1880s–1920s* (Toronto: Women's Press 1979), 164–6; Diana Pedersen, ' "Keeping Our Good Girls Good": The YWCA and the "Girl Problem," 1870–1930,' *Canadian Woman Studies* 7, 4 (winter 1986): 20–4; 'Report of the Corresponding Secretary, Ontario Union,' in *The Report of the WCTU's Annual Convention* (1911); and *Canadian White Ribbon Tidings*, Dec. 1924.

42 Cynthia Wright, ' "Feminine Trifles of Vast Importance": Writing Gender into the History of Consumption,' in this volume.

43 *Ladies' Garment Worker*, April 1912

44 The anti-Semitic quotation is from *Jack Canuck*, 29 June 1912. On the strike fund see *Jack Canuck*, 23 March 1912.

45 Ibid., 24 Feb. 1912

46 Ibid.

47 Ibid., 24 Feb. 1912. See also 23 March 1912.

48 Ibid., 9 March 1912
49 Clipping from the *Toronto Empire* in the Strikes and Lockouts Files, vol. 299, file 3446
50 Archives of Ontario (AO), T. Eaton Collection, series 35, box 5, no. 131, 'An Open Letter to the Trades and Labour Council,' from T.L. Wilkinson, 15 April [1912]
51 On John C. Eaton's anti-union attitudes see, for example, the newsclipping on him in the Strikes and Lockouts Files, vol. 299, file 3446. On the company's recruitment of strikebreakers see, for example, T. Eaton Collection, series 35, box 5, no. 131, J.H. Macdonald to J.J. Vaughan, 16 Feb. 1912; the report on the strike by a Labour Department official in the Strikes and Lockouts Files, vol. 299, file 3446; and *Souvenir Journal, 1911–1936*, A. Kirzner's speech (in Yiddish).
52 *Souvenir Journal, 1911–1936*, A. Kirzner's speech (in Yiddish)
53 *Labour Gazette*, Sept. 1912, 228
54 The quotations are from the *Ladies' Garment Worker*, April 1912.
55 Canada, Royal Commission on Price Spreads, *Minutes of Proceedings and Evidence* (Ottawa 1935), 4384, 4396, 4417, 4494–5, and 4543
56 *Ladies' Garment Worker*, Feb. 1917
57 See, for example, F.R. Scott and H.M. Cassidy, *Labour Conditions in the Men's Clothing Industry* (Toronto: T. Nelson & Sons 1935), 5–35, and Canada, Royal Commission on Price Spreads, *Report* (Ottawa 1935), 109–111. This report declared: 'We cannot, in frankness, refrain from stating that the labour and wage conditions in [the needle trades] are such as to merit the most emphatic condemnation.'
58 See, for example, Royal Commission on Price Spreads, *Minutes of Proceedings and Evidence*, 4444, 4463, 4501–10, 4803, and 4811–12.
59 See, for example, 'Evidence given by Miss Winifred Hutchison before the Price Spreads Commission on Violations and Evasions of Minimum Wage and Factory Acts,' File: 'Price Spreads Commission,' AO, Records of the Department of Labour of Ontario, Office of Deputy Minister, General Subject Files, 1930–1949, box 15; Records of the Department of Labour of Ontario, File: 'ILGWU, 1933,' box 9, deputy minister of labour to J.D. Monteith, 12 Sept. 1933.
60 Deputy minister of labour to J.D. Monteith, 12 Sept. 1933
61 Royal Commission on Price Spreads, *Minutes of Proceedings and Evidence*, 4520

62 Ibid., 4462 and 4520

63 *Ottawa Morning Citizen*, 17 Jan. 1935

64 Royal Commission on Price Spreads, *Minutes of Proceedings and Evidence*, 4559

65 Eaton was quoted in Alexander Ross, 'What It's Like to Live in Toyland,' *Maclean's* (June 1968), 15, reprinted in Michiel Horn, ed., *The Dirty Thirties: Canadians in the Great Depression* (np: Copp Clark 1972), 135.

66 See, for example, Correspondence Scrapbook, 1934, T. Eaton Collection, series 9, and Royal Commission on Price Spreads, *Minutes of Proceedings and Evidence*, 3057. On the company's profits and losses see *Minutes of Proceedings and Evidence*, 4579; *Star*, 12 June 1934.

67 Cornell University, M.P. Catherwood Library, Labor-Management Documentation Center, International Ladies' Garment Workers' Union Collection, David Dubinsky Papers, box 75, file 1b, S. Kraisman to D. Dubinsky, 12 March 1934

68 See, for example, *Montreal Gazette*, 18 Jan. 1935; *Ottawa Morning Citizen*, 17 Jan. 1935; and *Toronto Mail and Empire*, 17 Jan. 1935.

69 *Globe*, 11 June 1934. Also see similar articles on his speech in the *Telegram*, the *Mail*, and the *Star*, on the same date.

70 On the unionization of the cloakmakers in early 1934 see S. Kraisman to D. Dubinsky, 12 March 1934. On the fact that the 1934 strikers were non-Jews, see, for example, David Dubinsky Papers, box 75, file 1b, S. Kraisman to D. Dubinsky, 18 July 1934.

71 Royal Commission on Price Spreads, *Minutes of Proceedings and Evidence*, 4492 and 4573. See also Toronto *New Commonwealth*, 4 Aug. 1934.

72 On the 1932 strike see Toronto *Der Yiddisher Zhurnal*, 8, 21, and 29 Aug. 1932. The phrase 'the Jew/Gentile problem' is from David Dubinsky Papers, box 88, file 1b, H.D. Langer to D. Dubinsky, 6 July 1937.

73 The quotations are from S. Kraisman to D. Dubinsky, 12 March 1934. See also Multicultural History Society of Ontario, Papers of the Toronto ILGWU, S. Kraisman to F. Umhey, 27 June 1934.

74 David Dubinsky Papers, box 75, file 1b, S. Kraisman to D. Dubinsky, 18 July 1934

75 On the other women in the same department who failed to join the strike see Royal Commission on Price Spreads, *Minutes of Proceedings and Evidence*, 4525.

76 On the cloakmakers' strikes see, for example, *Labour Gazette*, Aug. 1934, 738 and 741, Sept. 1934, 810 and 813. The lengthy cloak strike involved a large cloak factory that was violating the union agreement by running away to a nearby small town. Since the ILGWU was extremely concerned about the threat of runaways, the union's strategy was to pour extensive resources into combating this particular firm so as to nip the problem in the bud.

77 On the difficulties in organizing non-Jewish women see, for example, *Der Yiddisher Zhurnal*, 4 July 1919, and International Ladies' Garment Workers' Union Collection, box 2, p. 24, Toronto Joint Council, Dressmakers' Union, Local 72, Grievance Committee Minutes, 6 Sept. 1938. These difficulties are also discussed in the interview with Ida and Sol Abel, Toronto, 1983.

78 On the basic change in Communist party policy in the late 1920s, see, for example, William Rodney, *Soldiers of the International: A History of the Communist Party of Canada, 1919–1929* (Toronto: University of Toronto Press 1968), 116. For a detailed discussion of the factionalism within Toronto's Jewish labour movement see Frager, 'Uncloaking Vested Interests,' chap. 7.

79 Toronto *Worker*, 11 Aug. 1934. See also ibid., 8 Aug. 1934, and Kraisman to Dubinsky, 18 July 1934

80 The quotation about Stevens is from the *Toronto Star*, 21 Sept. 1934. The quotation about the flag is from the *Toronto Telegram*, cited in Eileen Sufrin, *The Eaton Drive: The Campaign to Organize Canada's Largest Department Store, 1948 to 1952* (Toronto: Fitzhenry & Whiteside 1983), 30. See also *Worker*, 15 Sept. 1934; leaflet of 10 Sept. 1934 in the Strikes and Lockouts Files, vol. 364, file 187; and *New Commonwealth*, 11 Aug. 1934.

81 The quotation is from *New Commonwealth*, 4 Aug. 1934. See also ibid., 11 Aug. and 1 Sept. 1934; memo dated 2 Aug. 1934 in the Strikes and Lockouts Files, vol. 364, file 187; and *Hush*, 18 Aug. 1934.

82 On Laing and Henderson in the CCF see Joan Sangster, *Dreams of Equality: Women on the Canadian Left, 1920–1950* (Toronto: McClelland and Stewart 1989), 111, 143, and 203.

83 The quotation is from *New Commonwealth*, 1 Dec. 1934. See also 11 Aug. 1934.

84 The quotation is from AO, Local Council of Women of Toronto Papers, Toronto Local Council of Women, *Forty-second Annual Report, 1932–1933–1934*, 16–17.

85 See, for example, *Industrial Banner*, April 1912, and ILGWU leaflet reprinted in the *Worker*, 15 Sept. 1934.

86 Quoted in Lorna F. Hurl, 'Overcoming the Inevitable: Restricting Child Factory Labour in Late Nineteenth Century Ontario,' *Labour/Le Travail* 21 (spring 1988): 106

87 Local Council of Women of Toronto Papers, Minutes of the Toronto Local Council of Women, 3 Aug. 1934

88 For an extensive discussion of left-wing women in the years before the First World War see Janice Newton, ' "Enough of Exclusive Masculine Thinking": The Feminist Challenge to the Early Canadian Left, 1900–1918' (PhD thesis, York University 1987).

89 Minutes of the Toronto Local Council of Women, 3 Aug. 1934, and Royal Commission on Price Spreads, *Minutes of Proceedings and Evidence*, 4796–849

90 Information on Margaret Gould (previously known as Sarah Gold) is available, for example, in the interview with Joe Salsberg, 1984.

91 Records of the Department of Labour of Ontario, Office of Deputy Minister, General Subject Files, box 10, File: 'Eaton, T., Co., 1934,' A.L. Hynes (president of the Toronto Local Council of Women) to A.W. Roebuck (Ontario minister of labour), 7 Aug. 1934. Hynes pointed out that the workers' average wages in the dress department had been reduced from 46 cents per hour in 1929 to 26 cents per hour in 1934. See also Minutes of the Toronto Local Council of Women, 3 Aug. 1934, and *New Commonwealth*, 4 Aug. 1934.

92 Records of the Department of Labour of Ontario, Office of Deputy Minister, General Subject Files, 1930–49, box 10, file: 'Eaton, T., Co., 1934,' two leaflets issued by the ILGWU's dress local [July or Aug. 1934]. The two other women's organizations listed on the leaflets were the Women's International League for Peace and Freedom and the United Women's Federation.

93 Minutes of the Toronto Local Council of Women, 21 Aug. 1934. See also 10 Aug. 1934.

94 *New Commonwealth*, 4 and 11 August 1934 and 1 Sept. 1934; *Labour Ga-*

zette, Nov. 1934, 996 and 998; and Royal Commission on Price Spreads, *Minutes of Proceedings and Evidence*, 4525 and 4642

95 *New Commonwealth*, 3 and 24 Nov. and 1 Dec. 1934
96 As Joe Salsberg explained, the Jewish left did not see cooperative shops as a solution to the whole system of class oppression. This is apparent in the interview with Joe Salsberg, 1984.

7 'Feminine Trifles of Vast Importance':

Writing Gender into the History of Consumption

Cynthia Wright

In 1928 The T. Eaton Company Limited began construction of Eaton's College Street, a major new store located at the southwest corner of Yonge and College streets in downtown Toronto.[1] Devoted largely to home furnishings, it was the first attempt to build a modern, city-oriented department store in Toronto. The College Street store was conceived as the culmination of a new merchandising strategy for Eaton's. Under the management of John Craig Eaton, founder Timothy's youngest son and successor, Eaton's began to go after the so-called carriage trade, Toronto's upscale market. In this regard, Eaton's was influenced by similar changes in retailing initiated by leading department stores in New York and London.[2] Not coincidentally, this was the same period in which the Eaton family, socially and financially, became the equivalent of a local Canadian aristocracy, particularly after John Craig Eaton was knighted in 1915 for his contribution to the war effort.[3]

While planned as early as 1910, the first stage of Eaton's College did not open until 1930.[4] Because of the Depression and certain building problems, the other stages were never built: only seven storeys were actually constructed, and the skyscraper remained an architect's dream.[5] Yet, whatever the difficulties of its conception, the opening of Eaton's College Street resulted in a tremendous amount of fanfare in the press, with such headlines as 'Imposing New Store of Eaton Company Acclaimed by Public.'[6] The *Star* referred to Eaton's College as a 'symphony in silver,'⁷ and *Canadian Homes and Gardens* declared it 'one of the few great stores of the world.'⁸ Eaton's College Street would operate for years as *the* arbiter of distinction and correctness for urban bourgeois women. This article will use Eaton's College Street as a case study from which to reflect on the historiographical and theoretical problems of writing about consumption, specifically shopping, in a gender-critical manner.

The department store has traditionally been the territory of the business historian. However, business-oriented studies of department stores have been narrowly defined and preoccupied with the question of entrepreneurship.⁹ Recently, breaking with the constraints of business history, new writing by American and British social historians has identified the department store as a key bourgeois cultural institution.¹⁰ These historians have pointed to some of the ways in which the department store can be understood as a business whose concern precisely was the dissemination of a class-defined taste and culture. Benson, for example, argues that 'Department stores were ... the agencies of a class-based culture, carrying the gospel of good taste, gentility, and propriety to those who could afford its wares.'¹¹ Understanding the department store as a bourgeois cultural institution also enables us to see the gendered character of middle-class consumption, a perspective that the business history approach misses altogether.

The history of mass consumption is arguably central to an analysis of class and gender relations in twentieth-century Canada. Remarkably little Canadian work has been done, whether by labour, social, or feminist historians, to research and to theorize the impact of consumer culture.¹² This is striking given that Bryan Palmer, for example, argues strenuously in *Working Class Experience* that by the 1920s a mass commercial culture had supplanted many aspects of local working-class culture, including the political traditions of the working class.¹³ Along with some American writers, Palmer sees the development of mass consumer culture as an effective brake on the class struggle.¹⁴

Yet Canadian labour and working-class historians have concentrated for the most part on the productive sphere of social relations, investigating the history of factory and shop, the labour process, and the structure of labour relations. By contrast, as American historian Jean-Christopher Agnew argues, writing on consumer culture remains a 'conspicuous absence' within historical scholarship.[15]

A history of consumer culture is necessary for an understanding of the specific experience of women. With industrialization, women were excluded from many areas of paid production, while consumption increasingly became a particular responsibility of women. By the twentieth century, shopping had come to form a major part of most women's lives.[16]

This article will begin by surveying some of the theoretical and methodological issues in the history of consumer culture, including some feminist perspectives. I will then turn to the Canadian context to explore how Eaton's department stores and mail-order catalogues were central to the formation of a national market. Along with national advertising, particularly for the new brand names, and the media, Eaton's reorganized local retailing practices and transformed women's shopping routines. Finally, drawing on my own work on the history of the Eaton's College Street store in Toronto, I will suggest how an account of mass consumption demands a rethinking of traditional approaches to source material.

The Politics of Longing: Gender, Class, and Consumption

Theoretical work on mass culture is often burdened with elitist or conspiratorial assumptions. There has been a tendency in some analysis to focus on the irrationality of the consumer rather than on the irrationality of the way consumption is organized under capitalism.[17] Feminists have tended to be hostile to elitist formulations of consumer culture. In an early feminist polemic, 'Consumerism and Women,' for example, Ellen Willis scathingly attacked the sexist assumptions in a lot of what passed for cultural critiques, both radical and conservative, of postwar American affluence. 'Consumer-as-idiot' theory, she argued, was essentially 'woman-as-idiot' theory.[18]

Meg Luxton acknowledges the influence of Willis's essay on

her own analysis of consumption as women's work.[19] Indeed, the dominant tendency within existing work on women and consumption has been to reject the popular, sexist construction of women's shopping as self-indulgence and to call attention to the fact that consumption management is an important, and socially unrecognized, aspect of women's domestic labour.[20]

Both Willis and Luxton were in explicit disagreement with the argument put forward by Betty Friedan in the early feminist text, *The Feminine Mystique*. Friedan basically posits women as the dupes of 'the manipulators' – of advertisers and motivational researchers. For her, consumerism is nothing less than the mass deception of the middle-class American housewife, and certainly Luxton is correct to reject the behaviourism of this simplistic model of women and consumption.[21]

Luxton's own model of the housewife as ever-rational consumer in the face of the demands placed upon her by permanently dissatisfied household members is, however, not entirely convincing. For one thing, how is it that the housewife is able to remain impervious to the lure of advertising at the same time that the rest of the household, according to her analysis, is enthralled by it? Luxton does argue that wage levels in working-class households set real limits on the housewife: financial considerations, and her responsibility as consumption manager, force her to be 'rational' in a way that other household members need not be.[22]

Luxton's approach assumes that consumption in the working-class household can be understood by what the woman actually buys. This assumption is shared by historians who, for the most part, have thought about consumption in terms of goods produced or the standard of living. One problem with this approach is that it interprets consumption as a series at *completed* acts.[23] It does not encompass window-shopping, consumer desire, or what Agnew refers to as 'mental consumption.'[24] From the point of view of experience, it may be just as important to understand what a woman desired but could never afford to buy.

For the working-class woman, the privileged object of desire was frequently fashionable clothing.[25] Social historian Carolyn

Steedman's biographical account, *Landscape for a Good Woman*, details the structuring of one woman's unfulfilled desire for a single stylish item. Her working-class mother's longing for a Dior skirt runs powerfully throughout the text; indeed, Steedman writes, it 'symbolizes the content of my mother's desire.'[26] Steedman's mother, a weaver's daughter from the north of England, 'came away wanting: fine clothes, glamour, money: to be what she wasn't.'[27] Despite her roots in 'a traditional Labour background,' she became a working-class Conservative, 'for the left could not embody her desire for things to be *really* fair, for a full skirt that took twenty yards of cloth.'[28]

What are we to make of Steedman's account of her mother's longing? Should we see her mother as a victim of false consciousness, or as 'bought off' by consumerism, despite the fact that she was never able to afford any of its benefits? Should we see her as a woman who, after her move to South London, was cut off from her working-class kin and the political culture of industrial Lancashire, and therefore susceptible to all the distractions of clothing and glamour? Such an approach is suggested by Palmer, who dismisses the mass culture of the 1920s as lacking the redeeming political value of the entertainments put on by the Knights of Labour.[29]

Steedman herself rejects these suggestions, arguing instead that in a curious way her mother's longing was an extension of her class traditions rather than an abandonment of them. Indeed, her class background shaped her longing in particular ways. As Steedman writes of the political culture out of which her mother came:

> The legacy of this culture may have been her later search, in the mid-twentieth century, for a public language that allowed her to *want* ... But within the framework of conventional political understanding, the desire for a New Look skirt cannot be seen as a political want, let alone a proper one. We have no better ways of understanding such manifestations of political culture than they did in Burnley in 1908, when they used to say dismissively that 'a motor car or carriage would buy a woman's vote ... at any time.'[30]

Steedman's discussion might apply to a brief account of working-class women and their longing for clothes that appeared in the Canadian left journal the *Woman Worker* in the 1920s:

> Two working women walked out of a big departmental store. Passing the big store front, one of the women stopped. She gazed enraptured at the window. Then she exclaimed with great fervour in her voice, 'I do like that!'
>
> 'That' meant a beautiful evening dress made of a delicate soft yellow material and highly bespangled. Of course she pictured herself in it – what woman wouldn't? But this is as far as working women get. They see the clothes they like always on wax models waiting for the woman who has the money.[31]

One of the things that is noteworthy about this passage is that it assumes that all women, regardless of class, want such things as diaphanous yellow evening dresses, an item of clothing every bit as extravagant as a Dior skirt. There is a kind of democracy of desire here, but class position sets clear limits on who will have access to the objects of desire.

I am not here arguing for a politics of consumption in which window-shopping and consumption are seen as acts of resistance on the part of working-class women. Rather, I want to suggest that the intersection between the world of clothing and working-class women was far more complex than any of the existing theoretical models can suggest. To date, most existing historical work on gender and consumption has concentrated on middle-class women, in part because they were at the centre of a key institution of late nineteenth-century consumption, the department store.

'Go Out and Buy': Middle-Class Women and the Department Store

In any account of modern, mass consumption, the department store and the middle-class woman shopper must figure prominently. Yet women have generally been absent in accounts written from a business history perspective. When women were studied at all, it generally was as department store workers.

Yet, historically, department stores have been a site *par excellence* of pleasure and social life for women, and, above all, middle-class women. As historian William Leach comments: 'Feminization so marked the life of the stores that a twentieth-century historian of Macy's could write in 1943 that a department store was not a department store unless it "catered primarily to women."' [32] This observation is echoed by the 1969 popular history of Eaton's, *The Store That Timothy Built*, which declares: 'A department store is ... a woman's world, where she reigns supreme.' [33]

Indeed, the first department stores were a new kind of public space for bourgeois women. In addition to selling goods, many stores featured reading rooms, art galleries, and lounges where women could rest and socialize with friends. Benson suggests that department stores operated as the equivalent for women of the downtown men's club, and included many of the features of the bourgeois home.[34] For this reason, some middle-class, nineteenth-century feminists celebrated the department store as an arena of freedom for women.[35]

Give The Lady What She Wants! a popular history of Marshall Field's first published in 1952, an era committed to the gospel of freedom through consumption, is explicit about the links between department stores, shopping, and feminism, for the nineteenth century: 'An offshoot of the Feminist movement was a vast buying spree in the early 1850's, led not only by the radicals but by the more numerous conservatives who wore crinoline hoop skirts.' [36] The authors attribute this to the fact that no other places but the dry-goods and department stores would receive women and allow them to linger for hours: 'Here an unescorted woman was received with deference, catered to, waited upon. Few other such retreats existed, even in Chicago. No lady would dare venture without an escort into a downtown restaurant, for she would not be served. There were no beauty shops, tearooms, club-rooms.'[37] The ultimate goal of feminism, the pinnacle of freedom for women, is the right to buy without interference from husbands and fathers.

Give The Lady What She Wants! extols leading suffragist Elizabeth Cady Stanton for her militant defence of women's 'right to buy for themselves, their children, and their households.' The account of Stanton's story of 'The Congressman's Wife' is worth quoting at length:

> To dramatize her appeal that women were partners in the family and should have the privilege of sharing the family purse, Mrs. Stanton invariably told her audiences her tremulous tale of 'The Congressman's Wife.' This unfortunate lady, she related, had an ill-equipped kitchen, with a faulty stove. Whenever her husband returned from Washington, he chided her about her poor cooking and miserable meals. The woman had been hysterical when she asked Mrs. Stanton for advice. 'Of course you can't cook here!' Mrs. Stanton shrilled as she replayed the scene before avid crowds. 'Go out and buy a new stove! Buy what you need! Buy while he's in Washington!'
>
> The housewife was horrified, Mrs. Stanton declared. It would never do! Her husband would be enraged! He bought everything, even her clothes! He might beat her!
>
> At this point Mrs. Stanton always paused to pierce the nearest male in her audience with an angry stare. Then she cried, 'I told her – and I tell this to you women – "Go out and buy! When he returns and flies into a rage, you sit in a corner and weep. That will soften him! Then, when he tastes his food from the new stove, he will know you did the wise thing. When he sees you so much fresher, happier in you new kitchen, he will be delighted and the bills will be paid." I repeat – GO OUT AND BUY!'[38]

A similar set of links is made in the official history of Eaton's, *The Store That Timothy Built*, where we read that 'the fact that the largest stores developed in North America was due to a singular phenomenon: the earlier emergence of American and Canadian women from the bondage which afflicted their sex in other parts of the world.'[39] Again, women's freedom from 'bondage' is measured in terms of *freedom to consume*. It is taken for granted that cultures that do not offer women many shopping opportunities are not only backward but patriarchal.

At least some first-wave feminists did indeed become enthralled by the possibilities of consumption as a yardstick of freedom. The nineteenth-century American dress-reform movement countered what was seen as the sexual enslavement of women by fashion with a rationalist commitment to physical hygiene and natural simplicity in clothing. But that critique proved no match for the allure fashion continued to hold for some feminists. Nor did it seem creditable in the face of the department store's promise of freedom for the middle-class woman and employment for her working-class counterpart.[40]

If the late nineteenth century had already seen the emergence of consumption as the definition of middle-class femininity and freedom for women, it was probably not until the 1920s that these sets of links became more widely circulated. There is now a substantial body of work which establishes that, by the 1920s, advertisers targeted women as the shoppers at the centre of the world of consumption.[41] 'The proper study of mankind in *man*,' declared a journal of the American advertising industry in 1929, 'but the proper study of market is *woman*.'[42] Advertisers were able to translate and rechannel early twentieth-century demands for more freedom and choice for women into a consumerist model of choice. An advertisement from a 1930 edition of the *Chicago Tribune* makes this link explicit: 'Today's woman gets what she wants. The vote. Slim sheaths of silk to replace voluminous petticoats. Glassware in sapphire blue or glowing amber. The right to a career. Soap to match her bathroom's colour scheme.'[43] As a number of feminist historians have argued, we need to understand the rise of consumerism in the 1920s within the context of the defeat after the First World War of feminist visions of collective housekeeping.[44]

This is not simply a feminist variant of Palmer's argument that consumerism was a brake on working-class militancy. Palmer argues, as have others, that the expansion of consumption in the

1920s resulted in the withdrawal of workers from their immediate community and their preoccupation with the narrower unit of consumption represented by the family.[45] Certainly, in many respects he is correct, as the middle-class craze for ideal homes and interior decorating testifies. But again, we need to pay attention to the contradictions and class differences in this process, for consumerism also gave women 'public definition as consumers.'[46]

Canadian feminist historians have pointed to the many ways in which both working- and middle-class women were involved in political activism from their position as consumers.[47] Moreover, for working-class women, and single women in particular, the allure of commercial culture was precisely that it was a route out of the confines of the household.[48] For some middle-class women with the means, the prospect of exercising some power within the arena of consumption was appealing. The department store setting catered to the middle-class woman's 'sense of her class position and personal attractiveness'; as a result, some women used that class position to make what were frequently interpreted as unreasonable demands upon both saleswomen and male managers.[49]

Other middle-class women pursued careers as consumer experts; they advised manufacturers, retailers, and advertisers on how to appeal to women, but also acted as ambassadors for better living through consumption. By the late 1920s, 'efficiency expert' Christine Frederick, who had written on the application of Taylorism to domestic labour, argued that the problem with scientific management was that it couldn't give women the 'thrills' that shopping could. In her *Selling Mrs. Consumer* (1929), she wrote: 'One reason why so many women have failed to get a thrill out of scientific training in home economics or budget-keeping is because it is too strictly logical.'[50] The new route to feminine fulfilment was via consumption. Frederick's women wanted 'more kinds of food, more leisure, more athletics and sport, more education, more travel, more art, more entertainment, more music, more civic improvement, better landscaping and city planning, more literature, more social graces, more social freedom and more cosmopolitan polish and smartness.'[51] In Canada, the store that tried to embody all these aspirations was Eaton's College Street, the 'palace of consumption'[52] which opened in Toronto in 1930.

The College Street store was the culmination of a set of changes that had overtaken the Canadian retailing landscape in the decades before the store opened. In this next section, I will outline the role that department stores and mail-order catalogues played both in transforming retail practices and in the formation of a national market. From there, we will return to the College Street store.

The Canadian Department Store and the Formation of a National Market

Daniel Horowitz has argued for the American context that 'department stores and catalogues turned a series of local markets into integrated, national ones.'[53] Although Canada's first department store opened in 1866, and Eaton's launched a mail-order catalogue in 1884, it was not until the 1920s that we can speak of a national market in Canada.[54] The 1920s saw a major enlargement in Eaton's mail-order organization, with the opening of one hundred order offices that enabled customers to walk in, make their selection from the catalogue, and have the order sent in by the sales staff.[55] Eaton's first French-language catalogue was produced in 1927.[56] By the end of the decade, Eaton's had forty-seven department stores and a nationwide catalogue sales system.[57]

The process of creating a national market was uneven and not without conflict. For settlers in isolated areas of Canada, the catalogue was a lifeline; however, it was also part of a set of changes in the organization of distribution and retailing. Nellie McClung recalls in her 1945 autobiography: 'I remember very well the first ready-made dress I saw. A daring woman, Mrs. Bill Johnston, sent to Montreal for it and sent the money, fifteen dollars, mind you, and the neighbours cheerfully prophesied that she would never see the money again or the dress either. But the dress came and even the doubters had to admit it was a good-looking dress.'[58] McClung adopts here her familiar tone of gentle satire, inviting us to be amused by the 'backwardness' of Mrs Johnston's neighbours, but this should not distract us from noticing some of the changes in shopping routines and practices to which this passage points.[59]

These changes include, among others, a greater trend towards the buying of ready-made clothing, with the result that clothing made at home frequently came to signal poor or immigrant status;[60] the practice of paying a fixed price and cash only for purchases, rather than relying on combinations of credit, barter, and bargaining; and an increasing orientation towards national retailers instead of, or in addition to, local ones. Sending away for goods, with one's scarce cash, required trust in the process of buying goods not produced locally by people one knew.[61]

These incursions by national retailers into local markets were strongly resisted. As in the United States, where in some communities catalogues were publicly burned, there were those who thought department stores and their mail-order catalogues pernicious.[62] With less commercial development in Canada, one retail firm could quite conceivably monopolize the market. Newspapers refused advertisements from Eaton's to avoid the anger of local merchants. In small towns, where the general merchant was often the postmaster, mail-order catalogues would disappear or meet with destruction. For this reason, catalogues were sometimes mailed in plain wrappers. Ordering from a mail-order catalogue could provoke economic sanctions, particularly in the Maritime provinces.[63]

Mail-order catalogues were strongly resented by rural merchants, but the urban department store came under fire as well. In the late nineteenth century, department stores were vilified in tracts that accused them of feeding on the blood of women and children.[64] Referring to Eaton's, a writer in *Saturday Night* magazine declared: 'It is not necessary for me to give some recital of the shame practised by this or other department stores.'[65] Another issue of *Saturday Night* carried a mock department store advertisement that savaged department store retailing practices such as saturation advertising and constant bargain sales. The ad put the blame squarely on the gullibility of the woman shopper: 'Thousands of ladies visit our store every day, brought here by our cunning advertisements ... The ladies – bless 'em – are our game. If it wasn't for them we couldn't make the thing work at all. Men are not so easily caught, but the women just fall into our trap by the thousand ... Darling woman! It is you that makes the department graft a possibility.'[66] *Saturday Night* gave its support to the campaign by the Retail Merchants' Association of Canada for legislative restrictions on department stores, a campaign that met with little success.[67]

In the 1930s, at the height of the Depression, department stores would again come under fire when the Royal Commission on Price Spreads carried out an investigation of the chain-store phenomenon in Canada.[68] While the big stores continued to be heavily criticized by small retailers, the fact is that the large retail stores had undercut their critics by building an empire on a firm foundation: the newly created mass buying public.

The 1920s, particularly the latter half of the decade, were a period of major expansion for the department store in Canada. This was remarked upon at the time in an article in the Canadian architectural magazine, *Construction*. The article noted that expansion was noticeable in two ways. First, smaller communities were being pulled into the orbit of the department store:

> To the observer of building and business developments of today it is obvious that the department store, even in communities of modest magnitude ... is taking a continually larger and actually present place in their business life. This is occurring in a large number of centres. Even in the prairie cities such as Calgary, Saskatoon and Edmonton, to name no others, points which in the personal experience of men not over the threshold of middle age were little more than Hudson bay trading posts with a few satellite smaller stores and business establishments about them, the trend is evident.[69]

Second, in the city centres in which department stores had long been established, the big retail stores were 'extending their premises, and the scale and variety of their mercantile operations and services.'[70]

This expansion brought concentration: by 1929, three department stores (Eaton's, Simpson's, and the Bay) commanded 80 per cent of all department store sales and some 10 per cent of the retail market.[71] (There were an estimated twenty to twenty-five different department stores in Canada in 1930.)[72] After 1931, when they cornered a peak 12.6 per cent of the Canadian retail market[73] (12.8 per cent in Ontario[74]), department stores never again enjoyed a bigger share of the retail pie. Eaton's College Street was the last major store to be built before the department store began to lose ground, as the combined effects of the Depression and competition from discount chain stores such as Kresge's (particularly noticeable in Ontario and British Columbia) took their toll.[75] While the *Construction* article celebrated 'the metropolitan sense of things' that the department store brought to smaller centres, local retailers resented the competition intensely.

Many factors combined to account for the expansion of department stores for this period. Urbanization and population growth were certainly important. The Canadian population grew by 63.6 per cent (3.4 million people) between 1901 and 1921, and by 16.2 per cent between 1921 and 1930. Changes in transportation, most notably 'the production of a gasoline-powered automobile ... brought about a dramatic increase in the trading area (i.e., the number of potential customers) of department store customers.'[76] Certainly, the introduction of instalment buying, available to Eaton's customers beginning in 1926, was a major force for department store growth.[77] The significance of the extension of credit cannot be overemphasized. As Strong-Boag points out, 'given average annual wages that in 1929, for example, were $1200, and conservative estimates of the minimum budget required to maintain an average Canadian family, $1430 in the same year, domestic survival often relied on credit.'[78]

Although retailers such as Morgan's, Ogilvie's (both of Montreal), Simpson's (Toronto), and the Hudson's Bay Company were all growing in the interwar period, it was Eaton's that was unquestionably in the lead. For example, while the Hudson's Bay Company probably initiated the trend towards the building of branches, Eaton's rapid construction of branches in seven provinces within a space of two decades probably put it ahead of rival stores.[79] Moreover, Eaton's was the department store with the biggest sales in Canada. By 1930, Eaton's had 7 per cent of the Canadian retail share, making it the department store with the biggest sales in Canada and the eighth largest retailer in the world.[80]

Of course, Canadian regional differences made for an uneven growth process. For example, Eaton's did not open stores in British Columbia until 1948, when it bought out nine stores from David Spencer Limited.[81] It was not until 1955 that Eaton's had department stores in all ten provinces.[82] However, numbers of retail stores in the various provinces is not the only way of measuring the retail influence of a department store or its percentage of the retail market share, for Eaton's massive mail-order system ensured that sales would be generated even where the company had no department stores.

While I have focused on the importance of the mail-order catalogue and the department store for the formation of a national market, it would be a serious mistake to ignore other key contributors, among them the growth of a nationally distributed media, the development of saturation advertising, and the coming of nationally advertised name brands. In both the United States and Canada, the advertising agency and the brand name were part of the retail landscape by the last two decades of the nineteenth century. A nationally distributed media, however, lagged behind in Canada.[83]

Again, it was the 1920s that emerge as the decisive decade. For one thing, it was not until the early 1920s that, for the first time, the majority of Canadians lived in cities and towns, thereby providing one of the preconditions for the growth of nationally distributed magazines.[84] This period saw the first publication of new mass-market magazines aimed at women, including *Canadian Homes and Gardens* (1924) and *Chatelaine* (1928).[85] As we shall see, such magazines, together with the city newspapers, were particularly active in organizing relations to the urban department store.

'A Symphony in Silver': The Eaton's College Street Store

Of all the Canadian department stores, it was Eaton's that best defined a class-based 'taste.' Herbert Irvine, for example, who began to work in Eaton's College Street's decorating department in 1935, was an arbiter of distinction for the Canadian elite for thirty years. A journalist wrote of Irvine that 'his superior taste and feeling for period design were sought after by the cream of the country's architects and matrons ("If you didn't get Herbert Irvine," says a woman who did, "you didn't exist.").' Another individual commented 'Herbert taught everyone. He started the whole chain of taste in Toronto.'[86]

The newspaper account reads as if Irvine was able to influence so many by sheer innate 'taste,' but his career must be understood in relation to the department store's position as a bourgeois cultural institution. This does not mean that we simply replace an individual source of 'taste' and 'distinction' (Irvine) with an institutional one (the department store). Rather, it involves situating a store such as Eaton's College Street within a complex set of relations involving advertising, the media, the organization of credit, and the arrangement of space. In what follows, I will look at only two of these factors: Eaton's College Street and the media, specifically the new women's magazines; and the department store's interior design and architecture.

The department store is often studied in relative isolation, even by historians such as Benson who see the department store as a microcosm in which all the class and gender contradictions of the society are reflected and re-enacted.[87] It is also important to be aware of the ways in which the local media, primarily the daily newspapers and mass-circulation magazines, organized relations to Eaton's College Street. In the same way that advertising 'naturalizes' the commodity,[88] so the media operated to define and celebrate Eaton's College Street as an important site of social life, excitement, and taste.

While large-circulation women's magazines certainly existed in Canada before the 1920s,[89] it was this decade which saw the founding of important new periodicals, among them *Canadian Homes and Gardens* (1924–62), *Mayfair* (1927–61), and *Chatelaine* (1928–).[90] With the growth of nationally distributed media, magazines began to target particular audiences.[91] For example, while *Chatelaine* aimed for the broad middle class, *Canadian Homes and Gardens* and *Mayfair* both aimed for a more upscale female readership.

Interestingly, editors of both *Canadian Homes and Gardens* and *Chatelaine* had histories of working in department-store advertising. Samuel McIlwaine, editor of *Canadian Homes and Gardens* in the 1940s, had worked for Simpson's.[92] *Chatelaine* had a long-standing history with Eaton's. Bryne Hope Saunders, editor of *Chatelaine* for the years 1929–42 and 1946–51, worked as an advertising copywriter for Eaton's for three years.[93] Mary-Etta MacPherson, who replaced Saunders during the war years, wrote a popular account of Eaton's, *Shopkeepers to a Nation: The Eatons*, which was serialized in *Chatelaine*.[94] Doris Anderson, who became *Chatelaine* editor in the 1950s, was another 'graduate' of Eaton's advertising department.[95] But the relationship between the large-circulation women's magazines and the department store was more complex than simply one of overlapping personnel. One example is the relations among Eaton's College Street, upmarket magazines such as *Canadian Homes and Gardens*, and the modernist movement in furniture and design.

In the summer of 1925 the Exposition Internationale des Arts Décoratifs et Industriels Modernes was held in Paris. For the first time, 'the domestic interior was the subject of an internatinal exhibition of this size' and all 'the latest ideas in furniture and interior decoration' were on display.[96] Eaton's College Street, when it opened five years later, enthusiastically embraced the modernist movement. An advertisement announcing the opening of the store observed: 'Nowhere is the newness of the new era more apparent than at home ... In the minds of the homemaker and her husband is the common knowledge of decorative values; starched lace curtains and three legged tables could never have happened now.'[97] This 'common knowledge of decorative values' was located, at least in part, in textual sources.

Canadian Homes and Gardens, for example, devoted a special issue to the modernist movement in interior decoration, and observed in an editorial that 'true, Europe has been sending us warnings ... Now a thoroughly comprehensive exposition of *art moderne* has been given to us with the T. Eaton Company's enterprising show.'[98] A 1930 number of *Canadian Homes and Gardens* devoted several pages to Eaton's College Street's famous period furniture rooms, declaring: 'In this 20th Century, stores and their merchandise are news. Because of their definite and daily influence upon the lives and the taste of millions, it is essential that the public's buying centres show leadership and a sense of responsibility. Any shop that makes a sincere effort to lead its patrons along the paths of good taste and good values is worthy of consideration.'[99] Magazines such as *Chatelaine* and *Canadian Homes and Gardens* were part of the production of this common knowledge but they also identified Eaton's College Street as *the* site of taste in furniture and interior decoration, the link between Canada and the Paris-based modernist movement in design.

Eaton's, for its part, actively fostered the relationship between the store and American mass women's magazines that also had high circulations in Canada. Speakers from *House Beautiful* and *Ladies' Home Journal* were brought to Eaton's College Street to popularize the new ideas about home decoration.[100] Moreover, Eaton's College Street was itself, spatially and architecturally, a lesson in the modern decorative arts movement, as the advertisements for the store constantly emphasized. Indeed, the spatial organization of the College Street store provides a particularly fruitful source for historical analysis.

Space and the Department Store

The analysis of space is an important key to department stores, since it suggests a way to understand one of the most interesting of the big stores' structural contradictions: while based on the retail principle of free entry and the freedom to browse without obligation to buy, they are constrained to organize in various ways the thousands of customers who go through their revolving doors each day.[101] While the department store, in theory, was open to all, barriers of class and ethnicity were there. In the first pages of her autobiography, for example, Gabrielle Roy recounts with bitterness the humiliation that often accompanied her mother's attempts to negotiate service in French in the Eaton's store in Winnipeg.[102] Such experiences were no doubt reinforced by the refusal of department stores to hire among certain ethnic groups. 'Italians,' according to Robert Harney, 'knew that one needed to change one's name and hide one's origin to clerk in the big department stores.'[103]

The spatial organization of the department store can be understood at a number of levels. One approach is to examine the relationship between the department store and the city. Elizabeth Ewen has argued that department stores in New York City moved progressively uptown away from the downtown working class – that is, the primarily Jewish and Italian garment workers who made the fashionable clothes for the big stores.[104] In broad outlines, the same development occurred with Eaton's in Toronto. Eaton's College Street did not have adjoining factories, as did the earlier Eaton's, located further south on Queen.[105] Interestingly, according to Macpherson, the original plan was that Eaton's would relocate '*in toto* from the old downtown location.'[106] Aside from the building problems, Macpherson outlines two other factors which, in the end, went against the centralization of Eaton's at College Street. Both, significantly, related to women's shopping patterns.

Eaton's worried that women in downtown office jobs who shopped at Eaton's Queen Street store on their lunch hours would not transfer their business one mile north to College Street. Second, if Eaton's moved northward, it would be leaving behind the Simpson's store which, since 1872, had always been steps from its biggest competitor. It was 'the habit of several generations of Toronto women to visit both the department stores on every shopping-trip.'[107] Eaton's did approach Simpson's about sharing the Yonge-College corner but, according to former Simpson's president, C.L. Burton, they simply did not have the capital to take advantage of the opportunity.[108]

The architecture of the Eaton's College Street store also set it apart from its sister store on Queen. Timothy Eaton (in contrast to his contemporary, Robert Simpson) had been uninterested in the possibilities of architecture for creating an image for a department store. While the Queen Street store was a 'confused collection of buildings of varying dates,' the architecture of the College Street premises was planned with a view to 'the transformation of the store's image.'[109] Or, as a 1930 advertisement for the store put it, 'It will be something new in Toronto, won't it, to talk of Eaton's in the architectural terms of Greece and Rome ... While building on these noble, eternal principles the architects, withal, have not been unmindful that the store opens in 1930, in the restless age that wants change.'[110] Certainly the store was intended to be, in size and commercial terms, the leading Canadian department store of its time. It was also designed, and this was particularly true for the store's spectacular Art Deco interior, with a view to distinguishing it from anything else that had hitherto been the tradition for Canadian retail building.

At the level of the interior space of Eaton's College Street, the store's nonselling space is as central as its counters and cash registers. One of the most interesting arguments made by Benson in her *Counter Cultures* is that the key distinction between department stores and other forms of selling merchandise is in the nonselling arena, 'the world of bourgeois gentility and lavish service': 'Using an elaborate array of services to create an ethic of consumption that transcended individual sales, the palace of consumption was the department store's peculiar contribution to the consumer society.'[111] The nonselling arena was vital to Eaton's College Street. Its famous seventh floor ('the climax and showpiece of the entire store'[112]) consisted of the Eaton Auditorium (one of the most important concert and lecture halls in the city), the elegant Round Room restaurant, and a large foyer or lounge. The Eaton Auditorium was used for concerts, featuring musicians from Glenn Gould to Lady Eaton herself, many of which were broadcast on the radio. It was also the venue for lectures from leading couturiers and decorators.

Indeed, a 1931 advertisement for Eaton's College Street declared that the Eaton Auditorium was not merely a functional hall, but was meant to be an object of study: 'Come to a lecture, if only to see the EATON Auditorium. That alone will amount to a lesson in Interior Decoration. Study its lighting, its colour scheme, the placing of its mirrors, its exquisite simplicity and fine proportion and you'll have gained a good idea of what the modern movement stands for when interpreted by such brilliant exponents as Jacques Carlu, the designer of the Auditorium.'[113] This same advertisement begins with the headline, 'No, it isn't enough these days for a man or woman to talk books, art, music – one has got to be up on all the rights and wrongs of INTERIOR DECORATION,' and continues, 'One of the big purposes of the EATON Auditorium is to popularize this fascinating subject.'[114]

This College Street advertisement, interestingly, is one of the very few that addressed both men and women. Most advertisements assume a female audience, and structure the store as 'feminine space.' An advertisement that appeared in the *Globe* ten days before the opening of the store begins: 'Of course, there's a woman in the case. A woman's as essential to a store like this as Helen to the tale of Troy.'[115] *Construction* described Eaton's College Street as certain to become 'one of the most prominent rendezvous of the feminine Toronto.'[116]

'Feminine space' meant not just a place where women might comfortably browse and shop, but a sense that the spatial organization of the store's interior was feminized. A pre-opening advertisement of the Elevator Arcade of Eaton's College Street declared: 'each group of elevators is a different color ... How much easier to grasp "Take the Green Elevators, Madame" than the old befuddling reference to the points of the compass or the right or left hand. Moreover, for the usual mirror of the elevator de luxe has been substituted a clock – a bit of optimism on the part of the designer to the effect that punctuality is a keener instinct than vanity.'[117] In a short description of elevators, this text manages to suggest that women are both vain and unable to orient themselves spatially without the use of colour (rather like elementary school children). Another advertisement from the same period, this time for the small shops within Eaton's College, cries: 'Little Specialty Shops – isn't the mere sight of them to the smart woman as the song of the lark to the poet or the scent of the fox to the pack?'[118]

Department store managers have long assumed certain principles of the spatial organization of gender; for example, it is rare to find the men's clothing section above the main floor in major department stores because it is thought that men will not plunge into 'feminine territory' much beyond the first floor.[119] Examples such as these from Eaton's College Street suggest that historians must learn to read 'against the grain' the spatial dynamics of class and gender in the department store.

Conclusion

We need a history of consumer culture in Canada, not just because it is a 'gap' that urgently needs to be filled, but because it is a key component of understanding the reorganization of class and gender relations in the twentieth century. The existing theories and approaches to consumerism and the department store are inadequate, given the complexity of the material the historian has to analyse. We need to think in some new ways about the sources, in view of the limitations of approaches based largely on quantitative data and archival materials. This is not to suggest that we abandon these two traditional sources since, for one thing, the full holdings of the huge Eaton's archives have never been analysed and, second, we need much more concrete information than we have about real incomes in the 1920s and about who, in fact, was able to afford the consumer goods then available. But we also need to pay attention to evidence such as spatial organization or relations between the store and the media because they enable us to get at the full complexity of gender and class relations within and without the department store.

Finally, for historians of women, the study of consumer culture is a rich site for research into gender relations apart from the more common subject areas of work and family. Not only is consumption gendered in fundamental ways, historically and in the present, but there is a vast diversity in what women subjectively make of that fact, from women who hate shopping to those wearing T-shirts with the slogan, 'A woman's place is in the mall.' This explicit turnaround of the anti-feminist notion that 'a woman's place is in the home' suggests the continued resonance of the nineteenth-century idea that shopping is the ultimate feminine pleasure and liberation.[120] From the first department stores to the contemporary mall, feminist historians of consumer culture have a great deal of fascinating links to uncover.

NOTES

I want to thank the other conributors to this volume for their support and for incisive and invaluable comments on earlier drafts of this paper. Franca Iacovetta and Mariana Valverde also provided crucial editorial assistance for which I am very grateful. This article was written before the full holdings of the Eaton's archives were made available to researchers.

1 The phrase, 'feminine trifles of vast importance,' is from an advertisement for Eaton's College Street that appeared in *Canadian Homes and Gardens* 7, 12 (Dec. 1930): 86.

2 William Dendy, *Lost Toronto* (Toronto: Oxford University Press 1978), 157

3 Mark Starowicz, 'Eaton's: An Irreverent History,' in Wallace Clement, ed., *Corporate Canada* (Toronto: James, Lewis and Samuels 1972), 9–13. See also Lady Eaton's memoirs, *Memory's Wall: The Autobiography of Flora McCrea Eaton* (Toronto: Clarke, Irwin 1956).

4 As early as 27 March 1912 the *Toronto World* made the plans for Eaton's College Street front-page news, revealing that Eaton's had been secretly buying up land at the corner of Yonge and College streets for the purpose of building a ten-storey store. The date of 1910 for the first plans for Eaton's College Street is cited by Hilary Russell, 'Eaton's College Street Store and Seventh Floor,' unpublished paper, Canadian Parks Service, 1983, 395.

5 Russell, 'Eaton's College,' 395–6
6 Toronto *Globe*, 31 Oct. 1930, 13–14
7 *Toronto Daily Star*, 29 Oct. 1930, 27
8 *Canadian Homes and Gardens* 7, 12 (Dec. 1930): 85
9 Michael B. Miller, *The Bon Marché: Bourgeois Culture and the Department Store, 1869–1920* (Princeton: Princeton University Press 1981), 6
10 Ibid., 3. For other examples of this recent work see Susan Porter Benson, *Counter Cultures: Saleswomen, Managers, and Customers in American Department Stores 1890–1940* (Urbana and Chicago: University of Illinois Press 1986); Rachel Bowlby, *Just Looking: Consumer Culture in Dreiser, Gissing and Zola* (New York: Methuen 1985); Elaine S. Abelson, *When Ladies Go A-Thieving: Middle Class Shoplifters in the Victorian Department Store* (New York: Oxford 1990); William Leach, 'Transformations in a Culture of Consumption: Women and Department Stores, 1890–1925,' *Journal of American History* 71 (Sept. 1984): 319–42; William Leach, *True Love and Perfect Union: The Feminist Reform of Sex and Society* (London: Routledge and Kegan Paul 1981), especially chap. 9. For one of the few studies of consumerism and working-class women see Elizabeth Ewen, *Immigrant Women in the Land of Dollars: Life and Culture on the Lower East Side, 1890–1925* (New York: Monthly Review 1985).
11 Benson, *Counter Cultures*, 4
12 For an exception see Veronica Strong-Boag, 'Keeping House,' in her *The New Day Recalled: Lives of Girls and Women in English Canada, 1919–1939* (Toronto: Copp Clark Pitman 1988).
13 Bryan Palmer, *Working Class Experience: The Rise and Reconstitution of Canadian Labour, 1800–1980* (Toronto: Butterworth 1983), 190
14 For an influential discussion of the impact of consumerism on class relations and political democracy in the United States see Stuart and Elizabeth Ewen, *Channels of Desire: Mass Images and the Shaping of American Consciousness* (New York: McGraw-Hill 1982). See also Stuart Ewen, *Captains of Consciousness: Advertising and the Social Roots of the Consumer Culture* (New York: McGraw-Hill 1977), and his *All Consuming Images: The Politics of Style in Contemporary Culture* (New York: Basic Books 1988). For an overview of theories of popular culture as the end of civilization and democracy see Patrick Brantlinger, *Bread and Circuses: Theories of Mass Culture as Social Decay* (Ithaca: Cornell University Press 1983).

15 Jean-Christophe Agnew, 'The Consuming Vision of Henry James,' in Richard Wightman Fox and T.J. Jackson Lears, eds., *The Culture of Consumption: Critical Essays in American History 1880–1980* (New York: Pantheon Books 1983), 67

16 For one account of this transformation see 'Consumption and the Ideal of the New Woman,' in Ewen, *Captains.*

17 Fox and Lears, eds., *Culture,* xv–xvi

18 Ellen Willis, 'Consumerism and Women,' in Vivian Gornick and Barbara K. Moran, eds., *Woman in Sexist Society* (New York: Basic Books 1971), 480–4. Compare Fredric Jameson, 'Pleasure: A Political Issue,' in *Formations of Pleasure* (London: Routledge and Kegan Paul 1983), 4.

19 Meg Luxton, *More than a Labour of Love: Three Generations of Women's Work in the Home* (Toronto: Women's Press 1980), 172

20 Ibid., 168–73. Daniel Horowitz notes that, 'in history of women as consumers, housework has received the most concentrated attention.' See his *The Morality of Spending: Attitudes toward the Consumer in America, 1875–1940* (Baltimore: Johns Hopkins University Press 1985), 200.

21 Betty Friedan, *The Feminine Mystique* (New York: Dell Publishing 1963), 218; Luxton, *More than a Labour,* 172

22 Luxton, *More than a Labour,* 162

23 Agnew, 'The Consuming Vision,' 69

24 Ibid., 73

25 Middle-class observers often associated working-class women's love of fashionable clothing with sexual immorality. See Mariana Valverde, 'The Love of Finery: Fashion and the Fallen Woman in Nineteenth-Century Social Discourse,' *Victorian Studies,* 32, 2 (winter 1989): 169–88; Kathy Peiss, *Cheap Amusements: Working Women and Leisure in Turn-of-the Century New York* (Philadelphia: Temple University Press 1986).

26 Carolyn Steedman, *Landscape for a Good Woman: A Story of Two Lives* (London: Virago 1986), 24

27 Ibid., 6

28 Ibid., 47

29 Palmer, *Working-Class Experience,* 197–8

30 Steedman, *Landscape,* 121 (second ellipsis is in the original.)

31 'I Do Like That!' *Woman Worker* 1, 10 (April 1927): 6. I am indebted to Janice Newton for referring me to this source.

32 Leach, *True Love*, 234

33 William Stephenson, *The Store That Timothy Built* (Toronto: McClelland and Stewart 1969), 142

34 Benson, *Counter Cultures*, 83. The construction of the department store as 'feminine space' may also be seen at work in nineteenth-century novels such as Zola's *Au Bonheur des Dames* (1883) and Dreiser's *Sister Carrie* (1900). For a discussion of Zola, Dreiser, and the department store see Bowlby, *Just Looking*, chaps. 4 and 5. For more on Zola see Miller, *Bon Marché*, and Rosalind H. Williams, *Dream Worlds: Mass Consumption in Late Nineteenth-Century France* (Berkeley: University of California Press 1982).

35 Leach, *True Love*, 26

36 Lloyd Wendt and Herman Kogan, *Give The Lady What She Wants! The Story of Marshal Field and Company* (Chicago: Rand McNally 1952), 30

37 Ibid., 32

38 Ibid., 29

39 Stephenson, *Store*, 141–2

40 Leach, *True Love*, 260

41 See, for example, Michael Schudson, *Advertising, the Uneasy Persuasion: Its Dubious Impact on American Society* (New York: Basic Books 1984), 61 and 173; Strong-Boag, *New Day*, 85 and 116; William Leiss, Stephen Kline, and Sut Jhally, *Social Communication in Advertising: Persons, Products and Images of Well-Being* (Toronto: Methuen 1986), 112 and 114.

42 *Printer's Ink*, 7 Nov. 1929, as quoted in Nancy F. Cott, *The Grounding of Modern Feminism* (New Haven: Yale University Press 1987), 172

43 *Chicago Tribune*, 1930, as quoted in Cott, *Grounding*, 172

44 Strong-Boag, *New Day*, 117 and 120. Dolores Hayden, *The Grand Domestic Revolution: A History of Feminist Designs for American Homes, Neighbourhoods, and Cities* (Cambridge, Mass.: MIT Press 1983), especially 281–9; Rayna Rapp and Ellen Ross, 'The Twenties' Backlash: Compulsory Heterosexuality, the Consumer Family, and the Waning of Feminism,' in Amy Swerdlow and Hanna Lessinger, eds., *Class, Race and Sex: The Dynamics of Control* (Boston: G.K. Hull 1983), 93–107

45 Palmer, *Working-Class Experience* 190–2

46 Leach, *True Love*, 213

47 Strong-Boag, *New Day*, 118; Ruth A. Frager, 'Politicized Housewives in

the Jewish Communist Movement of Toronto 1923–1933,' in Linda Kealey and Joan Sangster, eds., *Beyond the Vote: Canadian Women and Politics* (Toronto: University of Toronto Press 1989), 258–75; Joan Sangster, *Dreams of Equality: Women on the Canadian Left, 1920–1950* (Toronto: McClelland and Stewart 1989), 138–40; Christine Foley, 'Consumerism, Consumption and Canadian Feminism' (MA thesis, University of Toronto 1979)

48 Ewen, *Immigrant Women*, 106–7; Peiss, *Cheap Amusements*

49 Benson, *Counter Cultures*, 5. Other middle-class women used their ready access to department stores as a means to investigate saleswomen's working conditions. See, for example, Ontario Archives, Pamphlet Collection, *The Work of Women and Girls in the Department Stores of Winnipeg. Being the Report of the Civic Committee of the University Women's Club after a Study of the Condition of the Work of Women and Girls in Department Stores, 1914.*

50 Christine Frederick, *Selling Mrs. Consumer* (New York: Business Bourse 1929), 22. For a discussion of Frederick's shift in emphasis from efficient housekeeping to consumption see Annegret S. Ogden, *The Great American Housewife: From Helpmate to Wage Earner, 1776–1986* (Westport, Conn.: Greenwood Press 1986), 158.

51 Frederick, *Selling*, 31

52 The phrase is Benson's. See her *Counter Cultures*, 81.

53 Horowitz, *Morality*, xxvii

54 James Bryant cites Morgan's of Montreal as the first Canadian department store. See his *Department Store Disease* (Toronto: McClelland and Stewart 1977), 17. On the Eaton's mail order catalogue see 'The Scribe,' *Golden Jubilee, 1869–1919: A book to Commemorate the Fiftieth Anniversary of the T. Eaton Co.* (Toronto: T. Eaton Co 1919), 150–60.

55 Stephenson, *Store*, 89

56 Ibid., 186; 'as far back as 1899 Eaton's was inviting *canadiens* to correspond with it in Canada's other official language, assuring them of replies in the same tongue' (192).

57 Simpson's, of course, also began a mail-order business, but Eaton's catalogue dominated from the beginning. See Michael Bliss, *Northern Enterprise: Five Centuries of Canadian Business* (Toronto: McClelland and Stewart 1987), 292.

58 Nellie L. McClung, *The Stream Runs Fast: My Own Story* (Toronto: Thomas Allen 1945), 47. I am indebted to Alison Prentice for drawing my attention to this passage.

59 Strong-Boag, *New Day*, 113 and 114, emphasizes the unevenness of the transformation to consumer society, even for middle-class people, as does Susan Strasser for the American context. See her *Satisfaction Guaranteed: The Making of the American Mass Market* (New York: Pantheon Books 1989), 110. Barter, for example, remained a reality for many cash-poor Canadians right into the twentieth century. See Enid Mallory, *Over the Counter: The Country Store in Canada* (Toronto: Fitzhenry and Whiteside 1985), 55, 57.

60 Mary Antin, an Eastern European Jewish immigrant, recalls in her autobiography: 'A fairy godmother to us children was she who led us to a wonderful country called "uptown," where, in a dazzlingly beautiful palace called a "department store," we exchanged our hateful homemade European costumes, which pointed us out as "greenhorns" to the children on the street, for real American machine-made garments, and issued forth gloried in each other's eyes.' *The Promised Land* (London: William Heinemann 1912), 187

61 For a discussion of these changes in the American context, much of which is relevant for Canada, see Strasser, *Satisfaction Guaranteed*. See also Bliss, *Northern Enterprise*.

62 On catalogue burnings see Robert Hendrickson, *The Grand Emporiums: The Illustrated History of America's Great Department Stores* (New York: Stein and Day 1979), 214. 'There were even firebombings of department stores across the country' (32).

63 Stephenson, *Store*, 48. According to a document probably prepared by the Eaton's Archives, there was far less resentment of mail-order catalogues in Canada than in the United States. City of Toronto Archives, Business Firms (pre-1900) File, Anonymous, 'Some Information on the Beginning of Eaton's Catalogue and Mail Order,' nd

64 One example is an unsigned tract, 'Departmental Stores. The Modern Curse to Labor and Capital. They Ruin Cities, Towns, Villages, and the Farming Community.' It is undated, but the Canadian Institute for Historical Microreproduction, from which I obtained a microfiche, places it in the 1890s.

65 *Saturday Night*, 31 July 1897, as quoted in Fraser Sutherland, *The*

Monthly Epic: A History of Canadian Magazines 1789–1989 (Markham, Ont.: Fitzhenry and Whiteside 1989), 89

66 *Saturday Night*, 27 Feb. 1897, as reproduced in Sutherland, *Monthly*, 89
67 Sutherland, *Monthly*, 89. The final line of 'Departmental Stores. The Modern Curse to Labor and Capital,' states: 'Read the Barnums of Business as to the trickery of Departmental Stores, Published by "Saturday Night." ' On the lack of success of the anti-department store campaign see Bliss, *Northern Enterprise*, 363, for Canada, and Strasser, *Satisfaction*, 215, for the United States. Sutherland notes that, by the early years of this century, *Saturday Night* was carrying 'numerous ads for the Eaton Company.' *Monthly*, 92. This no doubt was interpreted by the anti-department store forces as further proof that department stores controlled the press through massive injections of advertising revenue.
68 There are no book-length or even substantial accounts of the Royal Commission on Price Spreads, although many Canadian social historians mention it in passing. For two brief discussions from different perspectives see Starowicz, 'Irreverent History,' 13–20, and Bliss, *Northern Enterprise*, 425. Short excerpts from workers' testimony have also been published in various anthologies. See, for example, Irving Abella and David Millar, eds., *The Canadian Worker in the Twentieth Century* (Toronto: Oxford University Press 1978), 184–94.
69 'Department Store Growth in Canada,' *Construction* 21, 12 (Dec. 1928): 401
70 Ibid.
71 Statistics Canada, Merchandising and Services Division, *Department Stores in Canada, 1923–1976* (Ottawa: Queen's Printer 1976), 9. This was one of the findings of the Royal Commission on Price Spreads.
72 Ibid., 9
73 Ibid., 25
74 Ibid., 74 (table 10)
75 Ibid., 17. For evidence that Ontario and British Columbia lost the most ground, see 28.
76 Ibid., 15
77 Ibid., 16
78 Strong-Boag, *New Day*, 114
79 Statistics Canada, *Department Stores*, 14
80 Ibid., 16

81 Stephenson, *Store*, 106

82 Ibid., 118

83 'The first Canadian advertising agency, Ansom McKim, was set up in 1889; others followed to promote the emerging name brands and department stores. But, though there might be national advertising, there was a dearth of nationally distributed media.' Sutherland, *Monthly*, 113

84 Ibid.

85 Indeed, Sutherland suggests that Canadian women's magazines were among the first and most important mass periodicals in the country. *Monthly Epic*, 153. Compare Leiss et al., *Social Communication*, 80.

86 Adele Freedman, 'A Master of Tradition: Life for Herbert Irvine Is a Matter of Taste,' *Globe and Mail*, 8 Nov. 1986

87 Benson, *Counter Cultures*, 8

88 Agnew, 'The Consuming Vision,' 72

89 According to Sutherland, *Canadian Home Journal* (1905–59) was 'the first modern women's magazine.' It later merged with *Chatelaine*. *Monthly Epic*, 156 and 206

90 Sutherland notes that, 'Between 1928 and 1933, the circulations of *Canadian Home Journal*, *National Home Monthly* and *Chatelaine* had all roughly doubled. That the increase and onset of the Depression were simultaneous was one signal that a strongly supportive mass audience was in place.' *Monthly Epic*, 160

91 William Leiss et al., *Social Communication*, 79–82

92 Ibid., 163

93 Ibid., 160. Sutherland calls her Byrne Hope Sanders, but I believe he has incorrectly spelt her name. Compare Alison Prentice et al., *Canadian Women: A History* (Toronto: Harcourt, Brace, Jovanovich 1988), 297.

94 Sutherland, *Monthly Epic*, 163; Mary-Etta Macpherson, *Shopkeepers to a Nation: The Eatons* (Toronto: McClelland and Stewart 1963). Macpherson was also an editor with *Mayfair, Canadian Homes and Gardens,* and *The Canadian Home Journal.*

95 Sutherland, *Monthly Epic*, 246

96 Witold Rybczynski, *Home: A Short History of an Idea* (New York: Viking 1986), 180

97 *Globe*, 28 Oct. 1930, 18

98 *Canadian Homes and Gardens* 5, 11 (Nov. 1928): 15

99 Ibid., 7, 12 (Dec. 1930): 85. For a description of the period rooms see Ellen E. Mackie, 'And So to Eaton's – College Street,' in the same issue, 85–91, 107.

100 See the Eaton's College Street advertisement of speakers on home decoration, *Globe*, 27 March 1931.

101 Susan Porter Benson, 'Palace of Consumption and Machine for Selling: The American Department Store, 1880–1940,' *Radical History Review* 21 (fall 1979): 200–1. This article has been central to my understanding of space as a source for analysing the department store.

102 Gabrielle Roy, *Enchantment and Sorrow: The Autobiography of Gabrielle Roy*, trans. Patricia Claxton (Toronto: Lester and Orpen Dennys 1987), 3–8

103 Robert F. Harney, 'Ethnicity and Neighbourhoods,' in *Gathering Place: Peoples and Neighbourhoods of Toronto, 1834–1945* (Toronto: Multicultural History Society of Ontario 1985), 15. While working-class and immigrant people often had a conflicted relationship to department stores, this does not mean they did not patronize them. See Varpu Lindström-Best, 'Tailor-Maid: the Finnish Immigrant Community of Toronto before the First World War,' in Harney, ed., *Gathering Place*, 221

104 Elizabeth Ewen made this point during the 'Women as Department Store Customers, 1870–1940' workshop at the Sixth Berkshire Conference on the History of Women, 1–3 June 1984, Smith College.

105 Indeed, the prospect of Toronto's retail centre of gravity shifting northward particularly animated the *Toronto World*, 27 March 1912: 'What The World is most concerned about is telling the people of Toronto that the down town district has been settled as the financial part of Toronto and that there will be, in a very few months, little or no retail business below Richmond-st [sic] ... the seat of the retail business of Toronto must go up town with the same forcefulness that it has gone up town in New York, and is now going up town in Montreal.'

106 Macpherson, *Shopkeepers*, 83

107 Ibid., 84

108 C.L. Burton, *A Sense of Urgency: Memoirs of a Canadian Merchant* (Toronto: Clarke, Irwin 1952), 214–5. Burton was a former president of Simpson's.

109 Dendy, *Lost Toronto*, 157

110 'Eaton's Daily Store News,' *Globe*, 18 Oct. 1930

111 Benson, *Counter Cultures*, 81

112 Dendy, *Lost Toronto*, 159
113 *Globe*, 27 March 1931
114 Ibid.
115 Ibid., 20 Oct. 1930
116 Sinaiticus, 'Eaton's College Street Store, Toronto,' *Construction* 23, 11 (Nov. 1930): 356
117 *Globe*, 23 Oct. 1930
118 Ibid., 25 Oct. 1930
119 Stephenson, *Store*, 140 and 142–3
120 For an interesting account of contemporary cultural representations of 'feminine' pleasures see Rosalind Coward, *Female Desire: Women's Sexuality Today* (London: Paladin 1984).

8 Making 'New Canadians':
Social Workers, Women, and the Reshaping of Immigrant Families
Franca Iacovetta

In the spring of 1958 Mrs Garuba, a Hungarian refugee, entered the office of the International Institute of Metropolitan Toronto, a social agency offering aid to the city's non-British immigrants. With her husband employed out of town, Garuba came to the institute hoping to find a job and locate a daycare for her two small children. The Hungarian-speaking counsellor assigned to the case promptly placed her client in private service and the children in a Catholic nursery. It soon became clear, however, that a seemingly straightforward case of job placement masked a turbulent history of marital cruelty.

Staff workers first learned of Garuba's unhappy home life when she returned to the institute in mid-summer and recounted the following story. Earlier that week, two men claiming to be government inspectors had come to her flat demanding 'to investigate her private life.' While searching her place, they claimed to be looking for 'evidence of immorality' as her husband wished 'to get a divorce and take the children.' The next night they returned, this time admitting they were private detectives hired by the husband to discredit her reputation.

It was not until weeks later, after Garuba had been served a divorce writ and the agency had found her a lawyer, that the counsellors discovered the full extent of the woman's problems. According to a pretrial statement, the husband for years had been abusive, 'very often' committing 'physical violents' (sic) on his wife and children and flaunting his adulterous affairs. The couple had actually separated in the fall of 1956, when the Hungarian revolution broke out and the husband fled to a refugee camp. But he later convinced his wife to join him and, a few months later, the family arrived in Toronto. Domestic life did not improve, however. Soon after they arrived in the city, an ugly scene transpired when Garuba's husband, accusing his wife of flirting with a neighbour, slapped and kicked her until she fled and found refuge in the home of some Hungarian friends. By the winter of 1957 the couple was legally separated and the husband, now working out of town, was obliged to pay her child support, which he did irregularly. Thus it was that when Garuba first came to the institute, she was especially eager to secure work.

Following her encounter with the private detectives, Garuba had moved in with a Hungarian woman. But this arrangement proved to be disastrous, and when she returned to the agency in the winter of 1958 she was distraught. According to the notes taken by the professional social worker who now took on her case: 'She was very upset ... told me ... [the roommate] is often drunk and she and her boyfriend are rough ... and asked several times for money, which [Garuba] cannot give ... [Garuba] was afraid [the roommate] would be a witness against her in the divorce proceedings.'

Although aware of her plight, none of the institute staff could have guessed that Garuba, terrified of losing her children, would attempt suicide by swallowing poison. The attempt failed, however, and in hospital she agreed to undergo psychiatric evaluation and to place her children with the Catholic Children's Aid Society until her situation improved. At the time of her release in January 1959, the children were still living with Garuba's roommate. Garuba now became determined to get her children into a temporary foster home so that she could return to work and thus eventually provide a better home for them. This strategy would also offer her a defence against her husband's allegations that she was an unfit mother. For days, she phoned the institute repeatedly, asking for help in finding a home for her children. As the case comes to an end in the spring of 1959, she has learned that the placement process was being stalled by her husband's interventions. In response, Garuba, having just landed a job, defiantly takes matters into her own hands and registers her children in an orphanage located outside the city.[1]

Mrs Garuba's file is especially bulky and relates an unusually complicated tale, but it is one of hundreds of case histories contained in the confidential records of the Department of Individual Services of the International Institute. The professional and volunteer counsellors who staffed this department sought to play an interventionist role in the lives of their immigrant clients so as to ensure the newcomers' 'integration' into postwar Canadian society. In the immediate post-1945 era, as the world entered the nuclear age and the Cold War, there was much anxiety about the crisis facing Canadian families as well as considerable discussion regarding the need to ensure the social and political integration of the postwar European arrivals. There was also much agreement among the nation's middle-class professionals that, after two decades of depression and war, Canadians be encouraged to return to the privacy and comparative calm of a 'normal' family life.

The construction of the family that underlined the dominant rhetoric assumed a gendered arrangement in which husbands supported a wage-dependent wife and children, and women took on the task of running an efficient household and cultivating a moral environment for their children. The response of institute counsellors to Mrs Garuba and the other clients we shall encounter in this paper reflected a desire to preserve family life and, moreover, to reshape 'foreign' or otherwise deviant families according to a North American, middle-class model that combined patriarchal ideals of family and motherhood with the notion of a modern, companionate marriage. This aim was in keeping with the larger goal of assimilation. Notwithstanding the social workers' respect for the folkloric traditions of the European immigrants, many of the professionals saw their institutions primarily as instruments of 'Canadianization,' a view reinforced by the Cold War. That the institute counsellors were not usually successful in reshaping their clients' lives reflects in large part both the limited contact caseworkers had with their clients and the selective and pragmatic approach many clients adopted towards the agency.

This article is a preliminary look at the complex nexus of class, racial, and gender relations that characterized the encounter between social workers and their immigrant clients during the 1950s and early 1960s. It begins with a discussion of the literature on immigrants. Next, it turns to the institute itself and the family perspective the counsellors shared with others in this period. Finally, the paper turns to the case files. It draws on a sample of 320 files (from the years 1956–62) where women were the primary clients or co-clients. Rather than offer statistical generalizations or typologies, I have used the cases selectively to illustrate themes or approaches, and I have described the clients not as statistical categories but as individuals thrust into particular situations. The case files deal with those immigrants who actually sought assistance from sources beyond their family and kin networks, and thus they are more likely than other kinds of historical sources to highlight personal tragedies and conflicts. Because they were drawn up by counsellors trained in social work techniques, the records are themselves constructions reflecting the biases of a group of middle-class professionals and volunteers. And yet, even while the files are obviously biased texts, we can find in them significant clues that tell us something about the strategies and responses of the clients themselves.

The Scholarly Literature

The past two decades has witnessed the proliferation of exciting new work in immigration history in Canada and the United States. Heavily influenced by social history, immigration historians have sought to rescue the immigrant from being viewed merely as the object of host society policy makers and observers or as simply a victim of economic forces. Central to this shift in perspective has been an emphasis on capturing the immigrant perspective – on reconstructing the motives, strategies, and experiences of the immigrants themselves, as well as documenting the internal dynamics and efforts at community-building within their respective groups. In recent years immigration specialists have also stressed the remarkable resiliency of immigrant newcomers as they re-created culture and community amid a hostile and exploitative environment.

Efforts to rewrite the history of immigrants in North America have been successful. The new immigration history has largely discredited earlier pessimistic and ethnocentric models that por-trayed immigrants as destitute and downtrodden and depicted the immigrant experience as one of social dislocation and indi-vidual alienation. In Canada, the recent literature has also posed a challenge to traditional Whiggish interpretations evident in the work of scholars of the nation-building school, wherein the value of immigration was measured in terms of the contribution the newcomers could make to national development, and the rapidity and thoroughness with which the 'foreign-born' became assimi-lated. However, in seeking to redress past biases, some scholars have gone far in the opposite direction, writing insular histories of family and community. The immigrants emerge as heroes in some of these studies, and little is said of either the casualties of the process – the wives left abandoned in the old village, the men dead from unsafe jobs – or the physical or emotional scars the migration experience engendered even among the more suc-cessful migrants.

Furthermore, few immigration specialists have paid serious at-tention to women or gender relations. This gap is particularly glaring given that the literature has highlighted the role played by family and kin-networks in easing the transition from old world to new. As in the work of family historians whose insights they have borrowed, ethnic historians have obscured women's lives. Women tend to be subsumed under the rubric of the family and are thereby rendered invisible. The family itself is depicted as an indistinguishable unit, as a nongendered and reified collec-tivity that acts in a self-interested manner.[2] At the same time, however, this lack of a gendered perspective has not precluded most scholars from in fact highlighting, and thus prioritizing, the experiences of men. Such assumptions leave unexplored the no-tion that the family was both an arena of negotiation, usually between unequal partners, and, as Garuba's story so dramatically illustrates, an arena of conflict.[3]

Until very recently, most scholarly work on immigrant women in postwar Canada could be found in the contemporary studies of social scientists. Feminist social scientists have played a particularly critical role in uncovering the lives of non-British immigrant women and women of colour who entered Canada after 1945. However, there is a tendency among these scholars to portray immigrant women primarily as victims. This literature is dominated by a triple oppression model that depicts minority women as the victims of exploitative labour markets, racist societies, and domineering husbands who are themselves viewed as the product of deeply embedded patriarchal cultures. While these are indeed important insights, a perspective that focuses exclusively on the structural and cultural determinants of women's oppression leaves little room for agency. It obscures how the women themselves might have responded to their predicaments and, moreover, how they gave meaning to their own lives.[4]

While the case files of the International Institute hardly offer a complete portrait of the varied lives of immigrant and refugee women, they do provide a useful starting point for developing an approach that avoids the dichotomy of immigrant victims/immigrant heroes. This false dichotomy has similarly plagued the literature on women's history, and, in this regard, the evidence contained in the institute case files can also be used to support the more general claim that the complex nature of women's lives defies simplistic portrayals of women as either downtrodden victims or invincible heroines. The case files point to a wide range of situations experienced by minority women and reveal the relationships that women forged, or eschewed, both within and outside the family or ethnic colony. As such, they provide a window on those complicated and, at times, even contradictory, aspects of women's lives.

From the Point of View of Integration

When the International Institute opened its new downtown Toronto office in October 1956, the staff were aware of the formidable task they faced. The declared aim of the agency was 'to foster and promote the integration of "New Canadians."'' Its staff workers found themselves in a city where tens of thousands of immigrants had settled. They came from a wide variety of backgrounds but, overwhelmingly, in the period before 1965, the immigrants were British or European. 'From the point of view of integration,' explained a staff supervisor, 'the purpose of the Institute is to serve as a bridge between the old world and the new.'5 In seeking to be such a bridge, the institute was not an isolated agency. Rather, it was part of the complex and sometimes bewildering amalgam of public and private support services that existed at the national and local level.

In contrast to their predecessors a half-century before, the immigrants who came after 1945 potentially had access to a fairly wide network of services associated with the postwar welfare state. Notwithstanding their shortcomings, the immigrants benefited from a national system of unemployment insurance, mothers' allowances, and improvements in health, welfare, and workers' compensation schemes. They could also tap the more traditional forms of aid offered by charitable agencies, churches, and volunteer groups that had long served immigrant and working-class families. In Toronto, middle-class women's organizations, such as the Young Women's Christian Association (YWCA), the Woman's Christian Temperance Union (WCTU), and the Toronto Junior League, organized clothing and food drives and baby clinics, hosted child-rearing lectures, and dispatched volunteers to meet women arriving by train at Union Station. Both nationally and locally, the Imperial Order Daughters of the Empire (IODE) was involved in citizenship work, educating immigrants in Canadian government and encouraging them to become naturalized citizens. Many local branches regularly 'adopted' needy families, who were then supplied with emergency funds and had their house bills paid. Toronto's settlement houses acted as job placement centres and offered English classes and recreational activities. So, too, did Catholic, Jewish, and Protestant organizations. In addition to long-standing ethnic organizations, some new ones also emerged at this time. Through their referral services, all of these groups were in frequent contact with government departments, including the local offices of the National Employment Service (NES), the Immigration Branch, and the provincial Department of Public Welfare. Clients were also referred to hospitals, family court, and a host of family and child-protection agencies that, as in the case of the Children's Aid Society, were semi-autonomous but nevertheless an integral part of the apparatus of the welfare state.

The International Institute, which received charitable moneys through the city's United Appeal fund as well as private donations, belonged to this elaborate network of services. The agency was itself an amalgam of several organizations that had been involved in immigrant aid work since 1952. At that time, St Andrew's Presbyterian Church and the Toronto Welfare Council (later the Social Planning Council) agreed to run the church's old St Andrew's Memorial House as a friendship house, serving immigrants with the help of funds obtained through the Community Chest. Soon afterwards, a group of well-to-do Torontonians established within the house a counselling and orientation service for immigrants. Called the New Canadians Services Association, this organization became in the fall of 1954 a fundraising project of the Junior League of Toronto. Initially, its only full-time and professional staff member was Mrs W.E. (Nell) West, a social worker who had served as assistant deputy minister of public welfare in Ontario during the Depression and as a senior official with the United Nations Relief and Rehabilitation Administration (UNRRA) after the war. In 1956 the service officially amalgamated with St Andrew's House to form a multifaceted immigrant aid society.[6]

The International Institute differed from many of the city's agencies in that its clientele was exclusively immigrant. More specifically, it served non-British newcomers, which, in these years, meant predominantly European-born arrivals, including Displaced Persons from central and Eastern Europe and, later, Hungarian refugees, Germans, and Mediterranean groups like the Italians, Greeks, and Portuguese. It was not until the late 1960s that the institute attracted many immigrants of colour. While an awareness within the agency of the need to combat racism against people of colour was evident as early as 1963, when the institute joined forces with the Ontario Human Rights Commission to launch an anti-racism campaign,[7] the institute before 1965 worked mainly among white Catholic, Protestant, and Jewish Europeans.

Considering itself a 'specialized, non-political and non-sectarian agency,'[8] the institute sought to answer the needs of the newcomers it attracted by performing three major services. The mostly volunteer staff of the Department of Group Services ran the institute's reception centre and conducted community advocacy work. At the reception centre, staff workers organized a variety of cultural, educational, and recreational activities. These ranged from movies, afternoon teas, and Saturday night dances, to English instruction, bridge classes, and, for married women, lessons in nutrition, child-rearing, and the operation of domestic appliances. Amateur Nights showcasing talented immigrant musicians were designed to offer newcomers an opportunity not only to learn about Canada or to meet one another but also to mingle with the Anglo-Celtic Torontonians whom the institute staff sought to attract to these events. In this way it was hoped that, as one staff worker put it, 'the newcomers may be encouraged to become adjusted to the new culture and add to it by meeting, observing, and understanding their Canadian friends.'[9]

Although staff members frequently noted their failure in attracting more married women to the reception centre, they considered the reception programe, which drew both fee-paying members and casual attenders, a success. Writing years later, a former institute president recalled the events held at the reception centre with obvious fondness: 'Hundreds of people came virtually every evening ... They made music, played games, danced, talked with one another, or just enjoyed sitting in a decent surrounding instead of the sad and shabby rooms in which newcomers live ... That did not exclude that during the day they were counselled and referred, and what not.'[10] His view mirrored the sentiments of the supervisor of group services, David H. Stewart, who, a decade earlier, had described the program in these terms: 'Every activity ... is designed to foster and promote the integration of Old and New Canadian.' 'It is interesting to observe,' he added, 'that historical conflicts are resolved in this setting, within the special groups and in the general activities, as they could not be resolved elsewhere. The atmosphere ... is such that all members, through fellowship, avoid the expression of prejudice in pursuit of their common goal as Canadian citizen. Deliberately we cultivate freedom of expression and try to show that this personal freedom can thrive only in mutual self-respect. This general philosophy we foster as the groundwork for the Institute member when he eventually drops his membership to integrate into the community at large.'[11]

Second, while the institute staff adopted a model of cultural pluralism that assumed respect for some of the cultural traditions of immigrants, they hoped, ultimately, to Canadianize them. Amid the Cold War, staff workers, like many other Canadians, associated the willingness of newcomers to adapt to a Canadian lifestyle and adopt Canadian citizenship as a victory in the struggle against the Soviet union and as proof of the moral superiority of Western democracies like Canada. Such an orientation fit neatly with the broad program of the Canadian government during the early years of the Cold War. Immigration officials welcomed applicants likely to be anti-communist because of their European experiences and established screening processes to block the entry of 'Communists.' And, in 1950, the Liberal government set up the Citizenship Branch within the new Department of Citizenship and Immigration. Building on earlier practices of the wartime Nationalities Branch, the Citizenship Branch monitored Canada's ethnic communities and supplied organizations with materials depicting the Soviets negatively and Western democracies positively. Many of the movies, lectures, and other educational materials presented by the institute were designed to celebrate Canadian traditions and to reveal the horrors of communism.[12]

This interest in remaking immigrants into Canadians also explains why the institute staff viewed ethnic organizations with suspicion even while they cooperated with them. It was assumed that while such organizations gave immigrants 'a feeling of belonginess,' they retarded the process of assimilation. As one institute supervisor advised: 'The ethnic halls and clubs do good work in the sense that they help preserve the cultural heritage, but they do bad work in that they, unwittingly, I am sure, create national ghettoes and thus slow the integration, the Candianization ..., of the newcomers.' By contrast, he maintained, 'the Institute produces a mix of groups, of oldtimers and natives. In that respect, it is comparably more beneficial than any ethnic organization.'[13]

The third major service offered by the institute was undertaken by a specialized staff of professional social workers and trained volunteers who, under the guidance of a supervisor, ran the Department of Individual Services. It was their responsibility to provide information, a referral service, and counselling, when this was deemed appropriate. Although it is difficult to pinpoint precisely the number of counsellors employed at the institute in these years, the evidence suggests that at any given time there were between eight and ten, divided more or less evenly between men and women and between professional social workers and volunteers. While the supervisor held a master's degree in social work, most of the professionally trained personnel had obtained a bachelor of social work. All the professional social workers were men, whereas the volunteers, with one exception, were women. Most of these women appear to have been married. They also represented an ethnically diverse group; about one-half were Canadian-born while the remainder were either the Canadian-raised children of immigrants or themselves recent immigrants. In the latter case, all were Eastern Europeans from families with professional backgrounds. The one male volunteer, a refugee from Eastern Europe, was similarly a professional. Altogether, the staff could offer counselling in nineteen different languages.[14]

If the caseworkers belonged to the middle class, the clients generally belonged to the ranks of the economically disadvantaged, the working class, and even the poor. The vast majority of the clients in our sample (and virtually every southern European) came from a peasant or rural artisanal family background but had now joined the ranks of the urban working class. A small number of clients, approximately 15 per cent, were skilled factory workers who now found themselves underemployed or out of work. A tiny minority (6 per cent), most of them Eastern Europeans, were either professionals or married to professionals. In each case, they were facing difficulties in obtaining a Canadian licence or establishing a local practice, and were thus experiencing downward mobility. The clients came to the institute from various sources: while some were referred to the service from government departments, the courts, other agencies, or even the institute's own Group Services section, others came on their own, having heard of the institute by 'word-of-mouth,' usually from kin or neighbours.[15]

The Ordinary Family in Extraordinary Times

The institute's counsellors differed from each other in training or specialization, but they shared a basic commitment to the case-work approach that by the 1950s was a widely used social work technique.[16] When it came to considering how best to address their immigrant client's needs, they also shared a family orientation that placed much emphasis on the promotion of a stable familial environment, one in which, ideally, working husbands kept family finances relatively secure and housekeeping mothers maintained a loving and moral home. In an address to a local IODE chapter, Dr Robert Kreem, a social worker and West's successor as institute director in 1965, argued that along with 'financial success,' a 'happy family life' was an essential ingredient in the successful adjustment of immigrants. He added that as 'family tensions and discord' had 'a hampering effect on adjustment,' the institute staff had been committed to resolving intra-familial conflict and supporting struggling families, as well as attacking other barriers, like unemployment, that impeded the immigrants' successful adjustment. In making a case for the value of his agency, he used the metaphor of the family, calling it a 'home-away-from-home,' where the immigrants 'can discuss all their problems or share their joy.'[17]

In showing concern about the nuclear family and for the preservation of family life, Dr Kreem and his colleagues were scarcely alone. Indeed, their views reflected a family ideology that pervaded not only the social work profession in this period but most elements of society. In the immediate postwar years there was much hand-wringing about the challenges facing Canadian families. An educational specialist voiced the concerns of many when, in an address to the Toronto Local Council of Women in 1952, he declared: 'Children are growing up in an anxious age, where there is a threat of war. Homes are broken or both parents work. Modern life stresses specialization and scientific advancement has outrun comprehension.'[18] There was also considerable debate about how best to preserve, indeed, strengthen the family in a rapidly changing, modern world.

It was generally acknowledged that following two decades of suffering and devastation owing to the Great Depression and the Second World War, many Canadians were eager to resume their private lives, to marry, and seek happiness in a 'normal' family life. The plight of Displaced Persons, especially the children, was held up as a reminder of the havoc that war wreaked on family life and the misery experienced by those without families. Contemporary observers and social experts also pointed to the alarming evidence that families in Canada, as elsewhere, were facing extraordinary pressures. Rising rates of divorce and juvenile delinquency, an increase of married women in the paid workforce, the lack of affordable housing for newly married couples and young families, and the new fears unleashed by the threat of nuclear war were all viewed as indicators that the family was in need of bolstering.[19]

In an address entitled 'The Ordinary Family in Extraordinary Times,' a casework supervisor with the Family Welfare Association of Montreal provided a gendered analysis of her times:

[F]amily life has been taking a beating during the past 20 years ... [T]he great depression ... [meant the] postponement of marriage for many young people because of lack of jobs, which was extremely serious, both biologically and psychologically ... Many husbands and fathers appeared to be failing in their role as breadwinner and consequently in the eyes of their children to be total failures ... Then came the war ... Couples were flung apart to have widely different experiences. When the war was over, they had to begin all over again, but the situation was not the same ... For men there was the difficulty of settling down to a humdrum life. For women too, who during the war had to rally and do many things that they had never done before, there was a letdown ... A very special hazard to family life has been the extreme housing shortage [so that] young people have been unable to find a place of their own ... Overcrowding ... in the homes of relatives does not offer a natural opportunity for family life to grow and has contributed greatly to the development of strained and broken family relationships and subsequently less useful citizens.'[20]

As these comments suggest, the postwar discourse among middle-class observers and experts regarding family life was predicated on a model of the family that posited a strict gender-based division of tasks. The claim that men and women had different but complementary roles to play could also be accommodated to the ideal of a companionate marriage. Ideally, wives were perceived to be happy homemakers fulfilling their destiny to create a loving and stable home for a hardworking husband and children. In the words of the Reverend Dr W.J. Gallagher of the Canada Council of Churches, 'homelife, social standards and moral behaviour are the responsibility of women.'[21] Marriages were expected to be loving partnerships. It was nonetheless clear, as Ruth Pierson has recently shown, that the dominant rhetoric, and, indeed, the welfare policies of the day, assigned economic primacy and final authority to the man on the grounds that he supported a household of dependants.[22]

Such socially conservative assumptions were evident in the arguments of even progressive social workers who called for greater state intervention on behalf of the unemployed and poor. In a 1954 article that appeared in the *Social Worker*, official organ of the Canadian Association of Social Workers, three female community workers argued that male unemployment remained a serious threat to family life. Like many of their colleagues, the authors saw unemployment as essentially a crisis in masculinity and thus ignored the growing numbers of wage-earning wives who were keeping family finances afloat. In their discussion of the 'evil effects' of unemployment, wives are portrayed unsympathetically: 'the growing and persistent feeling of inadequacy of the man ... unable to supply his family's needs, the tensions arising between husband and wife, and the nagging that even the most understanding wife occasionally indulged in ...'[23]

In positing a return to a 'normal' family life, Canada's family and medical experts, like the American and British colleagues whose viewpoints they shared, were simultaneously expounding a familiar, middle-class ideal of womanhood that reaffirmed women's domestic orientation. Women, it was argued, possessed the moral capacity to provide their families with an emotional haven in an uncertain world, and it was precisely through their selfless contributions to home and family that they found true happiness and fulfilment. Both popular commentators and social scientists of the day affirmed the view that women were primarily responsible for creating a happy marriage as well as for child care and parenting. The ideal portrait of the married woman, then, was of a cheerful wife and good mother who accepted her social responsibility and reaped the benefits in the form of a contented husband and well-adjusted children. There was, however, a darker side to the argument for, as Veronica Strong-Boag has observed, those women who deviated from or defied such conventions were blamed for producing society's 'misfits,' be they deserting husbands, homosexual sons, juvenile delinquents, or the mentally unstable.[24]

As the contributions of community and agency workers to the the *Social Worker* document, Canada's postwar volunteer and professional social workers sought to reform the behaviour of their troubled clients by encouraging them to conform to the prevailing notions of 'normal' family life and 'healthy' gender relations. Thus, for example, while family agency workers counselled against pressuring unmarried mothers to give up their babies, they applauded when the desired outcome occurred. As one caseworker observed, through adoption the illegitimate child was given a two-parent family and 'economic and emotional security,' while the young woman was freed to form 'an attachment to another man leading to marriage.'[25]

Social workers who served an immigrant clientele similarly saw the process of assisting their clients' 'adjustment' as primarily a process of reshaping 'deviant' families according to the prevailing, North American model that combined patriarchal ideals of family with the notion of a companionate marriage. Arguing the merits of a 'socio-cultural approach' to social work that recognized the role of cultural background in explaining certain behaviourial traits among people, Benjamin Schlesinger, a lecturer at the University of Toronto School of Social Work, explained the objectives of his profession in relation to the postwar immigrants: 'Public agencies are asked to investigate deviations and social workers are faced with interpreting community standards to the "New Canadian."' Such community standards, as the remainder of his article made clear, included a more 'egalitarian' view of the family that placed limitations on the husband's domineering attitude towards his wife, including his right to beat her, and a more indulgent form of child rearing.

In making his case, Schlesinger was expressing the view of many Canadians, including the institute counsellors, that the newly arrived families from Eastern and southern Europe lagged behind the more modern North American family. But in seeking to reshape the immigrants' lives, they were not so concerned to eliminate the patriarchal organization of 'traditional' European families – many of which were peasant or rural artisanal families that had long combined traditions of masculine authority with a cooperative work ethos – as to alter its character and give it a more modern or North American basis. While immigrant men thus were expected to acquire sole responsibility for the economic support of their family, and be companionable partners to their wives, married women were expected to adapt to Canadian standards of domestic life in everything from cooking to child-rearing methods, and thereby provide a 'well-adjusted' home for their husband and children. Social workers saw themselves as gatekeepers of a modern, socially progressive society, with a right to intervene in the lives of their needy or unruly immigrant clients. As Schlesinger explained, the newcomers had come to a country that sanctioned 'the community's right to protect children, to regulate family disorganization, and to interfere in difficult family relations.'[26]

The case records of Toronto's International Institute provide a fine opportunity to consider how these approaches and ideals were translated into daily practice. Did the counsellors stick rigidly to prevailing notions of women and femininity and, for that matter, men and masculinity? To what extent did the clients themselves frustrate the aims of their counsellors? Did the demands and behaviour of the clients force their caseworkers to reconsider their objectives or at least to tolerate some deviance from the hegemonic ideal?

Tending to the Battered and Deserted Wife

Even while they made up only a small percentage of the institute's heavy caseload, the plight of women like Mrs Gabura and the other battered and deserted wives reinforced in the minds of the counsellors the association of minority women with victimization by men who came from cultures that sanctioned the harsh treatment for women and children. Their perceptions of how best to tend to the needs of such women was correspondingly influenced by their adherence to prevailing North American notions of gender and family.

We can see these factors at play in the Gabura case. In responding to Mrs Gabura's call for help, the caseworkers were initially most concerned to bring about a reconciliation between husband and wife. When Gabura first reported the incident involving the private detectives, the staff were genuinely alarmed. They also acted promptly, alerting the police to the situation and sending a stern letter to the husband. Convinced that the marriage could eventually be mended and the family reunited, however, the staff also encouraged the man to return home and seek therapy. 'If you have family problems,' read the letter sent to him, 'there are community agencies from whom you may get advice and counsel. We will be glad to help you make contact with them.'

Thus, Gabura's definition of her own problem – to be rid of an abusive husband and to raise the children on her own – became redefined by institute workers as a family problem. But in seeking to preserve her family, the caseworkers had not been interested merely to bring the husband back into the household. Rather, they had also hoped to reform him and thus reshape the dynamics of this deviant family along a more companionate model. It was only when caseworkers were completely convinced that there was no chance of reconciliation – the point being made painfully clear when her husband's continuing harassment drove Gabura to attempt suicide – that they abandoned the idea of reuniting the family and began to think of Gabura as a single mother. The sympathy they showered on her also reflected their conviction that she was indeed 'a good mother,' as one caseworker described her, and thus a worthy client.

Gabura's file stands out from most of the other cases involving violence against women in the considerable length of time that the institute counsellors were involved in her affairs. For a period, the woman developed a trusting relationship with the female volunteer who became her chief caseworker. Even this case, however, ends abruptly when Gabura ceased relations with the agency apparently because she no longer found it useful to herself and her children. Indeed, while they might have hoped to play a more profound role in all their clients' lives, the institute counsellors often found themselves confined to providing their woman clients with material aid – donating food and clothing vouchers or referring them to the local Welfare or immigration office for emergency handouts. At the same time, institute caseworkers, like their colleagues elsewhere, sought to avoid encouraging a family to develop a permanent dependency on state and community services. Thus, their desire to help a truly needy client was tempered by the belief that, in the long run, families ought to be economically independent. Such a conviction, as Linda Gordon has documented for the United States, has pervaded the profession of social work since the turn of the century. In the 1950s, social workers discovered the 'multi-problem family' that could not escape the vicious cycle of dependency. Such families absorbed a disproportionate amount of attention and financial assistance. It was thus all the more important, the professionals argued, that they be discriminating.[27] How, then, did these competing demands affect the institute caseworkers' response to the problems confronted by the battered or deserted wife?

Before venturing an answer to these questions, let us consider a few more illustrations. The following four case histories involving abused and/or deserted women offer different variations on a similar theme.

The client in our first example, Bella Schiff, was a young Jewish woman from Eastern Europe who came to the institute in the spring of 1959. The caseworker's initially guarded response to Schiff can be attributed largely to the fact that she had been referred to the agency by her probation officer. However, as the woman's story unfolded, the caseworker, yet another of the female volunteers on staff, became more sympathetic. On arriving in Canada two years previously, Schiff, it turned out, had entered into a common-law marriage with a man whom she had met on the voyage over. For much of the time she had been supporting him, until she was laid off from her factory job in October 1958. Though she had reported regularly to the local office of the Immigration Branch, she had repeatedly rejected the jobs assigned to her until the placement officers, convinced she was not serious about finding work, stopped the small handouts normally offered to immigrants who did not qualify for unemployment insurance. The resulting financial difficulties left the couple in considerable debt, prompting them to orchestrate a forgery scam in which they tried to cheat a friend out of his savings. The effort failed and landed both of them in jail for a few months. When she was released on probation, Schiff became determined to leave her partner, who, she now disclosed, had been abusive towards her 'most of the time.' Although she had tried to leave him on several occasions, each time he had forced his way back into her home. 'She is frightened,' wrote the caseworker after hearing the woman's story, 'and wants to separate from him.' In respond-

ing to Schiff's predicament, the caseworker agreed to cooperate
with the woman's probation officer, who had already made arrangements for her to acquire a legal separation from her common-law husband. The institute counsellor also set about trying
to find her client a job and convinced her to register in English
classes. She also referred Schiff to the Jewish Family Agency for
additional counselling, where it was hoped the woman might benefit from talking with a social worker who would better understand her racial background.

As promised, Schiff returned to the institute several days later,
informing the caseworker that the Jewish Family Agency had
helped her to qualify for welfare benefits (amounting to $17.00
each month) and to move her into a new flat. She declared that
she was now ready to look for a job. As the following file entry
suggests, the caseworker was pleased with the woman's progress
but remained sceptical that the client, having already shown herself to be a poor judge of men and a woman of low morals, might
easily be seduced into another relationship with a man she barely
knew. 'She talked to me clearly and sensibly,' the entry reads,
'and I had the impression that she was really glad about the
separation. It could be also possible that she will cling to another
[man] because of loneliness.'

Over the course of the next month, as Schiff was fired from
one job after another, her caseworker's attitude towards her re-
verted to one of suspicion. Typically, the caseworker had found
her client domestic service work. Within a week of obtaining her
first job, the employer who had hired Schiff as her cleaning lady
let her go. 'I heard,' the caseworker recorded in her file, accepting the employer's explanation of matters, 'that she was not
interested to work and took it too easy. Smoked cigarets all the
time and was slow.' When Schiff was fired again, this time from
a hotel where she had been employed as a chamber maid for
three weeks, a frustrated caseworker barked: 'It seems to me that
she cannot hold any employment.' To make matters worse, the
woman, by this time, had done the expected and taken up with
another man. While the caseworker tried a few more times to

place the woman in jobs, Schiff moved in with her new lover and subsequently disappeared.[28]

If the caseworker's perception of Schiff was clouded by the woman's less than sterling reputation, the converse could be equally true. As we saw in Garuba's case, the women who appeared as virtuous wives in no way responsible for their unfortunate predicament elicited a far more sympathetic response. Another Jewish woman, Mrs Karlinsky, for example, had been referred to the institute from family court, where her husband was in the process of obtaining a divorce. In the interim, however, he was making life miserable for her and she wanted to get out of the house as soon as possible. A pertinent case entry reads: 'He is treating her badly ... [T]hey are living together but everyday he tells her to get out of the place. [She] wants to find work to earn some money because the husband refuses to give her any ... [She] was in tears ... said that she has to find work to be on her own and not to ask for every penny from her husband.' Her eagerness to get on with her life was further evident in her eagerness to accept the domestic placement her caseworker secured for her in a nursing home. Two years later, when the caseworker reopened the file to find out what had become of her client, she found that, to her obvious delight, the woman was still employed at the same place.[29]

The counsellor's readiness to accept Karlinsky's version of events – that her husband was unredeemable and the marriage definitely over – was linked to the fact that a colleague on staff had acted as the court interpreter during the divorce proceedings and could confirm the client's claim that the husband was an unrepentant brute and the woman was better off without him.

In two cases taken from the early 1960s and involving Italian women, the institute staff were similarly convinced that there was little possibility of reuniting a wife with a husband who deserted the family. In the first instance, Mrs Caruso, a forty-two-year-old mother of five young children, came to the agency after she found herself abandoned by a husband to whom she had been married for fifteen years. The husband, who had a history of mental illness, had also been abusive towards his wife. Caruso had been referred to the institute by a social worker employed with a local community agency, the Neighbourhood Workers Association, in the hopes that the Italian-speaking volunteers might establish 'a friendly relationship' with her and enlist her into the reception centre's program. At the institute, the professional social worker assigned to the case agreed with his colleague's assessment, noting that the woman ought to be encouraged to break out of the isolation of her home and become more involved in her wider community. The pertinent file entry reads: '[She] is culturally isolated and is not involved with either the English or Italian community ... She seems to be interested in learning English but is hindered because she has three children at home. The three eldest children are attending [an elementary school].' Over the next few years, the institute acted much as a surrogate family, dispatching Italian volunteers to visit the woman, encouraging her to register her children in summer day camps, and even enlisting her in English and 'kitchen' classes while volunteers watched her children.[30]

The institute caseworkers apparently did not consider the possibility that Caruso might enter the workforce. She had neither experience in the labour force nor relatives with whom she might leave her young children, and as an older woman she was not an attractive prospect to employers. The caseworkers seemed resigned to the fact that, at least until her children grew up, she would remain dependent on government welfare benefits and other social services. This situation contrasts sharply, however, with the second Italian case in which the deserted wife had been a working woman with considerable experience in the workforce. Thus, when this woman, the mother of four teenage boys, found herself abandoned by her husband shortly after she experienced a workplace injury, the thrust of the caseworker's response was to secure the woman compensation payments until she could return once again to the workforce.[31]

As these cases suggest, the institute counsellors often found themselves having to recommend or accept remedies to a particular situation that they considered less than ideal. While they might have preferred that a woman compelled by circumstance to abandon a marriage might one day remarry and resume a 'normal' two-parent family arrangement, their daily experience also taught them that the chances of this happening were slim. They recognized there had to be some alternative for these female-headed households lest they become seduced into dependency. A single mother's entry into the workforce, especially when it might help to keep her family from either poverty or dependency, was considered far the lesser of two evils.

In seeking to find appropriate solutions to their clients' predicament, the institute caseworkers did not always respond in a consistent fashion. While a model of the ideal family influenced their assessments, other factors, such as the fear of fueling a racist backlash, were at times equally compelling. Thus when in the spring of 1958 a Hungarian woman who had been raped by a compatriot living in the same boarding house came to the institute wanting to lay assault charges against the man, the counsellors persuaded her and her husband to keep the matter quiet. A statement, filed some days after the event, reveals the caseworkers' motives: 'Acting on the premise that the more publicity given to such cases, the more difficult would be our general job, we decided to try to settle this out of court.' In the end, they convinced the woman to drop the charges on the condition that the institute find the couple 'better accommodation.' The case ends with a familiar, class-specific explanation of male aggression. 'As with so many cases,' the entry reads, the incident 'had arisen out of the frustrations of poor lodgings, lack of employment for the men, and the general insecurity.'[32]

Although they required a great deal of attention, the cases of abandoned wives, as noted earlier, made up a small proportion of a counsellor's workload. More typically, when the institute intervened in the life of a family whose husband was absent, the man had been only temporarily removed on account of illness or injury. In these instances, as the following case involving Mrs De Rosa demonstrates, it was quite common for the institute staff to see themselves as stepping in temporarily until the husband could resume his position as the head of the household and family breadwinner. De Rosa was a Portuguese woman whose husband contracted tuberculosis and was hospitalized in the Ontario Sanitorium in 1958. Her husband's illness left De Rosa, a young mother who had recently given birth, facing outstanding mortgage payments on a house the couple had recently purchased.

During the course of the next two years, the institute staff kept tabs on the woman, referring her to a lawyer who helped her to sell the house (though at a substantial financial loss to the couple), dispatching volunteers for home visits and English lessons, filling out application forms for welfare benefits, as well as helping her to move to a location nearer the hospital so she might visit her husband regularly. When it became clear that her welfare benefits were insufficient for her family's needs, her institute caseworker, a professional social worker, and the staff supervisor also recommended her to a local chapter of the IODE, which agreed to pay the woman's grocery and outstanding gas and heating bills. By offering De Rosa regular support, the institute staff were in effect helping her to continue to fulfil her domestic responsibilities and to maintain close relations with her husband. As the file comes to an end, it seems clear that her caseworker expects the husband will soon be on his feet and the family reunited.[33]

The priority that prevailing notions about family gave to women's domesticity were amply illustrated by those cases where illness or injury took the wife, rather than the husband, away from the household. Consider, for example, how caseworkers responded to the problem posed by an Italian family when, in the fall of 1959, the mother was hospitalized for 'nervous exhaustion.' She was a forty-year-old women who, since her arrival in Toronto three years previously, had been combining full-time factory work with raising a family. Convinced that the father could not adequately care for the children, his counsellor advised that the children, some of whom had become disruptive at school, be temporarily placed in a Catholic orphanage until his wife recovered. Such a response not only reflected prevailing notions about women's proper role but also the assumption that men alone could not be responsible for parenting.[34]

Men, Women, and Parental Responsibilities

Women, of course, were not the only sex to whom particular gender roles had been assigned. While men were generally given far greater rein than women, they, too, were expected to meet carefully delineated family roles as hard-working husbands and authoritative but fair-minded fathers. Typically, as we have seen, the men who defied the rules did not make themselves available to social agencies, nor did they show much interest in reforming their behaviour and reintegrating themselves into their families. This makes the few occasions when husbands did receive such counselling particularly significant.

Only one case could be found in the current sample where institute caseworkers considered themselves successful at saving a marriage and reuniting a family by reforming the husband's behaviour. The client in question was Mr Podoski, a Polish man and father of four teenagers who, in 1955, had abandoned his family to care for a sick mother. It was not until five years later that institute caseworkers encountered Podoski. He actually came to the office looking for work, but he was soon telling his story to the professional social worker who had been assigned to the case. Since their arrival in Canada in 1948, Podoski explained, his wife and mother had been unable 'to get along' while living under the same roof. When his mother had become mentally ill, he had chosen to move the two of them into a flat rather than place his mother in a nursing home. At present, she was in hospital but he explained that he would continue to care for her when she was released. The caseworker tried, in vain, to encourage Podoski to return to his wife and children. A statement filed some time after the interview describes what transpired: '[He] stressed ... that according to his cultural values, children are responsible for the welfare of [their] parents and that old age homes are designed simply for the 'poor and rejected' people. We explored possible plans together, but his own plan remained unchanged. Accordingly, his mother returned to him from the hospital. We recognized [his] immediate need was financial security and found him a job for which he was thankful. However,

he had been asked by his wife to return home and he was torn
between his responsibilities to his mother and to his family.'

No sooner had Podoski's mother returned home, however,
than the woman died, prompting him to return to his caseworker,
who now took the opportunity to counsel him on his duty to the
family he had abandoned. After several meetings, Podoski agreed
to return home. When, a month later, he sent his caseworker an
appreciative note, telling him that while his relations with his wife
and children were strained they were definitely improving, the
caseworker was decidedly pleased. In responding, the counsellor
assured the man that he had made the right choice in resuming
his responsibilities as husband and father. 'You and your family,'
he added, 'will need time and effort to get used to each other
again. A period of eight years can't be bridged in 1 or 2 months.
The most important factor is, that you and your family have the
courage to tackle the problem.' Instructing him to contact 'a
proper agency' should they 'face too difficult a problem,' he ended
with the following advice: '[R]emember, that no battle ever has
been won without sweat and tears.'[35]

As the institute staff workers never actually inspected Podoski's
family home, they could not determine for themselves the state
of affairs in that household. More typically, when clients were
suspected of being irresponsible, uninformed, or neglectful parents, the women took much of the blame. When, for example,
institute caseworkers suspected one family of taking a disproportionate share of the agency's weekly food voucher and clothing handouts, they decided to visit the family to determine the
root of the problem. The visitor was an experienced female volunteer who conducted many of the agency's home visits in these
years. Reporting on the sorry state of the household, she filed
the following report:

> The family has two rooms, kitchen and bathroom. When visiting
> them I found only Sonya (16 years) with the rest of the children.
> Helena [8] is suffering from chickenpox. Sonya mentioned the
> doctor and the medicine costs lot (sic) of money. The place was
> depressing, the rooms untidy, though furniture is new it looks

like old because it is very badly kept. The floor was dirty. It was morning and the courtains (sic) were still in the same position as were during the night. On account of the untidiness the girl (Sonya) was very embarrassed and she didn't know where she could have an interview. In the children's room was a bed where the sick Helena sleeps together with Sonya. The boy [11] has another bed and Melissa [3] sleeps in the crib. We couldn't have an interview in the kitchen either because the floor was to[o] dirty and many unwashed dishes laying around. Finally we went into parents['] bedroom. Even though the bed was covered it was still [noticeable] the dirty bedding.

While the visitor's preoccupation with dirty bedding and unwashed dishes smacks of middle-class prejudice, her report was generally sympathetic and confirmed the client's story that her family was in a tight financial spot, a situation made worse by medical bills and the outstanding debts owed to a furniture company. In the end, however, she concluded that the mother needed 'help for budgetting,' thereby laying a large part of the problem on the woman's supposedly inefficient running of the household. In positing a recommendation that reaffirmed women's domestic role, the caseworker also engaged in some victim blaming.[36]

In contrast to the twelve deserting or abusive husbands in our sample, only three files expose an unfaithful wife and one case an abusive mother. Not surprisingly, the caseworkers were particularly nasty in their evaluation of women who left husbands, took up lovers, or had illegitimate children. While caseworkers might attribute the physical abuse of children by fathers to their cultural background, immigrant mothers were exempt from such explanations, presumably because motherly love was thought to be a universal attribute all women, regardless of race or class, ought to possess. While this general assumption smacked of sexism, the brutality of the abusive mother documented here goes some way towards explaining why the institute caseworkers were so condemnatory.

In discussing the case of the abusive mother, it should be noted that much of the evidence gathered against the woman came in the form of accusations from her estranged husband while the couple was going through a messy divorce and child custody battle. He had enlisted the help of the institute to try to get the child placed in a temporary foster home until after the legal battle. Many of his accusations, however, were later confirmed by neighbours and even one of the woman's former lovers. The husband's account of his wife's abusive behaviour towards their young daughter included engaging in sexual intercourse with men in front of the child, and sexually 'touching' the child. Although the wife denied the charges when institute staff workers approached her in family court, they were unmoved, largely because they had read a letter she had written to her husband in which she apparently revealed some damning evidence about herself. The case files do not contain the letter, but the response it evoked from one caseworker suggests the nature of its contents: 'It was terrible – disgusting the language she used. I hardly could believe that a woman was writing such things.' The caseworkers' general contempt for the woman might explain why, after the father absconded with the child in the middle of the divorce proceedings, there were no disparaging comments made about him in the file. The case ends with a lengthy letter that the husband sent to the local police department. 'I am not willing to leave the child with the mother,' he concludes, 'I tried to persuade my wife to educate the child in a normal way but it was useless. I will teach my daughter Canadian morals and not the morals of her mother.'[37]

Housekeeping Mothers and Married Women Workers

The case files often reveal a good deal more about the caseworker's approach or attitude towards the client than they do about the client. By contrast, only rarely are we treated to the unmediated voice of the client, usually in the form of a written note left for the counsellor. Even such evidence, of course, does not preclude the possibility that the client might be acting in a manipulative fashion or constructing herself as a deserving client. Most of the time we are compelled to read the version of a client's story as filtered through the caseworker's 'professional' eyes. But just as we tease from these files evidence regarding the ideological and methodological inclinations of the counsellor, so, too, can we glean valuable information about the clients themselves, even if we cannot always determine their emotional or psychological state. At times, even the silences and absences in the files speak volumes. A consideration of the files reveals, for example, that while the counsellors' professional biases might have led them to depict many of their female clients as victims lacking the where-withal or resources to tackle their difficulties, the women cannot simply be dismissed as either passive victims or passive recipients of the welfare apparatus. Even Mrs Gabura of our opening story, though obviously the victim of a cruel husband and materially disadvantaged as a single mother, cannot simply be labelled a passive victim who allowed herself to be processed by a team of specialists. While she benefited from the support she received from the institute staff, she chose, in the end, to take matters into her own hands, a decision that appeared to correspond with a new-found sense of confidence following her recovery from her suicide attempt.

If caseworkers might have found it difficult to see Gabura and the other battered and abandoned women they encountered in their office as protagonists, the same cannot be said for their response to the far more numerous women who came to them in search of work or other forms of short-term, practical aid. Hundreds of immigrant housewives, most of them mothers of young children, showed up at the institute in these years, ready to collect clothing donations, food vouchers, and other handouts. Mothers with newborns picked up baby layettes; others attended the institute's free picnics and Easter and Christmas parties so they could collect the food baskets and presents for the children. Often, the woman had been directed to the agency by relatives or neighbours who had themselves benefited from the services the institute offered. For many of these families, the institute was not a substitute for support from family and kin; rather, it was an additional form of support.

Apart from trying to weed out fraudulent requests for aid – a preoccupation that might lead them to conduct home visits – the institute staff found little difficulty in processing these cases. When they did express concern for these clients and their families, it was one born of a frustration that they were not more successful in recruiting immigrant housewives into their English classes, civics lectures, and other programs offered through the reception centre. As late as 1967, for example, staff workers identified as a primary goal 'a need to meet the house-bound wife, with small children.'[38] The interest they showed in immigrant housewives reflected a genuine interest in providing a forum in which non-English-speaking women living in the isolation of their homes might make some contact with the wider society. This, in turn, was linked to their larger commitment to encourage immigrant mothers to convert to Canadian ways. In these aims, however, they were thwarted by the clients themselves, many of whom adopted a pragmatic approach to the agency. Most of the housewives in our sample, for example, declined to become members of the institute or to enrol in any of the programs offered through its reception centre. No doubt, heavy domestic duties and cultural differences partially explain why these women did not participate. But their behaviour more accurately reflected the selective ways in which many of these women made use of available services.

In seeking such forms of aid, the immigrant housewives did not, of course, pose a challenge to prevailing notions about woman's domesticity. By contrast, however, the image of the married woman worker did not conform to the hegemonic ideal of womanhood. By far the most common reason prompting married women to approach the institute was to secure help in finding a job so that they could contribute to their family's limited finances. Married women who were living in two-parent households, most of them with children, made up a majority of the female job placement cases. Fully 70 per cent of our sample deal with women seeking paid work, of whom close to two-thirds were married. The vast majority of the placements, or 95 per cent, involved domestic service placements and factory work, where many immigrant women were already employed. Indeed, immigrant women accounted for a significant share of the growing numbers of married women who entered the Canadian workforce in the two decades after the Second World War. By 1961, European-born women represented more than one-third of Toronto's total female labour force.[39]

The high proportion of married immigrant women in the workforce or seeking paid work reflected, above all, economic need related to the inability of the husband to earn a wage sufficient to support a wife and children. As scholars have observed for earlier periods, women's role as the family's secondary wage earner was a dramatic illustration of the great gap between the ideology of family breadwinner and reality: most working-class (and some middle-class) men could not earn a wage sufficient to support their families. The immediate post-Second World War era was no exception, particularly as it pertained to immigrant wage earners. But whereas in an earlier era the family's additional wage earner might more commonly have been a son and/or daughter, the general youthfulness of immigrant families in these years, coupled with more stringent schooling laws and plentiful job opportunities for low-skilled women in cities like Toronto, largely explains the higher number of immigrant wives who took up the slack.[40]

That so many married women came to the institute seeking jobs further attests to this fact. As the case files indicate, married women's work was prompted by economic need and their movement in and out of the workforce was largely determined by the demands of their family. Some women sought jobs to augment the income being earned by husbands in low-skilled jobs. It was just such a predicament that prompted the wife of a Hungarian factory worker to come to the institute looking for work in the summer of 1959. Her caseworker, an East-European professional recently recruited onto the institute's volunteer staff, evidently considered it unfortunate that a young mother should be compelled to enter the workforce, but he nonetheless obliged. His response was based on a recognition that the woman's pay cheque could prevent the family from falling into serious debt: 'Husband earnings $0.80 per hour in a small factory. Can hardly live on his earnings. Needs urgently some work to help out. Very shy, helpless looking but pleasant personality.' She was placed as a domestic.[41] In other cases, the sudden injury or seasonal layoff of a husband prompted nonworking wives like Mrs Dos Santos to seek temporary jobs to keep family finances afloat. She was a Portuguese woman and mother of two children whose husband had been laid off from his construction job in November 1960 and received $36.00 per month on unemployment benefits. She landed a factory job earning $8.00 per day. Three months later, when the husband was again employed, she informed her case-worker that she was quitting work, saying that someone had to watch the young children. The following winter, however, when the husband once again found himself out of work, she returned to the agency and accepted a placement as a cleaning lady in a private home.[42] Similar scenarios appear again and again in the files, and they suggest the selective way in which many women made use of the institute.

Given the ideological predilection of the institute counsellors, one might have expected them to have expressed considerable anxiety, if not hostility, about the remarkably high numbers of married women they encountered wanting a paid job. And yet, just as the files involving single mothers described earlier indicate, their responses revealed a less rigid adherence to prevailing gender assumptions than we might expect.

To be sure, in their responses to working women, the institute counsellors did distinguish between single and married women. Unless it concerned some unrelated factor pertaining to the woman's apparently disagreeable personality or her allegedly poor work habits, none of the cases in our sample involving single women seeking paid employment were cause for comment. This tacit approval of the single woman worker in not surprising given that unmarried immigrant women were expected to seek paid employment. Large numbers of single immigrant women, after all, had been recruited by immigration officials precisely to fill labour shortages, especially in domestic service.[43]

By contrast, the case records of married woman workers suggest that caseworkers preferred that married women remain in the household. They shared the commonly expressed view that the working wife might threaten the delicate gender balance that defined relations between husband and wife. When, for example, a mother of two children enlisted the help of the institute to get a hospital job, her counsellor, a volunteer female caseworker, advised her client to stay at home with the children at least until they were old enough to begin school, 'as they need her to adjust to the new environment.'[44]

But this file also reveals a significant degree of tolerance for the working mother, for the woman's caseworker also advised her client that, while her sons were preschoolers, she learn English and thus improve her chances for a better paying job in the near future. Often, the tolerance they showed such clients was linked to the caseworker's perception that a wife's entry into the labour force was intended as a temporary (and in many cases, seasonal) intervention – to keep her family from falling over the brink of poverty or to enable her family to accumulate some savings and purchase a home. It was generally assumed that once a husband had established himself, the wife would return to the household. And if the home to which she returned was no longer the multiple-family dwelling so characteristic of the housing arrangements of recent immigrants, so much the better. At least in the short-term, however, the overall needs of the immigrant family – whatever was needed to ensure a more smooth economic adjustment – took temporary precedence over the concern that men and women be encouraged to fulfil their prescribed roles.

The following two case histories, each one of them depicting scenarios in which the wife had become the family's sole breadwinner, nicely capture this complex dynamic. In each case, the counsellor faced the task of advising the unemployed husband, who saw his breadwinner wife as a sign of his failure as a husband and father. The first involved a Hungarian couple who, in 1956, came to the institute looking to find the husband a job. While his wife had for months been employed in an office, he had been completely unsuccessful on the job market ever since their arrival in the country. In the absence of his wife, the husband explained that he had 'lost his confidence' and 'felt depressed' about having to depend on his wife's earnings. In responding to his client, the caseworker was sympathetic. However, rather than try to place the man in a job, the caseworker suggested to him that since his wife apparently did not mind working, he should consider registering in the centre's English classes to improve his chances of securing a better-paying job. Although the man agreed, he never returned.[45]

The same caseworker had more success one year later with a Yugoslavian man who was similarly upset after being laid off from his factory job. In complaining about his predicament, the client claimed he opposed his wife's working since he would 'lose prestige with his friends.' In response, the caseworker advised the client, who had been a university graduate back home, to ignore his friends and consider pursuing a trade degree while his wife supported him and their young son. In this way, he could, on graduation, land a well-paying job and support his family on his own. The man returned to school and, three years later, the final entry of the case history indicates that the expected had in fact occurred.[46]

The institute caseworkers, in their daily encounter with female clients, showed a far less rigid adherence to the dominant rhetoric regarding the inappropriateness of working wives than was evident in the writings and legislation of family and welfare experts of the period.[47] In explaining this pattern, economic factors clearly loom large. First-hand experience with hundreds of clients had taught the staff members of the institute's Department of Individual Services (and, for that matter, their colleagues elsewhere) the critical economic role that many women within immigrant and working-class families played as the family's secondary wage earner. Indeed, one might also argue that, notwithstanding the dominant rhetoric of the day, staff workers were well aware that the married woman worker was in these years becoming an increasingly familiar figure. While the immigrant working wife did not correspond to the hegemonic ideal of womanhood, she nevertheless did conform to an emerging alternative pattern of married womanhood in the post-Second World War era. It might also be worth recalling that a good proportion of the caseworkers were not only themselves working married women but also refugees and immigrants. Despite differences in class (or wealth) between them and their women clients, the European women volunteer counsellors might also have felt some empathy for their compatriots who came to them for help in getting work.

Conclusion

While a preliminary consideration of a few hundred case files belonging to one immigrant aid society cannot offer an exhaustive analysis of the busy and sometimes chaotic world of the social worker's office, the confidential case records of the International Institute of Metropolitan Toronto provide us with an opportunity to begin an exploration of the complex relations that developed between the economically disadvantaged non-British immigrants who entered postwar Canada and the middle-class professionals and volunteers who sought to intervene in and even regulate the lives of their ethnic clients. Strongly committed to the process of guiding the integration of the postwar immigrants into Canadian life, the men and women who staffed the institute's Individual Services operated within a decidedly gendered notion of what constituted the ideal family, and they also saw themselves as having the right to intervene in the lives of deviants. At the same time, however, they were concerned that the 'disorganized families' they encountered (to return to Schlesinger's phrase) did not in the long run become a dependent or 'multi-problem family.'

As the frustration they expressed over their inability to exert a more permanent influence over some of their clients suggests, the institute counsellors were not dealing with passive recipients who could easily be remoulded. To a considerable degree, their success or failure in a particular case was contingent upon many factors, including the client's willingness to cooperate with her caseworker. In this regard, the case files hint at the diversity of relationships forged between caseworker and women client, ranging from brief or hostile encounters to extended counselling sessions. This calls into question the easy generalizations of immigration historians who have assumed that the relations between newcomers and the host society's 'caretakers' were necessarily and irrevocably hostile. A battered wife might well prefer the company of her female counsellor to her husband. Nevertheless, as Gordon has astutely observed, the relationship between caseworker and client was always one between unequal players. The assistance of even sympathetic counsellors was offered in the hope that they might eventually be successful in imposing a North American and middle-class model of the family.[48] Far from exhibiting any inclination to adopt or mimic Canadian customs, many of the institute's women clients responded in a pragmatic fashion to the institute, taking advantage of its services to meet their own needs as they defined them. And on more than one occasion, the institute counsellors, in turn, were compelled by their clients to agree to assist them in ways that they, as the experts, did not necessarily condone.

NOTES

I would like to thank the other contributors to this volume for their insightful comments on earlier rambling versions of this article and for several years of support and encouragement. My thanks also to Jim Struthers for some enlightening discussions about social workers and the postwar welfare state, and to Ian Radforth who, as usual, pored over my manuscript and offered constructive criticism and editorial advice. My article is part of an ongoing project on social and political agencies and the postwar immigrants for which I have received generous financial assistance from the Ministry of Multiculturalism (Secretary of State) through its Canadian Ethnic Studies Grants Programme.

1 Archives of Ontario (AO), International Institute of Metropolitan Toronto (IIMT), Confidential Case Files, Series E-3, case 89. In order to protect the anonymity of clients and caseworkers alike, and to meet the terms under which I was permitted access to the records, I have used fictitious names and, in recounting case histories, have either eliminated or modified biographical detail. I have quoted verbatim from the files; unless otherwise stated, where a client is quoted, I have relied on the words recorded by the caseworker. In referencing the 320 case files that make up the data base for the paper, I have assigned each case a number from 1 to 320. My coding system bears no resemblance to that used

by the institute. For a valuable discussion of methodological issues concerning the historian's use of social-work files see Linda Gordon, *Heroes of Their Own Lives: The Politics and History of Family Violence* (New York: Penguin 1980).

2 The literature produced over the past twenty years, especially in the United States, is vast. For the United States see, for example, the pioneering work, Rudolph Vecoli, 'Contadini in Chicago: A Critique of the Uprooted,' *Journal of American History* 5 (1964), and the following community studies: Victor Greene, *The Slavic Community on Strike: Immigrant Labor in the Pennslyvannia Anthracite* (Notre Dame: University of Notre Dame Press 1968); Caroline Golab, *Immigrant Destinations* (Philadelphia: Temple University Press 1977); Thomas Kessner, *The Golden Door: Italian and Jewish Immigrant Mobility in New York City* (New York: Oxford University Press 1977); and John Bodnar et al., *Lives of Their Own: Blacks, Italians, and Poles in Pittsburg 1990–1960* (Urbana: University of Illinois Press 1982). A recent synthesis that draws on the new historiography is John Bodnar, *The Transplanted: A History of Immigrants in Urban America* (Philadelphia: Temple University Press 1985). For Canada, representative examples include Robert H. Harney, *Gathering Place: Peoples and Neighbourhoods of Toronto* (Toronto: Multicultural History Society of Ontario 1985); N.F. Dreisziger et al., *Struggle and Hope: The Hungarian-Canadian Experience* (Toronto: McClelland and Stewart 1982); Howard Palmer and Tamara Palmer, eds., *Peoples of Alberta: Portraits of Cultural Diversity* (Saskatoon: Western Producer Prairie Books 1985); John E. Zucchi, *Italians in Toronto: Development of a National Identity 1875–1935* (Kingston and Montreal: McGill-Queen's University Press 1988); and Franc Sturino, *Forging the Chain: Italian Migration to North America 1880–1930* (Toronto: Multicultural History Society of Ontario 1990). A valuable discussion of the aims of new immigration historians is Roberto Perin's 'Clio as Ethnic: The Third Force in Canadian Historiography,' *Canadian Historical Review* 64 (1983); and his introduction to Perin and Franc Sturino, eds., *Arrangiarsi: The Italian Immigration Experience* (Montreal: Guernica Press 1988). A detailed discussion of these themes is in my 'Tackling the Ethnic Factor in Canadian History: A Twentieth Century Perspective,' paper presented to the Canadian Studies Conference, University of Edinburgh, May 1990.

3 Apart from the small but growing literature focusing on immigrant

women in the pre-1930 era, there are some exceptions to the pattern I
have described. For a consideration of feminist analyses of immigrant
families and gender relations see Judith E. Smith, *Family Connections: A
History of Italian and Jewish Lives in Providence, Rhode Island 1900–1930*
(Albany: SUNY Press 1985), and Donna Gabaccia, *From Sicily to Elizabeth
Street: Housing and Social Change among Italian Immigrants 1880–1930* (Al-
bany: SUNY Press 1984). Monographs on women include Hasia Diner,
Erin's Daughters in America (Baltimore: Johns Hopkins University Press
1983); Evelyn Nakano Glenn, *Issei, Nisei, Warbride: Three Generations of
Japanese American Women in Domestic Service* (Philadelphia: Temple Uni-
versity Press 1986); and Varpu Lindström-Best, *Defiant Sisters: A Social
History of Finnish Immigrant Women in Canada* (Toronto: Multicultural
History Society of Ontario 1988).

4 For example, see Sheila Arnopolous, *Problems of the Immigrant Woman in
the Canadian Labour Force* (Ottawa: Ministry of Labour 1979); Laura
Johnson, *The Seam Allowance: Industrial Home Sewing in Canada* (Toronto:
Women's Press 1982); Alejandre Cumsille et al., 'Triple Oppression: Immigrant Women in the Labour Force,' in Linda Briskin and Lynda
Yanz, eds., *Union Sisters: Women in the Labour Movement* (Toronto: Wom-
en's Press 1983); Roxanna Ng and Tania Das Gupta, 'Nation-Builders?:
The Captive Labour Force of Non-English Speaking Immigrant
Women,' *Canadian Woman's Studies* 3 (1981). A fuller discussion of these
themes can be found in my *Such Hardworking People: Italian Immigrants
in Postwar Toronto* (Montreal: McGill-Queen's University Press 1992).

5 Both quotations are by David A. Stewart and are cited in AO, IIMT,
MU6444, File: Group Services, *Annual Report* 1958–9.

6 MU 6474, File: Immigrant Assistance 1957–61, Memorandum, 'History
of the Institute'; MU6447, File: Individual Services Department 1961–4,
Report on First Year 1956–7

7 MU6444 File: Human Rights, A. Sandberg to W.E. West, 18 April 1963;
West to Sandberg, 18 April 1963; Minutes of Meeting with Human
Rights Commission, 26 April 1963

8 MU6390, File: Personnel 1964–73, Personnel Code

9 MU6474, File: Reception Centre 1960, Progress Report, nd (c. 1960). See
also ibid., D. Stewart to W.E. West, 19 Jan. 1958; AO, Local Council of
Women (LCW) Collection, Local Council of Women of Toronto, *Minute
Books*, Minutes of Meeting, 15 Nov. 1949, 25 Jan. 1954

10 MU6390, J. Gellner to C. Gourquet, 19 Oct. 1973 File: Board of Direc-
tors, Executive Minutes

11 MU6444, File: Group Services, *Annual Report* 1958–9

12 On the institute see, for example, MU6474 File: Reception Centre 1960,
Minutes of the Meeting of the Executive, 5 Dec. 1960; MU6444, File:
Group Services General 1956–64, File on Students' Cultural Nights;
File: Current Programme 1955–63 Memorandum, nd. See also LCW *Minute Books*, Minutes of Meetings, 28 Jan. and 15 Nov. 1949, 17 Oct. 1950,
20 Nov. 1951, and 25 Jan. 1954; Woman's Christian Temperance
Union, *Annual Report*, Minutes of Provincial Annual Meeting, May
1953; National Archives of Canada (NA), Imperial Order Daughters of
the Empire, MG 28, file 14, vol. 24, File on IODE Anti-Communist Committee: NA, MG 26, Canadian Citizenship Council, File on Pamphlets and
Immigrant Education, Vol. 70. On the Canadian government and immigrants during and immediately after the Second World War see Regin-
ald Whitaker, *Double Standard: The Secret History of Canadian Immigration*
(Toronto: Lester & Orpen Dennys 1978); and the essays in Norman
Hillmer, Bohdan Kordan, and Lubomyr Luciuk, eds., *On Guard for Thee:
Ethnicity and the Canadian State, 1939–45* (Ottawa: Canadian Committee
for the History of the Second World War 1988), especially N.F. Dreisziger, 'The Rise of a Bureaucracy for Multiculturalism: The Origins of
the Nationalities Branch, 1939–1941.' My thanks to Ramsay Cook for
bringing this work to my attention, and to Fred Dreisziger for fielding
my questions regarding his research. As part of my larger study on postwar immigrants I am investigating the records of the Citizenship
Branch at the National Archives.

13 Gellner to Bourquet, 19 Oct. 1973, as in note 10 above

14 Unfortunately, no complete list of staff and volunteers appears to be
available. My observations are largely based on my reading of the case
files, but other materials proved helpful. For example, see MU6474, File:
Job Classification, Personnel Memorandum, nd, MU6390, File: Personnel, Memorandum on Policies and Duties of Officers; Minutes of the
Meeting of the Executive, 11 Sept. 1961, 17 May 1965; File Reception
Centre 1960, Counselling Service Report, 1 and 4 April 1960; MU6463,
File: Individual Services/Group Services, Reports of Individual Services,
1959–61; MU6446, File: Individual Services Department, Activity Reports 1961–4.

15 MU6384, *Annual Report* 1962, 1964

16 Historical studies of the social work profession in the early post-Second
World War era is scanty. Valuable material can be found in Gordon,
Heroes of Their Own Lives; James Leiby, *A History of Social Welfare and So-
cial Work in the United States* (New York: Columbia University Press
1978); Amitai Etzioni, ed., *The Semi-Professions and Their Organization:
Teachers, Nurses, Social Workers* (New York: Free Press 1969); James
Struthers, *'No Fault of Their Own': Unemployment and the Canadian Welfare
State 1914–1941* (Toronto: University of Toronto Press 1983); his recent
'How Much Is Enough? Creating a Social Minimum in Ontario,
1930–44,' *Canadian Historical Review* 72, 1 (1991); Caroline Andrew,
'Women and the Welfare State,' *Canadian Journal of Political Science* 17,
4 (1984); Allan Moscovitch, *The Welfare State in Canada* (Waterloo: Wilfrid Laurier Press 1983); Allan Moscovitch and Jim Albert, eds., *The Benevolent State: The Growth of Welfare in Canada* (Toronto: Garamond
Press 1987); Jacquelyn Gale Wills, 'Efficiency, Feminism and Cooperative Democracy: Origins of the Toronto Social Planning Council' (PhD
thesis, University of Toronto 1989).

17 Dr Robert Kreem, Address to the IODE, St George Chapter, Toronto 28
March 1966, MU6474, File: Immigration General 1964–7

18 LCW *Minute Books*, Minutes of Meeting, 20 May 1952

19 Ruth Roach Pierson, *'They're Still Women After All': The Second World War
and Canadian Womanhood* (Toronto: McClelland and Stewart 1986); her
' "Home-Aide": A Solution to Women's Unemployment after World
War II,' *Atlantis* 2, 2 (spring 1977); Alison Prentice et al., *Canadian
Women: A History* (Toronto: Harcourt, Brace, Jovanovich 1988), chap.
12; Yvonne Mathews-Klein, 'How They Saw Us: Images of Women in
National Film Board Films of the 1940's and 1950's,' *Atlantis* 4, 2 (spring
1979); Susan Bland, 'Henrietta the Homemaker and "Rosie the Riv-
eter": Images of Women in Advertising in Maclean's Magazine,
1939–50,' *Atlantis* 8 (spring 1983); Linda Ambrose, ' "Youth Marriage
and the Family": The Report of the Canadian Youth Commission's
Family Committee, 1943–1948,' paper presented to the Canadian Historical Association Annual Meeting, Queen's University, June 1991; Veronica Strong-Boag, ' "Getting on with Life": Women and the Suburban
Experience in Canada 1945–1960,' unpublished paper, Feb. 1990. My
thanks to Nikki Strong-Boag for sending me her paper. For contempo-

rary examples see M.J. Henshaw, 'UNRRA in the Role of Foster Parent,' *Social Worker* 15, 1 (Sept. 1946): 11–15; 'Entry of Displaced Persons to Canada,' *Social Worker* 16, 1 (Sept. 1947): 7–9; William Glen, 'Social Workers New Unity of Purpose,' *Social Worker* 18, 5 (June 1950): 22–5; Josie Svanhuit, 'Multi-Problem Family or Multi-Agency Problem?' *Social Worker* 31, 4 (Oct. 1963): 14–16.

20 Elinor G. Barnstead, 'The Ordinary Family in Extraordinary Times,' *Social Worker* 16, 2 (Dec. 1947): 1–9

21 LCW *Minute Book*, Minutes of Meeting, 19 Feb. 1952

22 Ruth Roach Pierson, 'Gender and the Unemployment Debates in Canada, 1934–1940,' *Labour/Le Travail* 25 (spring 1990): 77–103; her ' "The Married Woman Worker" and Canadian Unemployment Insurance Policy, 1934–1950,' paper presented to the Berkshire Conference on the History of Women, Rutgers University, June 1990; Prentice et al., *Canadian Women*, 311–14; Susan Prentice, 'Workers, Mothers, Reds: Toronto's Postwar Daycare Fight,' paper presented to the Canadian Studies Conference, University of Edinburgh, May 1990. See also Denise Riley, 'Some Peculiarities in Social Policy Concerning Women in Wartime and Postwar Britain,' in Margaret Randolph Higonnet et al., eds., *Behind the Lines: Gender and the Two World Wars* (New Haven: Yale University Press 1987).

23 Eva Kenyon, Eileen Titus, Alice Hall, 'The Perpetual Crisis,' *Social Worker* 22, 4 (April 1954): 30–3

24 Strong-Boag, 'Getting On With Life'; references in note 22. See also Shirley Tillotson, 'Government and the Privacy of Leisure: A Gender Analysis of Public/Private Dualisms in Ontario's Recreation Movement, 1945–1955,' paper presented to the Canadian Historical Association Annual Meeting, Queen's University, June 1991.

25 See the discussion in Betty K. Isserman, 'The Casework Relationship in Work with Unmarried Mothers,' *Social Worker* 17, 1 (June 1951): 12–17.

26 Benjamin Schlesinger, 'Socio-Cultural Elements in Casework – The Canadian Scene,' ibid., 30, 1 (Jan. 1962): 40–7. See also J. Kage, 'From "Bohunk" to "New Canadian," ' ibid. 29, 4 (Oct. 1961); his 'The Jewish Immigrant Aid Society of Canada (JIAS) Social Services for Immigrants,' ibid. 18, 3 (Feb. 1960): 21–5; Brigitta L. Ball, 'With a Hungarian Accent,' ibid. 26, 1 (Oct. 1957): 30–43. On Canada's earlier medical experts see Eleoussa Polyzoi, 'Psychologists' Perceptions of the Canadian

Immigrant Before World War II,' *Canadian Ethnic Studies* 18, 1 (1986); Barbara Roberts, 'Doctors and Deports: The Role of the Medical Profession in Canadian Deportation, 1900–20,' ibid. 3 (1986).

27 Gordon, *Heroes*, chap. 3; Leiby, *Social Welfare and Social Work*, 283–5; Svanhuit, 'Multi-Problem Family'

28 Case 121

29 Case 54

30 Case 311

31 Case 173

32 Report on case, MU6505, File: Case Histories (not restricted)

33 Case 143

34 Case 283

35 Case 158

36 Case 17

37 Case 41

38 MU 6339, File: K. Brown Staff Meetings 1966–7, Staff Minutes, 6 Jan. 1967. See also Edith Ferguson, *Newcomers in Transition* (A Project of the International Institute of Metropolitan Toronto, 1962–4).

39 As detailed in S.J. Wilson, *Women, the Family and the Economy* (Toronto: McGraw-Hill Ryerson 1972), 19, the percentage of married women in the Canadian female labour force grew from 4.5 per cent in 1941, to 11.2 per cent in 1951, and to 22 per cent in 1961. According to the unpublished census data for Metropolitan Toronto, in 1961 the total number of women employed in the labour force stood at 260,633. European-born women numbered 96,941. (The data does not provide marital status.) Dominion Bureau of Statistics, Unpublished Tables, 1961. A detailed table is available in my *Such Hard-Working People*. For demographic data see Warren Kalback and Anthony Richmond, *Factors in the Adjustment of Immigrants and Their Descendants* (Ottawa: Statistics Canada 1980); Anthony Richmond, *Immigrants and Ethnic Groups in Metropolitan Toronto* (Toronto: York University 1967).

40 For the pre-1930 era see, for example, Michele Barrett and Mary McIntosh, ' "The Family Wage": Some Problems for Socialists and Feminists,' *Capital and Class* 11 (1980): 51–72; Martha May, 'Bread before Roses: American Workingmen, Labor Unions and the Family Wage,' in Ruth Milkman, ed., *Women, Work and Protest: A Century of U.S. Women's Labor History* (London: Routledge and Kegan Paul 1985). On the post-

war period see Patricia Connelly, 'Female Labour Force Participation: Choice or Necessity?' *Atlantis* 3, 2 (spring 1978); Pat Armstrong and Hugh Armstrong, *The Double Ghetto: Canadian Women and Their Segregated Work*, rev. ed. (Toronto: McClelland and Stewart 1984). For an immigrant example, see my calculations regarding male and female incomes within Italian families in *Such Hard-Working People*, chaps. 3 and 4.

41 Case 72

42 Case 167

43 For the immediate postwar years see, for example, Milda Danys, *DP: Lithuanian Immigration to Canada after the Second World War* (Toronto: Multicultural History Society of Ontario 1986), especially her discussion of the domestic schemes. Several studies, including Makeda Silvera, *Silenced* (Toronto: Williams Wallace 1988), deal with a later period and document the racist aspects of the domestic schemes as they were applied to West Indian women and other immigrant women of colour.

44 Case 28

45 Case 14

46 Case 109

47 See, for example, Pierson, 'Gender and the Unemployment Debates' and her 'The Married Woman Worker'

48 Gordon, *Heroes*, chap. 3